Streetwalking

CRITICAL CARIBBEAN STUDIES

Focused particularly in the twentieth and twenty-first centuries, although attentive to the context of earlier eras, this series encourages interdisciplinary approaches and methods and is open to scholarship in a variety of areas, including anthropology, cultural studies, diaspora and transnational studies, environmental studies, gender and sexuality studies, history, and sociology. The series pays particular attention to the four main research clusters of Critical Caribbean Studies at Rutgers University, where the coeditors serve as members of the executive board: Caribbean Critical Studies Theory and the Disciplines; Archipelagic Studies and Creolization; Caribbean Aesthetics, Poetics, and Politics; and Caribbean Colonialities.

Giselle Anatol, *The Things That Fly in the Night: Female Vampires in Literature of the Circum-Caribbean and African Diaspora*

Alaí Reyes-Santos, *Our Caribbean Kin: Race and Nation in the Neoliberal Antilles*

Milagros Ricourt, *The Dominican Racial Imaginary: Surveying the Landscape of Race and Nation in Hispaniola*

Katherine A. Zien, *Sovereign Acts: Performing Race, Space, and Belonging in Panama and the Canal Zone*

Frances R. Botkin, *Thieving Three-Fingered Jack: Transatlantic Tales of a Jamaican Outlaw, 1780–2015*

Melissa A. Johnson, *Becoming Creole: Nature and Race in Belize*

Carlos Garrido Castellano, *Beyond Representation in Contemporary Caribbean Art: Space, Politics, and the Public Sphere*

Njelle W. Hamilton, *Phonographic Memories: Popular Music and the Contemporary Caribbean Novel*

Lia T. Bascomb, *In Plenty and in Time of Need: Popular Culture and the Remapping of Barbadian Identity*

Aliyah Khan, *Far from Mecca: Globalizing the Muslim Caribbean*

Rafael Ocasio, *Race and Nation in Puerto Rican Folklore: Franz Boas and John Alden Mason in Porto Rico*

Anke Birkenmaier, ed., *Caribbean Migrations: The Legacies of Colonialism*

Ana-Maurine Lara, *Streetwalking: LGBTQ Lives and Protest in the Dominican Republic*

Streetwalking

*LGBTQ Lives and Protest in
the Dominican Republic*

Ana-Maurine Lara

Rutgers University Press
New Brunswick, Camden, and Newark,
New Jersey, and London

Library of Congress Cataloging-in-Publication Data

Names: Lara, Ana-Maurine, author.
Title: Streetwalking : LGBTQ lives and protest in the Dominican Republic /
Ana-Maurine Lara.
Description: New Brunswick : Rutgers University Press, [2020] | Series: Critical
Caribbean studies | Includes bibliographical references and index.
Identifiers: LCCN 2020012087 | ISBN 9781978816497 (paperback) |
ISBN 9781978816503 (hardcover) | ISBN 9781978816510 (epub) |
ISBN 9781978816527 (mobi) | ISBN 9781978816534 (pdf)
Subjects: LCSH: Sexual minorities—Dominican Republic—Social conditions. |
Gay rights—Dominican Republic. | Dominican Republic—Social conditions.
Classification: LCC HQ73.3.D65 L374 2020 | DDC 306.76097293—dc23
LC record available at https://lccn.loc.gov/2020012087

A British Cataloging-in-Publication record for this book is available from the British
Library.

♾ The paper used in this publication meets the requirements of the American National
Standard for Information Sciences—Permanence of Paper for Printed Library Materi-
als, ANSI Z39.48-1992.

www.rutgersuniversitypress.org

Manufactured in the United States of America

Este libro lo dedico a Paloma Sody, Antonio E. de Moya, y a tod*s l*s activistas LGBTQ en Santo Domingo quienes—con valentía, pasión y amor—han puesto y continúan a poner sus cuerpos, sus corazones, sus mentes y sus espíritus en el centro de la lucha por las vidas y los derechos de tod*s y para un mundo libre de opresión.

Contents

Streetwalking

Introduction

WHERE THE LOCAS ARE

In June 2010, I arrived for what would be the first of several consecutive research visits to the Dominican Republic (D.R.). I was born there. I had lived there before as an adult. I had conducted ethnographic research there on many occasions, but never on or about gay people. The first time I did ethnographic research in the D.R. was in 1995, when I met with the first of what would come to be several dozens of rural, urban, and plantation *servidores* (tradition keepers) and spiritual leaders in the southern provinces and throughout the capital city of Santo Domingo. My research was focused on racial ideologies and resistance within rural Afro-Dominican and plantation communities (Lara 2005).

The first time I had lived in the D.R. as a lesbian (in 1995), I had managed to find a few other gay women, but just by chance. It happened at a music concert in the Ruinas de San Francisco—in the colonial city (La Zona Colonial)—and I noticed two women holding each other (Lara 2009). Once I got past the (joyful) shock of seeing them, I went up and introduced myself. They drove me home that night. We laughed in the night breeze blowing up from the sea as we drove down the seaside walkway, the *malecón*. But after I stepped out of the pickup truck, I didn't see any of these women for a long time. Some of them I have never seen again.

By 2003—the next time I lived in the D.R. as an adult—I had met other Dominican lesbians and gay men in the diaspora through LLEGÓ, the national Latino Lesbian and Gay Organization. There, I had learned about GALDE (Gay and Lesbian Dominican Empowerment Organization) in New York City and met Luisa Rondón Lassen, Francisco Lazala Mejia, Yoseli Castillo, and Dulce Reyes Bonilla. In the D.R., I heard about and sought to meet Jacqueline Jiménez Polanco. She was a very powerful influence. While I was in the D.R. that year, she invited me to join her and a group of young women at a monthly gathering in Gazcue called Divagaciones bajo la luna.[1] This was the first time I hung out repeatedly with other Dominican lesbians in the D.R. The stories we shared and wrote in that space later became part of an anthology by the same title, which Jacqueline published and circulated in both the D.R. and the diaspora. At the time, she was working at the Facultad Latinoamericana de Ciencias Sociales (FLACSO) and was also a founding member of CAP-LGBTIR (Coalición de Acción Política), a political interest group and listserv that was opening spaces for Dominican lesbian, gay, bisexual, trans*,[2] and queer/*quír* (LGBTQ) activists. I was part of and responsive to international Latino LGBTQ networks (through the LLEGÓ and Pa'Fuera, Pa'Lante conferences) and had just stepped off the International Gay and Lesbian Human Rights Commission board of directors, where I had met LGBTQ activists from all across the globe. Living in the D.R. in 2003 and 2004, I revisited many of the communities I had come to know early in my research life. Our relationships had transformed into ones that followed a more usual script. I lived *afuera* (in diaspora). I brought gifts from *afuera*. I continued to ask about the conditions of peoples' lives, to attend ceremonies and celebrations, to follow up on the children and elders who were born and who died. Spending additional time on the sugar cane plantations in the south and the east, I spoke with those Dominicans and Dominicans of Haitian descent who remained following the restructuring of the sugar industry in the late 1990s. I found people moving between communities and some who had disappeared; they had been deported to Haiti, were victims of other kinds of mysterious extrajudicial violences, or had simply died. Many of the folks on the plantations were also talking to me about the impact of their current statelessness, something that would later evolve into state-legislated denationalization (El Caribe 2013). While in the D.R., I wrote a novel and continued my ethnographic research. And then in late 2004 (after Jean-Bertrand Aristide's removal in Haiti), unable to economically sustain a life as an out lesbian with antiracist politics in what was a politically and economically unstable context, I returned to the U.S.

That morning in June 2010, the friend of the friend who picked me up at the airport warned me about La Zona. I was going to be staying close to La Zona, in an apartment owned by an Afro-Dominican lesbian artist who lives in the diaspora.

"La Zona is not like it used to be," she said.

"Oh really? How?" I asked.

"It's full of *locas*—you know . . ."

"*Locas*, how?"

"You *know*. *Locas*, men dressed as women, men who do things with other men. . . . You just need to be careful. Don't go by yourself. There's a lot of crime."

"Oh. OK," I replied.

I didn't say anything else. But I did take mental note of where to find folks. My research had begun. La Zona was exactly where I was headed. I took note of the rhetoric linking *locas* to sex work and crime and the linking of the streets to danger. I would hear this over and over again over the course of my research. I also noticed that in that moment, I seemed to pass as straight, or at least as "not *loca*."

This self-fashioning (Allen 2011) and movement between gender registers was and is a critical element in my research, affecting my positionality and how people responded to me at different times. During my research, I intentionally moved into more feminine registers at border crossings and in non-LGBTQ spaces and moved back into my more natural state of masculine femininity when I was "in the life." The one time I tested this, I gained insight into the kinds of experiences that *macha* (masculine) and gender-nonconforming people might experience daily in the D.R. In the summer of 2011, having decided to test gender boundaries in my day-to-day experiences, I traveled to the D.R. as my usual "butch"/*macha* self. I explicitly chose to cross borders this way in contrast to the more feminine tones I usually embody in my crossings. If the immigration officers had not seen my female name on my passport, more than likely they would have just let me go. But my passport signaled my identity as a woman, and this contrasted with my gender presentation and their understanding of womanhood. This gender ambiguity made me suspect.

The two female officers at immigration called me over. They pushed me up next to a man who had been in the line in front of me. He looked as confused as I felt. They ridiculed me, calling out to other officers that they had a little man with a woman's name, asking if I wanted to be like the man I was standing next to. They asked me to repeat my name several times as a way to emphasize that my name was a woman's name. They threatened to send me back. Employing Dominican cultural logics and the inkling of *tigueraje* inside of me, I responded to their ridicule by telling them they needed to get their eyes checked and must need glasses. Clearly I was a woman; couldn't they see that? They stopped harassing me, stamped my passport, and waved me through.

Whereas I could choose to enter into more feminine registers in order to access non-LGBTQ and everyday spaces such as banks, supermarkets, public transportation, university campuses, and churches, my Dominican lesbian and gender-nonconforming counterparts—who cannot, do not, or refuse to—have developed deft and subtle mechanisms to do just the same, and they live their daily lives at great risk. What I experienced at the border was nothing compared to the stories many LGBTQ activists shared with me. Not conforming to biblical binaries of femininity or masculinity in the D.R. has very real consequences: daily violences, murder, economic marginalization, isolation. People are thrown out of banks and stores; they are kicked off public buses. University campuses—especially classrooms—can be spaces of unpredictable verbal and physical violence. At the same time, LGBTQ activists' refusal to conform to gender and sexual expectations despite the violences is what drove me to think about their choices and their work in the first place. But that wasn't the only reason. In all my years working with and being "in the life" with Dominican *servidores de misterios* and healers, everybody knew that I was gay. And nobody cared. In fact, there were a lot of "us" in these communities. What "us" even meant was always

Spiritual Ceremonies but not accepted in public spaces

being challenged in those spaces anyway. And nobody cared. So why was it that nobody cared in the spaces of traditional ceremonies, yet so many people cared when it came to public spaces like La Zona Colonial or when it came to laws to protect us? There were a series of underlying social and cultural contradictions that I was determined to figure out.

So on that June night in 2010, I walked by myself through familiar streets in La Zona Colonial, streets I had walked down all my life. But I was entering a new direction of inquiry, something deeply personal. I was looking for the *raras*, the *mariconas*, and the *locas*. I went to where the *locas* were. It was 11 p.m. on a Monday night in June 2010. I had wandered through La Zona as much as I could. I had stopped at different public plazas to look for people, but La Zona was crawling with national police and Politur—the tourist police. Not one *loca*. It was late. I was tired, and I decided it was time to head home. As I wove back down El Conde, I saw her: a young butch woman who, like me, didn't follow the rules of public expressions of Christian feminine embodiment. So I stopped her. It was awkward. I kind of just stood in front of her to get her attention. She was obviously headed somewhere, but I felt like this was my chance.

"Hi, do you know where *la gente* (the people) go to hang out?"

She looked me up and down. I realized that the femininity that I had donned that day was masking my gayness. I couldn't presume she was gay either. So I would have to resort to inference.

"What do you mean?" she replied.

"I heard something about El Parque?"

"Oh, oh yeah. You want to go to El Parque? Sure. Yeah, *hay gente* who hang out there. But it's a Monday night. There won't be a lot of people there tonight. Try again on Thursday."

She pointed me in the direction of the park. I thanked her, we shook hands, and I made my way over to El Parque just in case. The park was empty. The church in front of the park was ominously dark. A few regulars were drinking by the *colmado* at the far end of the plaza, a couple of young people were on the benches, but then . . . *nada*. It was just Monday. I would have to wait until Thursday.

LA ZONA

Santo Domingo was the first Christian colonial settlement in the Caribbean and, subsequently, the hemisphere. Once completely walled and guarded, the colonial city lies at the edge of the Ozama River, linking Santo Domingo to Santo Domingo Este with two bridges that stem off the area's northern and eastern borders. As the larger city of Santo Domingo has expanded through the investment of international capital and the rise in population produced by neoliberal market forces and urban migration, the colonial city has become yet another neighborhood within the teeming cosmopolitan city and has been redubbed La Zona Colonial, or La Zona. La Zona contains all the architectural armature of Christian coloniality: a fort; the national cathedral; the ruins of the first monasteries, hospitals, and customs houses; and the many colonial houses and Catholic churches, monasteries, and convents rebuilt first in the wake of Sir Francis Drake's invasion in 1586 and subsequently in the wake of the many hurricanes and earthquakes that have shaken La Zona's structures. After the designation of the colonial city as a UNESCO World Heritage Site in 1990, investment in La Zona increased exponentially.

La Zona was the original site for the rehearsal of Christian colonial settlement. *Christian coloniality* refers to the discursive and material intersections of Christian theologies with the construction of colonial being/knowledge and power. Christian colonial institutions came into being through the development of the colony, and the colonial city came into being through the development of Christian institutions. These institutions included the founding of the Dominican monastery where Fray Antonio Montesinos delivered his sermon condemning the enslavement of indigenous peoples in 1511. Established in 1510 with the arrival of Dominican monks, the monastery was one of the first Catholic edifices in the New World, preceded only by the chapel to the Virgen del Rosario (1498)—built by Catholic military settlers—and the Ermita San Antonio (1502), built by and for the first *ladino* (enslaved Christianized Afro-Iberian) laborers. In 1538, the Dominican monastery became the first Christian colonial university, initiated under the mandate established by Pope Paul III through the *Bula Apostolatus Culmine*. The university specialized in theology, and it was here that many religious leaders were educated in preparation for the expansion of Christian colonial power throughout the Caribbean and the Spanish colonial empire. The monastery is close to the park where LGBTQ activists gather to hang out and spend time together. Next to it is the church to the Virgen del Carmen, where LGBTQ activists have staged numerous protests and public performances.

Throughout the sixteenth century, the colonial city was populated by multiple convents, monasteries, and churches. Different religious orders also established small plantations within and along the city's boundaries. Some monasteries, like that of the Hieronymite order, incorporated the labor of up to four hundred enslaved people (Sáez 1987). Together with Christian military forces and Christian colonial governors and legislators, the religious orders and secular priests enabled and battled for control over the legal and economic institutions central to the management of the tribute system (*encomiendas*), the trade in enslaved peoples, the mines, the sugar cane plantations, and subsequently, the cattle ranches surrounding Santo Domingo. With the establishment of the Real Audiencia in 1504, an institution protecting the interests of the Spanish Crown, the colonial city became the principal site of confrontation between the church, the Crown's representatives, colonial governors, and *encomenderos* (Rodríguez Morel 2011). The *joined forces to control indigenous*

Catholic Church had a powerful role in the architectural, political, and social structuring of the colonial city. Today, in part because of its historic architecture and also because this architecture serves as a powerful index of the success of the Christian colonial project throughout the Americas, La Zona is central to the Dominican Republic's Catholic Hispanic nationalist narratives.

When I was a young gay child in the 1980s—the height of the D.R.'s late twentieth-century economic crisis (Espinal 1995)—La Zona was a series of neighborhoods of abandoned buildings, shells of buildings torn down twenty years before, empty stores with overpriced (unsubsidized and highly taxed) goods, and informal labor. *Aviones*[3] abounded, high heels helping them hang on to their *gringo* companions. I remember playing in an aunt's house on the northern end of La Zona, the cement floors sticky with heat and sweat, the stifling afternoon contained by the old wooden structure held up by mere pressure on either side. I used to play by the door just to get air. I also remember, when I was a slightly older gay child, accompanying my parents to the sparsely furnished apartments of intellectuals, left-wing activists, and bohemians. Many of the Dominican men in these homes, including my father, were married to foreign women from North America and Europe. Many afternoons and evenings of my gay childhood were spent accompanying this circle of heterosexual, mostly Marxist adults in the palacio de la esquizofrenia. I would drink my papaya juice while they enjoyed their coffee, rum, or beer. Tourists floated in between tables, often searching for some semblance of Euro-American familiarity. It was in the *palacio*, when I was thirteen, that I first heard the song "El Gran Varón" by Willie Colón, released in 1988. Though I could not understand it at the time, I watched as the adults commented on the seriousness of the content: the as-yet-unspeakable HIV epidemic and the homosexual subjects at its center. Intuitively, I felt this song had something to do with me, but I did not yet have the language for it. This, in a nutshell, is my memory of what La Zona was then. I have no active memory of LGBTQ life in La Zona outside of my own gay personhood. I would be a gay adult before I started seeing how present LGBTQ life is in La Zona.

Since the early 2000s, La Zona has been a place where Dominican, European, and North American business owners have staked a claim in the global tourist market via transnationally franchised businesses and nationally owned hotels; it is a place riddled with banks, foreign embassies, and cultural centers; it is a place where bohemians, artists, intellectuals, and social activists live in studio apartments squeezed in between the expensively refurbished colonial homes; it is a place where the poor have been pushed out to other neighborhoods or hide in the patios along the periphery; it is a place full of galleries selling art, jewelry, and Dominican culture to Dominicans and foreigners alike; it is a place where bookstores are slowly falling into ruin; it is a place where sex workers find good business during the day and night; it is a place teeming with bars known as cafés and with LGBTQ nightclubs; it is a place where LGBTQ activists hang out in droves

vacated urban core

despite the discontent of La Zona's *Junta de vecinos* (neighborhood association). Among the *Junta de vecinos'* membership are Catholic clergy, including the now retired Cardinal Nicolás López Rodríguez.

Former Cardinal López Rodríguez was the president[4] of the institution responsible for the initiatives that refurbished many of the historic buildings in the colonial city in the 1990s and the early 2000s: the Patronato de la ciudad colonial. The Patronato is a governmental body that includes the archbishop of Santo Domingo, the local political leadership, and directors of cultural organizations. They collect millions of pesos each year from renters, buyers, and various international bodies located within La Zona, as well as from private investors; these monies enable the maintenance of colonial infrastructure. The Patronato was founded by President Joaquín Balaguer in 1993, and then Archbishop López Rodríguez was named as its president.

The primary role of the Patronato is to secure the Catholic Hispanic colonial memory of the D.R., specifically through language and the management of cultural artifacts and buildings. As part of its establishment, the Patronato oversaw the celebrations and activities around the five-hundred-year anniversaries of colonization in 1992 (five hundred years after Colombus's landing) and 1998 (five hundred years after the colonial settlement of Santo Domingo). The Patronato has been responsible for carrying out the Plan Cuna de América— the renovation of historic buildings—and the administration of a *fondo* (fund) for the protection of the colonial city, "whose function is mandated by a special [unspecified] regulation" (Balaguer 1993). And in 2012, the Patronato was one of the major sponsors of La Zona's "Colonial Fest."[5] The Patronato also provides oversight to numerous universities and learning centers in the D.R. as well as the publication of books and documents. To date, there have been no public records to indicate how the Patronato's funds are managed or disbursed, and there are none required. The cardinal sits on the *Junta de vecinos* as part of his dual role as a resident of La Zona and president of the Patronato. In his position, he carried out a public battle against those who are (or are associated with) LGBTQ people in La Zona. His targets included gay clubs and El Parque.

El Parque is a site where we rest for a bit, sitting down with each other to hang out, to *convivir*. To share a soda, or a beer, or a glass of water. To catch up on life and the day. To share stories. To interact. To film each other. To flirt. To pick someone up for sex. To spend time *en el borde*, with others streetwalking: the punk rockers (*rockeros*), the trans* and gay sex workers, the quiet men who like sex with men, the bawdy lesbians, the drug dealers, the drug users, the alcoholics, the scholars, the journalists, the graffiti artists, the writers, the painters, and the musicians. All of us streetwalking. The *colmadero* likes us because we keep the business going. Also because we aren't doing any harm. He lets us use the bathroom when we need to. And sometimes he sets out a few chairs under the big *flamboyan* tree shading the northeastern corner. The *rockeros* hang out on the Duarte statue. The sex workers perch on the northwestern benches, close to the street where cars are passing by. The men looking for other men occupy the benches on the western side of the park, where one can sit to read a book under the streetlight. The lesbians are under the *flamboyan*, near the *colmado*. And we walk and talk among and in between. The bisexual *rockera* comes over to the *flamboyan* for a cigarette. The lesbian who that day decided to cut off all her processed hair and declare herself "una lesbiana negra!" (a black lesbian) stands on the base of the Duarte statue. The police go to harass one of the men on the benches, and everyone flows over to witness and interrupt. There is no boundaried purity here—only encounters that rupture easy lines of definition and sameness. Everyone is hanging out, *conviviendo*. In this sense, "hanging out opens our attention to the transmutations of sense, borders of meaning, without the enclosures and exclusions that have characterized a politics of sameness" (Lugones 2003, 220). That is not to say that there is no conflict. There was a time when a *lesbiana* made fun of the *rockeros* and one of the guys pulled a knife on her, threatening to cut her for being "una puta lesbiana" (a lesbian whore). This moment of destabilization is also part of streetwalking: a moment of misrecognition. The rules of the street are different. The infractions lie not in the copresence of these two subjects in the same space but rather in their use of the power of language to demean difference—an infraction that results from the rupture in the logics of transgression that are streetwalking's creed and safeguard.

For me, hanging out with other lesbians, bisexual women, queers, and trans* folks in public at El Parque disrupted the neat construction of public space as always already heteronormative and Catholic Hispanic. This was also true about streetwalking throughout La Zona. La Zona is strategically constructed to give the impression of Christian colonial continuity, to draw from the colonial past into a Christian colonial future, and streetwalking within that space disrupts this totalizing narrative. Hanging out disrupts the public/private dichotomy: what is supposed to be private is made public. The process of hanging out in this public space creates a sense of home for those who cannot be who they are at home. They find that sense of home in each other. But for those invested in Christian colonial biblical manhood and womanhood, our presence was an affront to the *moralidad pública*—the ideological concept of public moral order, known in other contexts as moral propriety and/or public decency.

Backed by the Catholic Hispanic nation-state and a fundamentalist religious public, in 2010 the cardinal mobilized the concept of *moralidad pública* in carrying out the production of moral panic about the LGBTQ presence in the heart of the country's primary locus of its Christian colonial legacy (Padilla and Castellanos 2008). As Mark Padilla argues, López Rodríguez drew on the Patronato's mandate and its accompanying expectations of preserving La Zona as part of the "symbols of Spanish cultural heritage and Catholic religious tradition" (Padilla and Castellanos 2008, 35) and to substantiate his Easter Mass proclamations against the *lacras sociales* (social trash)—the homosexuals who had invaded La Zona and presented an affront to the *moralidad pública*. We knew that, and we chose to hang out anyway.

Lesbians in El Parque

It was 2013. I made my way down to El Parque from the palacio de la esquizo-frenia. I walked past the cathedral and then past the small storefronts filled with cheap souvenirs for sale. At El Parque, a group of young women stood in small clusters around the palm tree on the eastern end. We were there to spray-paint T-shirts for LGBTQ Pride. News had gone out through the social networks: *las gatas*[6] were gathering in the park. Yenny had made stencils and had brought spray-paint in all the colors. We brought the T-shirts. The goal? To have fun, to show our pride, and to hang out with the others streetwalking. By the time I arrived, there were about twenty other women. Izzi got there shortly after I did; she carried a large piece of cardboard and markers.

The T-shirt party was happening the Saturday afternoon before the Domini-can tribunal court's ruling on a case between a nonprofit reproductive rights organization, Pro-Familia, and the Catholic Church (Cruz Benzán 2013a; Mejía 2013). The church had sued the organization for its television campaign sup-porting reproductive and sexual rights, stating that the campaign was an offense to *la moralidad pública*. Second, the church representatives demanded that the campaign should also be considered illegal because it went against *moralidad pública and* Catholic Church doctrines. As members of La Colectiva Mujer y Salud pointed out, "Until only a few decades ago, in countries like ours, it was inconceivable that an institution—whether state-led or private—would openly display positions contrary to the Catholic orthodoxy. The church's social and ide-ological control was so totalizing—and the culture of democracy so weak—that public space simply did not allow for dissidence, which in fact was more often channeled in the margins of our small intellectual or the semi-clandestine leftist communities" (Paiewonsky 2013). In the Santo Domingo of a few decades prior (the 1980s, for example), the Catholic Church was supported by a much more authoritarian regime. In 2013, the campaign in favor of sexual and reproductive health was aired on television and radio. And unlike the D.R. of Balaguer's or Trujillo's years, the Dominican courts of law were willing to consider the case. A majority of public opinion was in favor of Pro-Familia's position and campaign. Ultimately, the judge ruled in Pro-Familia's favor (Cruz Benzán 2013b). But that Saturday, we didn't yet know the outcome of the trial. We were together to pub-licly take up space.

The group of folks around me that day was definitely *not* clandestine. Two *machas* sat on a bench, one with her hair in cornrows, the other with a button-down dress shirt on, her BlackBerry hanging casually in her left hand. Willy, a publicly self-identified trans* man, sat with them. Women sat on each other's laps, kissed each other on the lips, and held hands. We all shared bottles of soda, beer, and water. We helped each other with the stencils and spray-paint and then just sat around, catching up. Grace, a member of the Metropolitan Community Church (ICM) was recruiting women to join a new prayer circle. Mirla, back from a trip to Haiti, was filling us all in on what was happening over in Léogâne. We also discussed the court case.

As soon as the first round of T-shirts was finished, Izzi called out to every-one, "Photo, people! Photo!" We all pulled on our new T-shirts, complete with rainbow horseshoes and the double woman symbols, and stood around Izzi and her new poster, which read, "We support Pro-Familia." As soon as the image was taken, it was sent around to all the phones in the park and posted on social media. As new women joined the group, we each took turns posing with the sign. In the photos, it was obvious we were in El Parque. The familiar landscape served as a metanarrative of streetwalking: we were standing in the space of El Parque, of streetwalking sociality and life. Our painted T-shirts added an additional sym-bolic layer to the image. Our bodies became the grounds for the crystallization of meaning. The space where we gathered became layered with multiple registers of personhood that collapsed an easy reading of subjectivity. Our presence was then extended into the cybersphere through shared photos, tags, and messages. We finished the photoshoot and dispersed to hang out some more.

As I sat back down on the bench, I studied the church in front of El Parque. Several families were coming out of the chapel from what seemed to be a wed-ding. Men were dressed in suits. Women wore tight, elegant dresses and high heels. A woman dressed in white was surrounded by children, also dressed in white. I guessed that the man next to her, in a suit like the other men, was her newly minted husband. Grace sat down next to me. We silently observed the heterosexual charade for a little while. Grace sighed.

"What happened?" I asked.

"If only one day that could be me," she responded.

"Really?"

"Really."

I nodded, remembering a story I had been told the first time I sat in the park, back in 2010. In 2009, a group of three LGBTQ activists staged a gay wedding in that very same place, in front of that same church. The wedding involved two gay men, and the illegal ceremony / public performance was officiated by a les-bian representative of one of the local activist collectives. Just as the performance finished, the police broke up the celebration and hauled away two of the activ-ists. Later, when the incident was covered by the newspapers, a representative from the local *Junta de vecinos* was recorded as saying, "We are going to defend [El Parque] as a community gathering and recreation space, because for many months now we have tolerated the ostentatious presence of those citizens who

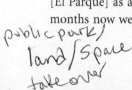

proclaim themselves to be *pájaros* and *pájaras volando*" (Sosa 2009).[7] LGBTQ activists pushed back, and the incident touched off several years of media and territorial battles between those who come to El Parque and the more conservative members of the local *Junta de vecinos* (Tavarez Mirabal 2011). At some point, security cameras were installed and trained on the "gay sections"—the parts of the park where LGBTQ activists hang out. And periodically, the church foments police harassment.

A year after the gay wedding ceremony, in April 2010, Cardinal López Rodríguez issued one of his famous homophobic statements to the press as a cardinal and as a member of the *Junta de vecinos* about the *delinquentes—jevitos* (playboys) and metalheads, homosexuals and drug addicts—who were engaged in "gross behaviors" in El Parque (Herrera 2010).[8] Immediately following his statement, the police rounded up many of the very same people who were standing around me this Saturday afternoon. The police took them into custody under charges of disturbing the *moralidad pública*. The folks spent a night in jail. A national debate ensued on TV and radio and in newspapers about the rights of LGBTQ people to occupy public space. While those in support of the LGBTQ community stated that those arrested are citizens just like any other, those against referred to LGBTQ promiscuity, immorality and general "atentos contra la buena costumbre de la sociedad" (affront to social respectability; Herrera 2010), and among the most conservative, the affront to national pride. After all, they argued, it was a park named after one of the country's founding fathers. We were still there. I looked around at all the women hanging out, laughing and sharing intimacy, learning and listening. They were there "to participate in communicative creations, to gauge possibilities, to have a sense of the directions of intentionality, to gain social depth" (Lugones 2003, 209).

Grace offered me some soda. I held out my cup. As she poured, I pondered what she had said about her dream to get married.

"Not me." I said.

"Why?"

"No—all that artifice? For what? So that others can tell me what I have is real? No."

"It's nice—to have your family and friends affirming your relationship."

"Yeah ... no. Too much production."

Grace slapped my thigh. "You are so cynical."

"I guess I am."

We both laughed.

"But Ana and Rosie's wedding was sweet," I offered.

"It was," she agreed. "We all helped them. Everyone came together to make that happen."

The heterosexual couple in front of us kissed as their photographer's camera flashed. I thought back to another event from 2010, when a heterosexual

role
media

Haitian-Dominican couple—Yoselin Guerrir and Nicodem Cony—kissed at a public intersection about two miles from El Parque. Their kiss was caught on someone's cell phone camera and made it into the national newspapers (Bonilla 2010). Within days, an official from the department of migration ordered an investigation into the couple's legal status, going so far as to attempt to deport them. The kiss was used as a measure of the couple's collective moral personhood, which the police official, in turn, used as a justification for his investigation. Police officers arrested the couple, and a series of xenophobic responses emerged in the public sphere—online, on the radio, and in newspapers—condemning the public display of affection. As a result, both Guerrir and Cony had to answer very public questions about their citizenship status, whether they worked (both of them sold cell phone cards on the street, yet another mode of streetwalking), whether they were married, had families, and so on. Their lives were completely invaded by the state and media *because of a kiss*—the same thing the couple in front of us was doing right then. In response to the state and public's racism and xenophobia, radical lesbian activists organized a national direct-action kiss-in—the Besatón.[9]

The Besatón, which took place on a rainy Saturday afternoon in June 2010, was a direct response to the repressive actions against Guerrir and Cony and by extension Dominicans of Haitian descent and Haitian migrants in the country. It also aimed to call attention to the ongoing harassment of LGBTQ youth by police in public spaces. At the Besatón, the protestors referenced the multiple occasions in which LGBTQ people have been harassed for kissing in public, directly making connections between day-to-day homophobia and widespread anti-Haitian discrimination. The protest also directly critiqued the local Catholic Church's role in promoting the abuse of vulnerable peoples by police authorities.

The Besatón procession traversed the Christian colonial symbolic geography of La Zona. Parque Independencia, a park dedicated to the national founding patriarchs, is located at one end of the pedestrian walkway (El Conde), known in more recent history as the place where tourists seek out male and female sex workers. El Conde is a site of gay male sociality and part of the gay sexual tourist economy (Cabezas 2009; Gregory 2006). But it is also the main thoroughfare into La Zona, where thousands of tourists come each year in their visit to "the first European city of the Americas." El Conde leads to the national cathedral and Parque Colón. In Parque Colón, Columbus stands in shiny brass, pointing to the west, an indigenous woman forever looking up at him from his feet. In Haiti, people have deposed Columbus's statue and thrown it into the ocean, but in the Catholic Hispanic D.R., he stands at the center of the colonial city world, directly in front of the national cathedral. The Besatón procession made its way across this symbolic geography, marking a path between the nation-state and the church, the general and the sexual tourist economies, the presumably heterosexual nation and its streetwalking underbelly.

As the Besatón activists marched down El Conde, protestors kissed each other and hugged and kissed strangers. One lesbian activist hugged a female tourist police officer. The officer did not respond but instead stood stiffly silent in the arms of the *macha* (masculine) lesbian. As the procession meandered forward, everyone commented on the officer's inaction, one lesbian protestor insisting that the officer was "so scared that she froze" (personal communication, Y.G. 2010). As I reflected on the officer's nonresponse, I also wondered if her bodily restraint aimed to diminish the action's importance or to render the state neutral rather than violent in the face of a homosocial gesture. Was she herself *del ambiente, de familia*—in the life? The Besatón procession passed other police officers, both tourist and national, and finally made its way to the endpoint. We crowded around the entrance to the cathedral, steps away from Columbus, and kissed each other in the rain: women, men, trans*, gay, straight, dark-skinned, light-skinned, Dominican, Haitian, and otherwise. It was almost utopian, except that the purpose of our gathering was to bring attention to church- and state-enacted violence while also attempting to make visible the banality of kissing. As activists took turns at the megaphone, demanding respect for ourselves and our relationships, others waved posters of the cardinal in protest.

In 2013, shortly after our afternoon in El Parque, another Besatón was enacted. This time, there was no catalytic event. It emerged out of a coalesced communal anger. As the activists themselves stated, "We believe the *Besatón* is an ideal political act to engage with each other and to repudiate [the violence we experience in the country], calling attention to the hostilities, the verbal and physical assaults we experience on the streets, as well as the physical, sexual violence and the racism that we live through day to day." Why, they asked, "are we prohibited from demonstrating affection in public in our country? Why, instead, is it not prohibited to shout at each other, insult each other . . . not have free secular and quality education? Why is it not illegal for the church and state to decide about women's bodies?" (Arias 2013). In this way, the two Besatón protests redirected attention away from the bodies and actions produced through streetwalking and toward the structural violence produced by ongoing Christian colonial sexual terror (Nuestro Tiempo 2015). Discussed in section 1, chapter 2, *sexual terror* alludes to the completely encompassing modes of violence that permeate the social body, striking against those whose desires, feelings, and erotic dispositions do not conform to Christian colonial morality—in particular, Christian colonial ideas of biblical manhood and womanhood.

On that Saturday afternoon, though, we sat in El Parque, facing a church, surveilled by cameras, spray-painting T-shirts, and making posters in defense of sexual education. As the sun set and it was no longer possible to see the colors on our T-shirts, our group dispersed. I carried my T-shirt on my shoulder, wanting to preserve it after all the effort that went into painting it. I looked around La Zona. There are at least sixteen church buildings—the cathedral, chapels,

[handwritten annotations: interrupts, move, through spaces as physicals of power, ACTIVE SUBJECTS]

smaller churches, and monasteries—in an area less than one square kilometer. From El Parque walking north, I passed three. Life in La Zona was and is defined by the Catholic Church. Life in coloniality is defined by Christianity. But Christian coloniality extends into and through the colonial geography maintained and extended throughout the nation-state. With the Pro-Familia case, we were a collective witness to the institutional and geographic exercise of Christian moral authority through social and political bodies, including the governmental institutions of the Dominican nation-state. The layers of stone and wood around us, restored and revived, were intentionally cultivated reminders of Christian colonial presence. The extensive apparatus of the Catholic Church throughout La Zona was both a vestige of the actual architecture of the colony and also a refraction of the centrality of a Catholic Hispanic mission that has been a central aspect of modern governance since 1498. As I streetwalked, I realized that I was navigating a complex geography in which streetwalking insistently interrupts Christian coloniality and the logics of the Catholic Hispanic state. Despite an ongoing campaign lasting more than five years, LGBTQ activists continue to congregate in El Parque, continue to visit the gay bars ensconced within the colonial city's architecture, and continue to make *la calle* our own.

Streetwalking

Streetwalking usually refers to those who walk the streets for money. Here I use the term to refer to "active subjects"—those whose person collapses the public/private dichotomy central to Christian coloniality, who experience home "as inseparable from other places of violence" (Lugones 2003, 219). Streetwalking, we are aware that our lives are fragile, we lack institutional legitimation, and as a result, we are often unintelligible to the agents of oppression. This position as "the outlaw, the despised, the useless, the insane, the hustlers, the poachers, the pickers of garbage, the urban nomads, [the *delinquentes* and *lacras sociales*] of the reconstituted spatiality of the cityscapes" allows us to "defy and unmask common sense" (219), to transform silence into action that in turn enables the mobilization of that action for liberation. Streetwalking could and does include the "home-shelter-street-police station/jail/insane asylum-cemetery circle, in ever so many permutations" (209) on equal footing: in none of these spaces do we make Christian colonial sense. We structure our lives as permeable, malleable, open to possibility—any possibility that might render us more intelligible to each other.

In ethnographic literature, the street—*la calle*—has often been configured as a space of sexual labor, economic hustle, and transnational tourism (Brennan 2004; Cabezas 2009; Gregory 2006; Padilla 2008). The street has also been discussed as a place that needs to be cleaned (for foreign tourists) and where women, in particular, are subject to heightened surveillance and police harassment. Across the Caribbean, the streets are a site for Carnival, excess, and the exercise of different registers of masculinity and femininity (Alexander 1994;

Edmondson 2003). As Jafari S. Allen writes, "*La calle* is where men are expected to provide for the family through labor, as well as to bond with other men. Implicitly also, men are expected to have sexual liaisons in this sphere, populated by men and 'fast women'" (2011, 180). The corner has particular resonance as a space of hypermasculine homosociality. Here, however, I will discuss how *la calle* serves as a space of *resistencia*—a space where people streetwalk in order to occupy public space by hanging out. *La calle* is where they produce demonstrations and parades to protest the Catholic Hispanic nation-state.

Under Rafael Leonidas Trujillo's thirty-year military dictatorship (1930–1961), known as the Trujillato, and Joaquín Balaguer's authoritarian regimes (1960–1962, 1966–1978, 1986–1996), the D.R. was constructed as a Catholic Hispanic nation-state. These regimes and their insistence on the D.R. as a morally Catholic nation-state foreclosed the possibilities of streetwalking within the official discourse or public spaces. What occurred as a result, however, was the construction of public spaces as sites of disappearance, loss, emptiness, hypersurveillance and social control, and subsequently the extension of Christian coloniality and its accompanying sexual terror into the interior spaces of homes, prisons, police precincts, and police cars. The state was able to realize its achievement of a Catholic Hispanic *moralidad pública* by expanding its presence through the rupture of public/private divides. The validation of the Trujillato by the Catholic Church became a key component in the extension of the authoritarian regime into the everyday lives and spaces of Dominicans. The Concordat of 1954,[10] which secured the church's relationship with the Dominican government, was but one element in a larger body of agreements, licenses, financing, and negotiations of power between the two bodies. In an effort to stave off the Dominican oligarchy's contempt against his person, Trujillo secured the validation of the Vatican through the vehicle of the Concordat.

Twenty years after the end of the Trujillo dictatorship, authoritarian president Balaguer achieved the discursive resurrection of ethno-racist ideologies in which he reconfigured nation, state, race, and sexuality. Reinscribing a centuries-long racist trope of the savage *negro*, Balaguer writes in his book *La Isla al Reves*, "The de-nationalization of the Dominican part of the border was no less alarming nor disturbing in its moral aspects. All of the zones near the Haitian territory had been invaded by exotic customs that not only undermined the morality of the Dominican people, but also against the unity of religious sentiment. Incest and other practices no less barbarian, contrary to the Christian institution of the family, are not rare in the lower extremities of the Haitian population and are a testament to their tremendous moral deformities" (1983, 83).

Writing between past and present tense, Balaguer effectively transcends the boundaries of time to keep the Trujillo regime's concerns ever-present, even now in the 2000s, more than thirty years since the book's publication. This statement captures how the nation is continuously written onto a territory with borders that are dangerous, porous, and invaded. Balaguer writes Christianity into the national body and across the territory. He reconstructs the familiar tropes of black savage sexuality onto an imagined (dark-skinned) Haitian body that is incapable of containing Christian morality or notions of family—something he contends the Dominican (Catholic Hispanic) body is capable of. This is despite his knowing participation in the Trujillato's many modes of sexual violence.[11] To that end, he emphasizes that the D.R., its territories, its families, and its morality must be protected. In this discourse, Balaguer collapses the containment of both the nation and the nation's sexuality into a moral and sacred national obligation.[12] We see this ideology play out in the continual disciplining of gender and sexuality. Balaguer's discourses, both mobilizing and reflecting public sentiment, enabled the consolidation of a racialized biblical manhood and womanhood as measures of national belonging. The disproportionate disciplining of those deemed outside or foreign to the nation also targeted bodies that were deemed incapable of bearing Catholic Hispanic souls. Balaguer's conceptualization of the Catholic Hispanic nation-state drew on popular understandings of Christian personhood.

Today in the D.R., the ongoing project of Christian coloniality as it developed through the Trujillista-Balaguerista regime is further troubled by neoliberal economic and political forces. Through globalized tourism, we see the replication of Christian colonial logics against and through streetwalking. The already constructed nature of the Caribbean region as feral and uninhabited, in which "wild and savage men who ate human flesh (Cannibals) and sexually precocious women (Amazons) who were to be tamed and controlled in the name of God and the Crown" (Kempadoo 2004, 1) serve as a backdrop to the neoliberal reordering of relationships between global forces as they traverse across ethno-national boundaries. Tourism, a large percentage of the gross domestic product (GDP),[13] expands across a landscape that is increasingly restrictive to rural and urban poor Dominicans. Tourists who go to the D.R. to experience the picturesque tropics (Thompson 2006), to imbibe rum, and to partake in the expansive Dominican sex trade do so in a context in which the Catholic and Christian churches collude with the nation-state to discipline the imagined lascivious behaviors of those deemed to be *lacras sociales*.

Over the course of my fieldwork, LGBTQ activists staged numerous protests in front of La Zona's churches. From performances of gay marriage to kiss-ins and demonstrations that traversed the city's geographies, many LGBTQ activists and their supporters ended up in front of churches. They often chose churches as their primary sites of protest because, as I was told over and over again, the Catholic Church's global moral authority positions it above the governmental authority of the state. Because of its global power, the Dominican nation-state often acquiesces to the church's demands, and the Dominican public is deeply shaped by the church's moral debates and positions. As a result, the problem for

Dominican LGBTQ activists is not just the lack of recognition and protection from the nation-state but also the church's investment in the *moralidad pública* as exercised through the vehicle of the state. Because of this, LGBTQ activists choose to confront the Catholic Hispanic nation-state in the staging of public demonstrations in front of Catholic churches—the majority and most significant of which are located in La Zona.

In 2004, after the cardinal had made proclamations (Associated Press 2004) that resulted in yet another series of police roundups in gay bars and arrests of LGBTQ activists on the streets, the LGBTQ community staged a public protest that, like the Besatón in 2013, disrupted the Christian colonial geography of La Zona. Thalia, a trans* activist and performer, shared the story of a protest LGBTQ activists staged against the cardinal:

THALIA: One time we staged a parody in which we confronted the cardinal. We went to El Conde and V— [a gay activist] dressed up as the cardinal. We all came out behind him, singing as a group—at the time, the cardinal had said that we should all be given visas to leave the country, that we should be sent to Europe, where we could get married and stuff.

And so we made up a song:

Señor cardenal mío,	My dear lord cardinal,
homosexual yo soy.	I am a homosexual.
Mándame pa' europa	Send me to Europe
o para nueva york.	or to New York.
Soy una raza mala,	I am a bad race
según el cardenal.	according to the cardinal.
que orina en las paredes	I urinate on the walls
de la catedral.	of the cathedral.

Because he said all the gay bars were down there, by the cathedral. And so V— went out on to El Conde, and all the crowds joined us. It was street theater. We finished at Parque Duarte. The police didn't do anything.

The protest chant is bold, collectivizing the voices of LGBTQ activists in a parody of the cardinal's power and authority. In particular, the chant inverts the cardinal's threats. Reading into the multiple layers of meaning and translating them into common parlance, the chant could be read as saying, "Yes, they say, we are homosexuals! We are! You want to send us to New York? To Europe? Please, cardinal—will you? You know I'd love to go." This last line is particularly cheeky in referencing the common desire among Dominicans to travel to these metropoles. Yet for decades, these places were inaccessible to HIV-positive people, and they are currently inaccessible to trans* people, who lack documents that correspond to their gender identities. They are generally inaccessible to many Dominicans who lack the kinds of funding, sponsorship, or paper work required to acquire visas to travel to the U.S. and Europe. This kind of streetwalking reimagines *la calle*, La Zona, as spaces where Christian colonial violences are confronted and flipped, where erotic orientations toward freedom undergird a desire for *resistencia* to the Christian colonial violence mobilized by the cardinal's speech.

Throughout this book, *las calles*—and specifically the streets of La Zona and the spaces in front of churches—figure as prominent and necessary sites and spaces of streetwalking, where streetwalking is protest. Whether in the case of lesbian activists organizing to condemn the church's role in promoting repressive reproductive policies or the state repression of particular modes of public expressions of intimacy, or LGBTQ activists protesting the cardinal, or the Caravana del orgullo (the annual LGBTQ Pride parade)—*la calle* is often overtaken by those who seek to mobilize an awareness and consciousness that both their presence and their message challenge concepts of the Christian moral authority embedded within the nation-state's governance structures. It is our erotic orientations, described in the next section, that guide us toward justice in the context of Christian colonial sexual terror.

Erotic Orientations

Streetwalking is rooted in the erotic and is guided by the erotic orientations that shape us. Audre Lorde defines the erotic in several ways. She writes, "The erotic is a resource within each of us that lies in a deeply female and spiritual plane, firmly rooted in the power of our unexpressed or unrecognized feeling" (1984, 53). In this definition of the erotic, Lorde points to the intangibility of power and yet the knowability of its potential within ourselves. Power here is tied into body, feeling, and thought. Coming together, these three distinct loci of knowledge enable the erotic to express itself through "the chaos of our strongest feelings" that in turn produces yet another knowing, that "having experienced the fullness of this depth of feeling and recognizing its power, in honor and self-respect we can require no less of ourselves" (54). That knowing, that satisfaction, and the power that comes with it extend to our relations to others. As Lorde writes, "The erotic . . . [provides] the power which comes from sharing deeply any pursuit with another person. The sharing of joy, whether physical, emotional, psychic, or intellectual, forms a bridge between the sharers which can be the basis for understanding much of what is not shared between them, and lessens the threat of their difference" (1984, 56). Lyndon Gill expands on Lorde's theorization. He proposes "that the erotic must be reconceptualized as a perspectival trinity that holds together the political-sensual-spiritual at their most abstract; in other words, 'the erotic' describes various formal and informal power hierarchies (the political), sexual as well as nonsexual intimacy (the sensual), and sacred metaphysics (the spiritual) simultaneously" (2018, 10).

[handwritten annotations: political / sensual / Spiritual — Trinity]

As we seek to experience the erotic through our daily acts and ways of living, we can no longer tolerate conditions that diminish that power. As Lorde writes, "Our erotic knowledge empowers us, becomes a lens through which we scrutinize all aspects of our existence, forcing us to evaluate those aspects honestly in terms of their relative meaning within our lives. And this is a grave responsibility, projected from within each of us, not to settle for the convenient, the shoddy, the conventionally expected, nor the merely safe" (1984, 57). When we are connected to the erotic, the "political-sensual-spiritual" perspectival trinity that Gill articulates enables relationships that are rooted in an appreciation for one's own and other's capacities to embody what Chela Sandoval (2000) describes as differential oppositional consciousness in order to foment the necessary tactical strategies toward the realization of liberation and justice.

Centering the Lordean erotic and Gill's elaboration of an erotic perspectival trinity within a conversation about streetwalking enables the articulation of how streetwalking intersects with political identities. This articulation enables us to think about how streetwalking is a malleable state, always shifting between sites/bodies, emerging and retreating as needed. As with same-sex desire, streetwalking emerges with the potential to be expressed. As with homophobic violence, streetwalking also coincides with the potential to be marked. To illustrate this relationship among erotic orientations, streetwalking, and political identities, I turn to Nina's story.

When I interviewed Nina, she identified as a lesbian, a Dominican, a feminist, and a healer. She was in her early sixties at the time. Nina breaks with a range of Dominican expectations of womanhood and femininity in her appearance, her desires, and her behaviors. She has facial hair, and she refuses to remove it. She wears loose clothing, usually pants, and does not use makeup. She is very light-skinned but understands herself as *Afro-descendiente*. At the time of our interview, Nina lived with her mother, whom she cared for both physically and financially. Nina is also a mother; her daughters both live in the U.S. Though at one time she was married to a man, Nina distinguishes between a time before and after she accepted (*asumio*) her desires for women and subsequently her identity as a lesbian. Nina was a teacher for many years and was active in the Dominican feminist movement throughout the 1980s and 1990s. After retiring from teaching, she decided to leave activism altogether and focus on healing work. Since the time of this interview, an oral history conducted in 2010, Nina has opened a national healing center and works with people in both the capital city of Santo Domingo and the northern provinces. Here she shares her experiences in taking on (*asumir*) a feminist identity, an identity that was both a precursor and simultaneous to the realization of her lesbian desire:

> When I went to my first Encuentro Feminista, I had not yet taken on the identity of feminist. I was deeply embedded within the Communist Party and the

Nina

women's committee in particular. See, that's how the political parties were
organized. The men ran as candidates for office, and women organized the
party press, meetings, and the logistics of the campaigns. But in 1981, the man
who was my mentor within the party changed my life. The United Nations
had announced the year of the woman in 1975, and in 1981, there was a Latin
American Feminist Encuentro. And the party felt that it was important to have
a presence at this conference, to ensure that there was party representation
within the larger hemispheric conversation. They also wanted me to strategize
with other women from the party who were also going [from other countries].
So I went as the Dominican Communist Party's women's committee representative. But when I got there, I was completely transformed by the conversation. Upon meeting feminist activists from across the hemisphere, I learned to
critique my position within the party. I became a feminist. And this [critical
development] occurred for many women who are part of the feminist movement here [in the D.R.].

Nina's feminist identity emerged through a process of transformation that
subsequently shifted the total range of possible desires on a deeply erotic level.
These shifts were mirrored in her realization of same-sex desire and in her critique of her own experience within her political party. After her return from
Colombia, Nina worked with the Communist Party for two more years until she
could no longer bear nor stand behind (*soportar*) the sexism of the *patriarcado*
(patriarchy). This first transformation in her erotic orientation was perhaps more
attainable than the realization of her same-sex desire, which would come many
years later, when, as Nina said, "I finally had the courage to leave my husband." As
she experienced the gradual and sometimes painful transformation in her political awareness, the personal toll emerging from the denial of her same-sex desires
and the perpetuation of a heterosexual marriage steeped in patriarchal political
mores (even left-wing ones) became too much for Nina. Though this is not the
case for everybody, the "chaos of [her] strongest feelings" (Lorde 1984, 54) about
her political possibilities produced through her shifting political consciousness
resulted in her identification as a feminist. Identifying as a feminist and seeking others who identified similarly produced additional political possibilities
that awakened her erotic orientations toward a feminist futurity grounded in a
broadened understanding of herself as an Afro-descendant woman.

Simultaneously, her shifting political consciousness intersected with her
attraction and desire for women, causing a profound shift in her personal
relationships—with her husband, her children, her mother, and all others.
Understanding herself as always in relation, Nina could no longer deny the
sources of her joy; she could no longer sustain the Christian colonial mechanisms that were diminishing her life and the potential lives of others. Nina's
story is a story of streetwalking—of an oppositional consciousness born out of

collective participation in *resistencia*, rooted in the shifts in erotic orientation produced through relationships.

Transforming Silence into Life and Protest

I have come to believe over and over again that what is most important to me must be spoken, made verbal and shared, even at the risk of having it bruised or misunderstood.

—Audre Lord, *Sister Outsider: Essays and Speeches*

Audre Lorde's talk "The Transformation of Silence into Language and Action" was first delivered at the 1977 Modern Language Association's Lesbian and Literature Panel in Chicago. The talk was later published in the seminal collection of Lorde's essays, *Sister Outsider*. In this talk, Lorde reveals how a recent cancer scare awakened her consciousness. This awakened consciousness produced a realization that she had to prioritize speech and speech acts in her struggle for liberation and truth. Facing death, Lorde states, "My silences had not protected me. Your silence will not protect you" (1984, 41). In other words, Lorde realized all that had yet to be spoken, to be said, to be articulated in a way that reached beyond her own internal conversations and consciousness. There were differences yet to be bridged and situations yet to be confronted. In a sense, this realization of the power of speech as action allowed Lorde to conceptualize that "within those weeks [of facing death] came the knowledge—within the war we are all waging with the forces of death, subtle and otherwise, conscious or not—I am not only a casualty, I am also a warrior" (41).

When I first embarked upon my research with LGBTQ activists in the D.R. in 2010, Carlos Decena's (2011) book *Tacit Subjects: Belonging and Same-Sex Desire among Dominican Migrant Men* was just going to press. Carlos and I had had the opportunity to meet, talk, share, and be a part of each other's lives as a result of our participation in the Transnational Hispaniola conference, which had taken place in the D.R. in June 2010. In addition to spending time together at the conference, we also went to scholar-activist Fatima Portorreal Liriano's house along with the art/literary critic and teacher Carolina González and the scholar Alaí Reyes Santos. At that gathering at Fatima's house, we pored over her copies of Rodolfo Kusch's (2007) *Obras completas*, ecstatic to encounter this out-of-print publication. As Fatima entertained us with raunchy stories of Dominican men and women negotiating sexuality in the *campos*, I prepared dinner (I like to cook), and Carlos spoke to me about his particular obsession with the idea of the subject as it is produced by language. I would later encounter his analysis of the differentiation between *ser* and *estar*, in which he builds on Kusch's arguments to generate the idea of the tacit subject, the subject produced through the quotidian navigation of respectability politics, masculinity, migration, and sex; the subject who becomes by being in the state of constant animation (*estar*) rather than by enunciation of being (*ser*); and tacit subjects as they are produced by silence and by the knowledge produced in that silence.

While I could relate to Carlos's theories and knew those subjects and had experienced these understandings of the world and states of being myself, I was also seeing and experiencing something else while in community with others in the D.R. Since 2000, when Jacqueline Jiménez Polanco and Mirla Hernández Núñez had come out on Dominican national television, since the first public LGBTQ gatherings in Santo Domingo, since the 2001 Feria Internacional del Libro, some Dominicans had been choosing to publicly articulate a visible and known LGBTQ presence. This is not to discount the previous two decades of LGBTQ community gathering, publication, and activism that had taken place in women's groups, at regional feminist conferences, through regional HIV advocacy, or between sex workers before the early 2000s. But there had been an explicit shift in Dominican society that produced the conditions by which small groups of people began to walk the street while mobilizing LGBTQ political identities. I wanted to understand this shift and, more explicitly, what our subjectivities could look like and what they could reveal about the potential for liberation in this present moment.

Those who are at odds with home

I build on Lorde's theorization of speech and the transformation of silence by adding Maria Lugones's theorization of streetwalking theorists as those "who are at odds with 'home'" (2003, 209). Bringing these two theories together enables me to present stories by and about Dominican LGBTQ activists to highlight the many ways streetwalking produces meaning and life. I build on the lessons I learned from Dominican LGBTQ activists about life and protest. For those of us who do not conform to Christian colonial biblical gender binaries and its attendant heterocomplimentarity, violence can erupt anywhere and at any time—at home (with our families), in institutional spaces (schools, hospitals, utility companies, borders), and on the street. In these ways, "home is lived as a place inseparable from other places of violence, including the street" (Lugones 2003, 209). Streetwalking ruptures and exposes Christian colonial public/private spatial dichotomies because those of us streetwalking bring into the public that which is supposed to be private, tucked away, masked, and unknown/unknowable: sex, sexuality, sexual desire, and unabashed sexual joy and multigendered possibilities.

Streetwalking also points to the ways in which subjectivity itself is a relational construct located in the everyday and everywhere—for example, when we walk down the street. It draws attention to how one "makes sense among and with others, and also how its absence [the absence of sense] renders one's words, gestures, movements nonsensical" (Lugones 2003, 219). Streetwalking includes those whose actions do not abide by the possibilities enabled by dominant institutions and discourses—in the case of the D.R., of the Catholic Hispanic nation-state and Christian colonial notions of personhood.

Streetwalking encompasses the lives and work of Dominican LGBTQ activists. Why, I asked myself, did LGBTQ activists emerge in the D.R.—a society in which multiple, often conflicting, understandings of gender and sexuality generate other possibilities, including tacit subjectivities? The idea of streetwalking opens up the possibility of conceptualizing how streetwalking functions "as a chemical catalyst so as to bring to light power relations, locate their position, and find out their point of application and the methods used" (Foucault 1982, 780). Streetwalking renders the many different power relations existent within Dominican society very visible. LGBTQ identities function as one of several strategies for the management and transformation of those same power relations. To engage in streetwalking is to refuse silence.

RESISTANCE, *RESISTENCIA*

Resistencia is a critical embodiment that is knowable through streetwalking, through the practices of actively transforming silence—verbal, bodily, spiritual—into power. Streetwalking is "the unspecified term that lies outside the binary configuration of domination and subordination" (Sandoval 2000, 162). Streetwalking elucidates existing relationships and exercises of power that can either perpetuate or constrain life, producing what Chela Sandoval calls differential oppositional consciousness. For Sandoval, "differential oppositional social movement and consciousness represent constructivist functions that perceive power as their world space, and identity as the monadic unit of power via subjectivity capable of negotiating and transforming power's configurations" (2000, 179). Streetwalking allows us to embody a mode of differential consciousness through life and protest, specifically and explicitly because we can upend and reconfigure Christian colonial expectations, boundaries, and structures central to maintaining the Catholic Hispanic nation-state.

Thinking about my experiences in community with Dominican LGBTQ activists and the reasons I returned again and again over many years to these places, spaces, and moments of community, I know that all I have to give in return for their generosity are stories: stories that seek to evoke a modicum of the electric collective effervescence of community spaces, stories that yearn to make sense of the powerful ways in which we move through the world. This book is merely that: a collection of historical, ethnographic, and theoretical stories that reflect my own experiences and what I have learned about power in the face of ongoing and multiple forms of violence. I would like to be able to say that my lesbian friends root their humanity solely in the intimate and collective moments of realized desire; I would like to be able to say that my trans* friends understand their personhood solely through the realization of their personal and collective truths; I would like to say that my gay friends understand life solely through the joy of unbridled *communitas*. And while it is certainly true that humanity, personhood, and life happen through desire, realization, and *communitas*, I also cannot deny the intensity of violence in shaping our experiences in the everyday and over lifetimes. As Gerardo, a gay interlocutor asked, "¿Si no nos tiran chinas, no somos maricones?" (If they don't pelt us with oranges, does it mean we are not gay?). His story is presented here in chapter 3.

I have thought about Gerardo's question for many years. The image of having oranges thrown at one's person is a metaphor for violence. However, it is also a metaphor that evokes the image of audiences throwing tomatoes at a failed performance. In this sense, orange throwing becomes a metaphor for the failed performance of Christian colonial manhood or womanhood and the failed performance of heterosexuality/normativity. This metaphor also indexes all the possible spaces in which one could have an orange thrown: on the street, on the stage, at home, at school, and so on. But what could Gerardo's question evoke for *maricconas* like me? One, I don't need to have an orange thrown at me to know I am a *maricona*—and a *marimacha* to boot. Two, *marimacha* is both something I am and something I do; it is others who have taught me that being and doing *marimacha* threatens something they hold dear. Thus the threat of having oranges thrown is always present because of the fear of my difference. Three, as a result of this interpellation, I learned early on that my likelihood of experiencing violence is high because I am unabashedly a *marimacha*. Four, being an unabashed *marimacha* and having oranges thrown at me has taught me valuable life lessons about both the forces that produced the orange throwing and my own capacity to resist the forces that produced the orange throwing. And finally, the many ways I choose to resist those forces has produced an erotic orientation rooted in oppositional consciousness: a different way of knowing, doing, and being "conceivable as an interrelating set of subjectivities and social movements in resistance to dominating powers" (Sandoval 2000, 145) that would otherwise not exist if one, two, three, and four were not true.

Resistance—and its Spanish iteration, *resistencia*—offers one broad possibility for conceptualizing the modes of oppositional consciousness I also name as streetwalking. Resistance and *resistencia* originate with the Latin term *resistire*, meaning "to remain firm." In English, resistance contains multiple meanings: it can be a refusal to accept or comply, and it can also imply the use of force in the opposition of one person to another or the ability to not be affected by the actions of others. In the sciences, it is used as a concept to describe the limiting action of one force or substance on another. *Resistencia* also signals the capacity—that is, the potential a person or group of people have to contain or endure the external oppositional forces or pressures imposed by others. *Resistencia* implies the capacity to act, which in Western epistemologies signals individuated personhood. But here I would like us to consider Lugones's theorization of how acting, as part and parcel of active subjectivity, "does not presuppose the individual subject and it does not presuppose collective intentionality of collectivities of the same" (Lugones 2003, 6). When we reconceptualize subjectivities beyond the idea of the individual/individuated subject, then *resistencia* must also be reconceptualized: the capacity to act is predicated on the capacity to conceptualize the self as always already in relation. *Resistencia* signals our capacity to endure the violences of multiple external forces and, through that endurance, to maintain the potential to live and protest as selves who are always already members of an imagined and/or actualized collectivity (Rodríguez Morel 2011).

Jafari S. Allen writes, "Whatever our vision for progressive or revolutionary politics, counterhegemony rests on the recognition of one's own self, intentions, and desires. In order for there to be resistance—whether in the form of a planned strategy or improvised tactic—we must have a thinking, desiring, decision-making subject" (2011, 80). But what happens when that singular subject articulates itself as always already in relation with others, as is the case with Dominican LGBTQ activists? The concept of the self as always already in relation is important to understanding the mobilization of *resistencia*. There are many theorizations of this kind of personhood. For example, the African philosophical concept of *ubuntu*, as a self "defined in relation to a larger social or ethnic group which encompasses not only the living but also the dead, the spirits, and the unborn" (Kochalumchuvattil 2010, 112), helps clarify our understanding of how *resistencia* is not only a question of individual agency acting on behalf of one's own interests only but also about the expression of multitudinous, pluralistic desire and thought.

In her speech "Transforming Silence into Power," Lorde locates the primary site of resistance in speech and writing. She argues that to speak goes beyond merely resisting: it produces the possibilities of shaping reality for ourselves and beyond ourselves. In this way, Lorde gives valence to speech as a central component of agentive action, an exercise of power that, as Michel Foucault states, "is a way in which certain actions modify others" (1982, 788). Lorde argues not only that speech is a form of action but also that for oppressed people, speech as an action that contributes to the shaping of reality is central to our survival. Speech—and the transformation of those silences produced through the endurance of violence—actualizes our potential to live and to survive. To speak is to render ourselves, our lives, and our struggles visible. The actualization of our speech as simultaneously individual and collective agentive action further enables individual and collective survival and life, producing new realities that were, though always there, existing while enduring violence. It is the collectivization of individual speech—through the multiple tactical strategies that will be discussed in this text—that enables us to register Dominican LGBTQ activists' use of protest as a mode of *resistencia*.

In anthropology, James C. Scott's theorization of resistance has been particularly reiterated. Scott's theories of resistance primarily address the "infrapolitical"—that is, the "subterranean world[s] of political conflict which left scarcely a trace in the public record . . . *the prevailing genre of* day-to-day politics for most of the world's disenfranchised, for all those living in autocratic settings, for the peasantry, and for those living as subordinates in patriarchal families . . . a politics that 'dare not speak its name,' a diagonal politics, a careful and evasive politics that avoided dangerous risks, a politics quite in keeping with the reputation of the peasantry for 'cunning'" (1990, 112). Within the infrapolitical, the powerless mask themselves in the face of power, enabling subjects to mobilize hidden transcripts that redirect, undermine, and resituate what he calls "public transcripts" (2).

The collective unmasking by Dominican LGBTQ activists is the primary subversion of the idea of sex and sexuality as something that is done in private between two people. That unmasking produces a "visibility that makes us most vulnerable [and] which also is the source of our greatest strength" (Lorde 1984, 42). In the Dominican context, to be elucidated here, the violences of the Catholic Hispanic nation-state have produced a series of counter acts by LGBTQ activists that break with culturally acceptable tacit subjectivities to produce a collective unmasking, streetwalking. In this sense, being seen and having visibility are strategies that seek to undo the harm produced by the violence that forced others like us to hide, to die, to change our names, and even to leave.

Resistencia among Dominican LGBTQ activists in many cases ruptures the infrapolitical through an unmasked appropriation of all spheres of sociality. This unmasking produces *confrontaciones* (encounters) with one's self, family, friends, communities, churches, and the broader Dominican society. These *confrontaciones*, in turn, produce new possibilities for LGBTQ life. What are these possibilities? Maybe Thalia can dress in a way that feels good to her every day, despite other's limited and incorrect perception that she is a man. Maybe Mirla won't have to fear that someone will find out she is a lesbian and, as a result, fire her from her job.

Maybe Gerardo won't be sent to jail because he was hanging out with gay people at the park. Maybe Deivis can go to church with his mother because he really loves the church he grew up in. Maybe Nairobi won't be spit on when she walks down the street. Maybe men won't threaten lesbians with rape when they walk down the street holding hands. Maybe none of us will have to worry that we will be jailed, beaten, or killed because of someone's misogyny, homophobia, or transphobia. These stories seem so cliché when written here. But they are real possibilities embodied in the experiences of real people who, unmasked, engaged in a multitude of strategies of *resistencia*. Their examples speak to how unmasking and the transformation of silence produces the possibility of naming the ways in which power produces everyday and structural violences—components of what I theorize here as sexual terror. Sexual terror relies on the mobilization of Christian colonial discourses about moral gender and sexual norms, about the nation-state's exercise and amplification of these Christian colonial discourses, and about contemporary negotiations among Dominicans about the place of these norms and discourses in the present and future of Dominican personhood.

Building on Lugones's concepts of active subjectivity as a subjectivity that relies on the multiplicity and relationality of the self and streetwalker theorists as those who "valorize the logics of resistance" (2003, 175) while simultaneously reconfiguring the relations of power, I suggest that streetwalking is a malleable disposition, an agency that shifts between sites/bodies, emerging and retreating as needed. It is not stuck in place to a particular body or set of bodies, to a specific site or set of sites, to the individual, or to the collectivity. It moves neither forward to a transcendent future nor unidirectionally toward a certain end. It is a potentiality because it signals the potential to agentively streetwalk or to incidentally be marked as someone who is streetwalking. Streetwalking enables us to conceptualize responses to sexual terror as part of a collective, temporally complex set of iterations and potentialities. Streetwalking allows us to see the acts of *resistencia* mobilized in collectivity against Christian colonial sexual terror that in turn produces new possibilities for personhood.

Etymologically speaking, the concept of *resistencia* is about our capacity to stand firmly in place. However, in the context of a Catholic Hispanic nation-state, *resistencia* has accumulated a different set of meanings, sometimes requiring standing firmly in place and at other times requiring mobilization, movement, and action. In this text, *resistencia* is also explicitly about enabling the perpetuation of life, sometimes at the cost of life. The concept recalls the histories and historicization of *quilombos, palenques, manieles,* maroon communities, and contemporary indigenous and Afro-diasporic land struggles;[14] the histories of black struggle against European colonial forces, resulting in manumission, emancipation, and abolition; the histories of Latin American communist struggles and revolutions; and the histories of armed struggle and collective resistance to authoritarian regimes. *Resistencia* also encompasses the multiple dimensions of refusal: the refusal to accept the conditions one finds oneself in, the refusal to accept others' categorizations of oneself, the refusal to comply with social expectations, the refusal to act accordingly. It requires an examination of our capacity to think, speak, and act through and against the forces of repression, oppression, and violence.

Therefore, an ethnographic work such as what is presented here, which seeks to challenge the premises of Eurocentrism and U.S. imperial dictates about what LGBTQ-ness (and Dominicanness) should be while also articulating the theoretical flesh of Christian coloniality, is about managing the multiple discourses of being and belonging that streetwalking *also* requires us to navigate. Streetwalking is a practice of the simultaneity of being, employing multiple discourses across multiple registers as we "learn, listen, transmit information, participat[e] in communicative creations, [and] gauge the possibilities" (Lugones 2003, 209) at our disposal. Through all these movements across register, discourse, and being, an "ethnography of refusal" (Simpson 2014) provides the methodological space from which to consider Dominican LGBTQ life and protest as streetwalking and streetwalking as a series of narratives that actualize what life and protest are, have been, or might be.

Streetwalking is about refusing to be silent, refusing to conform to social expectations, refusing to cave to stereotypes and violence, and refusing the Christian colonial moral proclamations *and* imperial categories and ideologies of personhood that emerge through Christian colonial processes. For the LGBTQ activists I worked with, life and protest are also about refusing to succumb to both Christian coloniality and the tragedies of Dominican historiography—a historiography that continues to collude with the impulses and futurities of a Catholic Hispanic nation-state. They are about a subtle dance between different discourses and political avenues that include rights, laws, and the human while also drawing from complex affective and spiritual understandings of relationship and personhood. As I will explore in this book, many of the strategies of *resistencia* among Dominican LGBTQ activists emerge from a "knowledge archive structured through prior languages and experiences of exclusion and inclusion that are tethered . . . to historical processes" (Simpson 2014, 15): as the descendants of enslaved Indigenous and African peoples, as continuously persecuted peoples, as peoples struggling to maintain family lineages under the oppression of a fundamentalist Catholic Hispanic nation-state, as peoples living in bodies that breach the codes of biblical manhood and womanhood. In this way, we can understand that the experiences of sexual terror are not just about sexuality but about how sexuality, gender, race, and nationalism are materially and morally co-constituted through Christian colonial ideologies. Streetwalking can be liberatory for all of us—if we dare to acknowledge the potential that anyone we encounter on the street has the capacity to rupture Christian colonial moral imperatives that constrain, rather than enable, life.

M. Jacqui Alexander reminds us that "activism is an ongoing process through which we create and re-create ourselves in community and have to learn, to practice and to think justice all at once" (2005, 130). Creating, re-creating, learning, practicing, and thinking justice implies that we are oriented toward liberation, toward a destabilization of the structures and modes of power that limit our lives in the first place. LGBTQ activists in the D.R. teach us about the power of transforming silence into action.

An "In the Life / On the Street" Methodology

As an author exercising scholarly authority, I am particularly attentive to the power of my words within the broader context of Dominican LGBTQ lives and protest. I find particular inspiration in Lorde's example. She states,

For those of us who write, it is necessary to scrutinize not only the truth of what we speak, but the truth of that language by which we speak it. For others, it is to share and spread also those words that are meaningful to us. But primarily for us all, it is necessary to teach by living and speaking those truths which we believe and know beyond understanding. Because in this way alone we can survive, by taking part in a process of life that is creative and continuing, that is growth. And it is never without fear—of visibility, of the harsh light of scrutiny and perhaps judgment, of pain, of death. But we have lived through all of those already, in silence, except death. (1984, 43)

Writing this book is about much more than the writing itself: it is about speaking my particular experiences of visibility and power in community and conversation with others who—like me—choose to assume a political identity as a lesbian (or gay, bisexual or trans*) despite all the forces that punish us or seek to eliminate us. It is taking seriously the implications of publishing a book with a title that places LGBTQ squarely in the center, just above my name. Central to this mobilization of authorial power is an engagement with the politics of refusal.

As Juana Maria Rodríguez points out, "A politics of refusal has a long history in feminist of color scholarship. . . . [It] remains an operative mode of analysis that demands, rather than forecloses, futurity" (2011, 333). Rodríguez draws on Jafari S. Allen's theorizations of refusal and rearticulates them as the very necessary "temporal, spatial, and relational orientations" (2011, 313) that produce real recognition for queer black subjects. She adds that refusal (i.e., negating what negates us) is both central and necessary to queer temporalities and subjectivities that counter the ongoing "violence of state and social erasure" (333). Adding to conversations about the politics of refusal, Audra Simpson demonstrates the many ways "accounts that became histories which dialectically informed theories, which then emboldened the laws of nation-states" (2007, 70), dispossess the very people who become objectified through those analytic processes. In other words, she points to how the production of knowledge within multisited colonial spaces fortifies ongoing colonial-imperial processes of absorption, assimilation, dispossession, and deterritorialization. In this sense, a "politics of refusal" and attention to the "ethnographic refusals" of my friends and interlocutors are central to the ways in which I narrate my research findings. I bring these analytics into my own work in order to consider how streetwalking is also about politically refusing Christian colonial categorical thinking and modes of being, even as some of those categories are mobilized in the service of liberation.

Relatedly, through my own ethnographic refusals—that is, a refusal to engage in particular conversations that would satisfy imperial-colonial gazes but diminish my own and others' autonomy—this book considers the management of silence/silencing and disruptions to silence.

In my research, I purposely followed the lead of LGBTQ activist interlocutors—specifically that cadre of radical lesbian activists who sat on benches with me, asking me to look elsewhere. Though eventually they did agree to and welcome my questions and my research, their agreement was conditioned by their ethnographic refusal of the anthropological project of objectification through the structuring of sexual subjectivities. They agreed to speak with me because I made it clear that I would be turning my gaze away from any sort of analysis about what Dominican sexuality or gender may be and onto the Christian colonial processes that contextualize and produce Dominican LGBTQ protest. Honoring our friendships, therefore, is about making visible my own location with regards to their local struggle. At stake in their refusals at the limits of discourse—the places where conversation stops, where enough has been spoken—are the very real lives of Dominican LGBTQ activists, people who have made an active decision to make their lives public, to unmask, to rupture society's gender and sexual expectations in order to make known that which is always known/unknown. At stake are the issues of life and death among my LGBTQ friends and other streetwalking friends, their families, and communities across the D.R.

In writing as a lesbian scholar born in the D.R. and currently based in the U.S., I am particularly attentive to how my words are being scrutinized and legitimized by the vetting authorities of the U.S. academy. Streetwalking myself, this process pains me, because I have a deep-seated, innate rejection of Western colonial processes of authentication and authorization. My sense of place in the world is born out of a differential consciousness that is always aware of "the fragility of sense, at every step conscious of recognition or lack of it, searching for back up, aware of the lack of institutional back up at every turn" (Lugones 2003, 219). Particularly because the U.S. academy relies on a limited set of frameworks that are reified over and over again, I struggle to be intelligible in the world where I (my existence) do not make sense. I say this even as I acknowledge that my own thinking is in part shaped by this system and its epistemological frameworks. My position is also informed by my experiences and formation as a lesbian: to be able to assume my own lesbian identity, I had to and continue to fly in the face of all the systems, institutions, and expectations imposed by U.S. and Dominican societies. I continue to walk the streets—on and off campus, despite all the violences present. So given my own attitudes about the U.S. academy and Western knowledge production, it wasn't surprising to me when those in the LGBTQ community in the D.R. also rejected being objectified.

I am deeply attentive to how my positionality and writing are being scrutinized by LGBTQ activists in the D.R.—folks who are critically attuned to and vocal about having authority over their own narratives. When I first began my research, lesbian activists met my desire to write about their lives and work with a simple retort: "Why don't you write about Dominican women returning to the island?" They were asking me to write about myself. Why did I return? they wanted to know. Why did I come back when I had an entire life off the island? I should scrutinize my own motivations, they said, and focus on myself. So we talked late into the night on public benches in the parks. I have access to intellectual and material resources, I said. What is the cost of accessing those resources for us? they retorted. The Dominican LGBTQ struggle is important to my own life—wherever I am in the world, I said. Why? they asked. We have a lot to learn from Dominican LGBTQ political discourses and strategies, I said. My friends laughed at me. We are just doing what we have to do to survive, Mirla said. *Interesante* (drawn out, quiet), said Elena. I laughed. Fine, I said. What do you want me to write about? What will help the movement? Anything that gets the church off our backs, they said. OK, I can try that, I responded.

So here I am—writing in English about a community that lives and protests mostly in Spanish, sometimes in Kreyol. Language is both a barrier and a stepping-stone. For years, Fatima and I have gotten into arguments about language. These arguments usually happen when we go to the movies together. Since most of the movies in Dominican theaters are from the U.S., they are usually in English and are often subtitled, requiring monolingual Spanish speakers to read while watching. This provokes Fatima to make proclamations about how she refuses to speak English because it is an imperial language. Though I agree with her political position, I usually retort that Spanish is too. We have been having this argument for twenty years. We eventually realize that we are both stuck with authorizing knowledge in imperial-colonial languages. And yet we also both know that there is an understanding, a knowing that is beyond language itself. At different phases of my writing, I have had to face the ways in which writing in English may make my work inaccessible to the very people that matter to me. Most of the activists I know and interact with do know and read English, even as they refuse to speak it. When I sent them copies of my dissertation (before it was submitted and after) or of articles (before they were published), these copies were in English. And they are read and responded to despite the fact that they were in English. But others will not be able to read my work—in some cases not just because it is in English but because it is written. Because the Dominican education system actively discriminates against children who do not conform to biblically binary gender norms or heterosexual expectations, some of my friends in the LGBTQ community cannot read or write. This makes the project of writing suspect and yet, as an action, even more necessary; it is a transformation of what is loudly shouted on the streets into the two-dimensionality of text.

Lorde reminds us that "in the transformation of silence into language and action, it is vitally necessary for each one of us to establish or examine her function in that transformation and to recognize her role as vital within that transformation" (1984, 43). This book is a midpoint between the many conversations and observations that took place between myself and Dominican LGBTQ activists between 2010 and 2015 and the many conversations that remain to be had in public fora, between friends, and into the future. Despite all my trepidation and the many risks I am taking in writing this text, this work is vital. It is not just vital in the sense of being necessary. It is vital in that it is full of life. It is vital in that it will live beyond this present moment when I sit writing it. And it will die too. There will come a point, hopefully, when this work is not necessary. When its arguments are of another time and place. When the realities of streetwalking reflect another set of truths and other horizons of power.

Streetwalking is my response to the many late-night discussions with Dominican LGBTQ interlocutors in 2010 and 2011. These discussions generally took place on the benches of public parks or while walking through the streets of La Zona. Surrounded by Catholic Hispanic architecture and institutions, we were constantly reminded of our own vulnerabilities. It is because of my friends' struggles with the Catholic Hispanic nation-state and the impact of that nation-state on their lives that I first took up questions about the relationship between Christianity and sexuality, Christianity and activism, and Christianity and nation-states. Because so much of the time spent in LGBTQ community was always in the literal shadows of the church, our conversations greatly informed the direction of my research. This is intentional. Informed by my use of an "in-the-life / on-the-streets methodology," I purposely focus on the priorities of the communities with whom I lived, played, worked, and streetwalked. An "in-the-life / on-the-streets" methodology allows me to create critical scholarship that broadens the scope of what our collective lives "in the life" can be from the point of view of what "being on the streets" can show me. Being in the life is being "in the life" on the street.

The concept of an "in-the-life / on-the-street" methodology emerges from an understanding of the streets as malleable spaces where meaning is constructed through interaction, relationship, exchange, and hanging out. The street, though mapped, is not determinate. Streets are also places and spaces of conflict, violence, and quotidian negotiations of authority and power. Life on the streets is both beautiful and dangerous. Making community on the streets inverts our relationship to home and disrupts the neoliberal logics that construct home as a space apart from the public, from others, and from broader social, political, and economic forces.

In his book In the Life: A Black Gay Anthology, Joseph Beam writes, "In the life, a phrase used to describe 'street life' (the lifestyle of pimps, prostitutes, hustlers, and drug dealers) is also the phrase used to describe the 'gay life' (the lives of Black homosexual men and women). Street life and gay life, at times, embrace and entwine, yet at other times, are precise opposites" ([1986] 2008, xviii). The phrase "in the life" specifically and intentionally centers black gay life as the primary lexicon of being. Juxtaposed with the quote "All the women are white, all the blacks are men, but some of us are brave" (Hull, Bell-Scott, and Smith 1982), the application of the phrase "in the life" indexes black gay life as a complex, holistic experience. It also points to the ways in which black(queer)ness is still silenced, invisible, criminalized, and marginalized—on a global scale.

For me, coming into gayness, into this life, was also about coming into blackness and, at times, Dominicanness and yet, at other times, Latinidad. It was all these things, sometimes concentrated in some respects more than others and, at other times, all at once. Therefore, when I decided to go to the D.R.—at first to study the work of lesbian artists—I knew no other way to be gay than to enter "into the life" as lived by young Dominican lesbian activists, hanging out. Being "on the street" allowed me to hang out deeply (Allen 2011, 7). Lugones writes, "Hanging out permits one to learn, to listen, to transmit information, to participate in communicative creations, to gauge possibilities, to have a sense of the directions of intentionality, to gain social depth. Unlike enclosures of the social that are conceived as less permeable, hangouts are highly permeable" (2003, 209). Hanging out was an active, engaged way of being and living with others (Lara 2014). This included hanging out at parks, going to clubs, going away together on the weekends, attending parties, and entering into the daily and exceptional dramas of lesbian couples. It included entering into the world of gay and trans* *supervivencia* (living against expectation) and activism, gay sociality, gay and trans* economies, and gay and trans* spaces, as well as separate women's spaces. It also included being in the life in *palos* drum celebrations, *velaciones* (prayer ceremonies), healing ceremonies, funerals, human rights forums, film festivals, political actions, and conferences. It was being my full self and manifesting the breadth of my spirit in the presence of other spirits. Being in the life was a way of breathing, of learning to recognize myself all over again as a person of diaspora returned home while also seeing and learning to recognize others who are in the life with me. I was returning with my "spyglass" (Hurston [1935] 1990), searching for insights into new questions about what it means to be black and a woman and gay and free in the twenty-first century. Hanging out not only allowed me to be "in the life" with others; it also contributed to my capacity to read and understand the many tactical strategies that streetwalking enables us to employ in our day-to-day (or night-to-night) lives. Some of the tactical strategies that I will explore in this book include *confrontación*, flipping the script, and telling *cuentos* (stories). At the center of each of these tactical strategies are embodied transformations of silence into action, conducted in a context that is also always under the Christian colonial gaze.

In the D.R., being in the life is living between the images of black queerness present (*RuPaul's Drag Race*) and absent within broader depictions of white gay sociality (*Will and Grace*) portrayed through international media, living between the expectations of an international LGBTQ human rights movement and the realities of a local Dominican understanding of sexuality, living between everyone else's ideas of development and the on-the-ground desires of Dominican people.

Measured against the Global North's colonial-imperial gaze, Dominicans—like their counterparts throughout the Caribbean—always fall short. For Dominican LGBTQ activists, then, this translates into never being the right kind of black, or the right kind of gay, or the right kind of modern. As one dark-skinned gay man expressed to me, "Gay men come from *afuera* and they think they are coming to a jungle" (interview, R.R., May 2013). Being in the life in the D.R., then, is not always legible along the same lines as black *quare* (Johnson and Henderson 2005) personhood in the U.S. E. Patrick Johnson theorizes that *quare* is "from the African American vernacular for queer; sometimes homophobic in usage, but always denotes excess incapable of being contained within conventional categories of *being*; 3. One who *thinks* and *feels* and *acts* (and sometimes 'acts up'); committed to struggle against all forms of oppression—racial, sexual, gender, class religious, etc.; 4. One for whom sexual and gender identities always already intersect with racial subjectivity" (2001, 125). *Streetwalking* traces the ways in which streetwalking disrupts distinct contexts and histories of Christian coloniality in the D.R. as LGBTQ activists move through *el ambiente*.

In Spanish, the idea of "in the life" gets transformed into *del ambiente* (interview, Junior, May 2013). Being *del ambiente*—of the environment—assumes being in the current of everyday life shared by everyone else while also entering *al ambiente* of LGBTQ sociality. Being *del ambiente* is about *supervivencia* as LGBTQ, as HIV-affected persons, as sex workers, and as activists while also *haciendo una vida* (making a life) within the special and specific spaces of the street, the club, the *enramada* (ceremonial arbor), the *palos* ceremonies, the church, and the park. Similar to the phrase "in the life" in English, *del ambiente* as used by LGBTQ persons, both activists and not, is a fierce declaration of living and belonging—being of a place where one finds oneself.

Being *del ambiente* is also about being *en familia* (in family), what Juana Maria Rodríguez (2003) describes as a queer community-building process. Metaphors of *familia* abound, and as I continued in the life / on the street, terms such as *hermana* (sister) and *prima* (cousin) emerged as relational identifiers to describe me in relation to others. At times, if I inquired about whether someone knew someone else, the response I would receive was "*Fulano*? He's my brother; of course I know him." Activists who work intensely together refer to each other in sibling terminologies not always because people are building alternate families but because relationships signaled by the use of these terms are understood to be intimate and productive of specific kinds of personhood. Together, being in the life and *de familia* create complex webs of relation based on spending time together, caring for each other, laughing together, dancing together, witnessing together, being together, and knowing this—together.

Throughout the time of my research, it was important for me not only to be "in the life" but to also be attentive to the boundaries set out by others "in the life" and "on the streets" with me and to be attentive to the ways in which

Dominican LGBTQ activists actively refused my categories, my questions, or my perspectives. Their ethnographic refusal was central to my own process of discernment. I would not go where others did not guide me to go, but I was also very self-reflexive in my negotiation as someone who had left—as someone who was "no longer Dominican," as one lesbian activist said to me. As a researcher in the life—even when I was recognized as a *prima* or *hermana*—I was also generally made aware of my difference. Sometimes because I used outdated slang words, or spoke with a slight American accent, or composed sentences strangely. At other times because my perspectives were so different from the collective perspectives of those around me. And yet at other times because I didn't follow social codes and cues. It didn't matter if I felt like I was home; sometimes if I challenged others just a little too much (something that would happen in the course of debates or conversation), the recognition of me as a part of the community was immediately revoked. These moments taught me about the boundaries of Dominican LGBTQ life—the places I could enter and the places I would never be able to enter because I had not grown up in the D.R. and because I could leave.

Because of these factors, even if I pushed against the boundaries of what was OK to talk about, I would do it with attention to the signs of when I had pushed enough. In other words, there were some streets I could not walk down as who I was in those moments.

Lastly, because I was in fact moving back and forth between the D.R. and the U.S., I also maintained my relationships long distance—through social media, email, and video calls. I kept abreast of news and incidents through the same vehicles but also kept an attentive record of news articles and reports. Many things are not reported on, especially events that have a major impact on my Dominican LGBTQ friends. Newspapers actively participate in spectacular displays of homophobic violence, including (and especially) the murder of famous gay men and those not so well known. However, the day-to-day abuses of police, doctors, business owners, university professors, and the general public and the deaths of trans* women, gay men and lesbians, and in some cases sex workers were largely unreported by the Dominican media. To find out about these experiences, I had to rely on LGBTQ media—disseminated through online video platforms and social media—and LGBTQ friends. These spaces of sociality and information sharing were important not just to me; they were ways in which we could keep abreast of each other's lives and work, mobilize for protests and gatherings, and learn language and frameworks for making sense of our experiences of quotidian and institutional violence.

On Naming

Naming is a complex task that always runs the risk of diminishing or mislocating peoples' understanding of themselves, their communities, and histories.

This task is made increasingly difficult in *Streetwalking* because I am traversing the landscapes of U.S. critical race theories, Latin American decolonial theories, Dominican historiography, and twenty-first-century ethnography. My naming schema is imperfect. It does not seek to be perfect. Instead, I have sought to be true to the language my interlocutors use, while also making some decisions on my own about the ways in which I am choosing to challenge contemporary racial, sexual, and gender discourses.

When I speak about Afro-descendant people in the D.R., U.S. hegemonic and Dominican ultranationalist ideas about blackness delimit the narrow boundaries within which Dominican conceptualizations of blackness can be articulated. Though elsewhere, I (as well as many others)[15] have attempted to rupture these boundaries, in this text, I choose to move through the complex iterations of Dominican blackness using a variety of terms. I use the term *negro* (in Spanish) to signal the language developed through Spanish Christian colonial discourse. I use *Afro-descendant/Afro-descendiente* to encompass black and *mulatta* identities, but there are times when I also use *black* or *Afro-diasporic* as synonymous terms for the ways in which "organizations, scholars, and activists reposition the Dominican Republic within the context of the African diaspora recognizing a common thread of global Blackness, and what it means, historically and contemporaneously" (Simmons 2012, 123).

When I make recourse to the term *streetwalking*, I am referencing my own theorization of Dominican LGBTQ lives and protest. Though some Dominican LGBTQ activists may refer to themselves as streetwalkers (*callejeras/callejeros/callejeres*) in a variety of contexts, they may reject this language too. This is a term I am using to theorize the many lessons Dominican LGBTQ activists have taught me about *resistencia*. I use the term *streetwalking* to encompass those who live, walk through, and make meaning at "the margins of common sense: the outlaw, the despised, the useless, the insane, the hustlers, the poachers, the pickers of garbage, the urban nomads of the reconstituted spatiality of the cityscapes" (Lugones 2003, 219). Streetwalking denotes how all those who walk on the streets carry within us the potential to become marginal to the social order. It also signals the transit between sites of being and knowing and refuses the categorical structuring of personhood—whether across gender, sexual, racial, national, class, or any other lines.

I explicitly use the acronym LGBTQ—lesbian, gay, bisexual, trans*, and *quír*—throughout this text because that is how Dominican LGBTQ activists refer to themselves. Because the use of LGBTQ is an intentional decision by activists, I have used this as the overarching term to identify those community activists who were my primary interlocutors. My intentional operationalization of streetwalking as the entry point into political subjectivity dislocates static identity as the starting point for conceptualizing being. However, my intentional use of LGBTQ signals my interlocutors' intentional use of that same set of categories as part and parcel of their political subjectivities.

INTRODUCTION 37

The activists I worked with explicitly rejected *queer* as an imperial imposition from the Global North.[16] In turn, *quír* functions as a reappropriation and resituation of the term *queer* in Spanish, similar to Johnson's use of the word *quare*. As in Johnson's definition, *quír*—as used by my interlocutors—relocates the center of Dominican LGBTQ beingness within a matrix of knowledge and being that stands outside of mainstream white, northern conceptualizations of queerness, even as it draws from and transits through global imaginaries. *Quír* signals what Cathy Cohen describes as "a new political identity that is truly liberating, transformative, and inclusive of all those who stand on the outside of the dominant constructed norm of state-sanctioned white middle- and upper-class [Christian colonial] heterosexuality" (2001, 441).

Dominican LGBTQ activists also use the terms *loca, maricona, macha, machorra, pájaro, rara, raro, patas,* and so on. These terms carry pejorative and violent meanings, so I only use them here when they are part of someone's speech act. Relatedly, trans* activists use "trans*" as a third gender identifier—as in man, woman, trans*. Therefore, at times, trans* may appear as "Dumont is trans*" (similar to Gerardo is gay or Mary is black), or as "Junior is a trans* activist." I use trans* with the asterisk as a nod to the many gendered possibilities within trans* iterations.[17]

The names of my interlocutors have all been changed with two exceptions: when their names have been used in public forums and films and when they have asked or authorized me to use their names. In a context where their real names are not legitimated by the Catholic Hispanic nation-state, trans* activists insisted that I use their real names. The understanding of self-chosen names as the point of realness speaks to the transformation of the terms through which life is produced. It is not the government name that determines one's name; it is *el ambiente* and one's relationship with others *en la calle* that produces the meaning under which one's self (and name) comes into being. As Dumont explained to me, "We are out and proud to be [*de ser*] trans*. We stand behind what we say" (correspondence, October 2014).

THE CHAPTERS

Streetwalking is divided into two sections. The first, "Street Smarts," deals with the broader discursive and social structures (in all their temporal dimensionality) that LGBTQ activists in the D.R. must also deal with. Here, I frame the streets as sites for the ongoing production of Christian coloniality and its attendant sexual terror. In the first chapter of this section, "Christian Coloniality," I delve into a Foucauldian archaeological discussion about Christianity and its relationship to the Catholic Hispanic nation-state. I provide context for the many incidents of sexual terror experienced by my LGBTQ friends and interlocutors. I argue that all our readily accepted categories of moral personhood are ensconced in

stian colonial notions of heterocomplimentary biblical manhood and wom-
hood. I locate streetwalking within the Christian colonial geographies of the
Catholic Hispanic nation-state. Within these geographies, discourses of *moralidad pública* are an important tool for the development and perpetuation of
sexual terror, especially when it is mobilized to control streetwalking within public spaces. This section is dedicated to providing a deeper contextualization for
the theorization of streetwalking and the articulation of the strategies used by
LGBTQ activists in the enactment of *resistencia*. In the second chapter of this
section, "Sexual Terror," I articulate the myriad structural formations that produce sexual terror. I discuss how Christian coloniality circulates through international, national, and local geographies to perpetuate the logics of sexual terror
produced through Christian coloniality.

In the second section of this book, "Streetwalking," I explore the various
strategies of streetwalking that enable *resistencia*. The three primary strategies
I discuss are *confrontación*, flipping the script, and *cuentos*. In "Confrontación," I
explore how violence permeates public and private spaces and how streetwalking
ruptures those distinctions. Looking at how LGBTQ activists navigate the various registers of sexual terror they experience in the everyday, this chapter traces
the contours of *confrontación* that includes self-acceptance, *supervivencia*, and
collective accountability. *Confrontación* references streetwalking negotiations
over internal subjective states alongside a wrestling and struggle with others over
the right to exist. In "Flipping the Script," I explore how shifting discourses are
mobilized by LGBTQ activists to restore and maintain respect and dignity. Flipping the script entails testifying, reading, and giving shade. It is about the inver-
sion of power relations in ways that subvert Christian colonial claims to moral
authority. In "Cuentos," I examine the interstices between tacit and streetwalking
subjectivities. In these interstices, *cuentos* enable distinct articulations of friendship, collective speech, and history making.

PART I

Street Smarts

As I was taught by my queer elders, in order to know where I am going, I need to know where I came from and where, exactly, I am standing. Walking through the streets of La Zona and beyond—to other less formal, unpaved streets, or streets locked in by high-rises, or streets that are really roads and paths to mountains—I am consistently reminded that the D.R. is a Catholic Hispanic state. Whether because of the multiple times that Christians bless me from point A to point B, or because of the ways God is invoked in day-to-day interactions, or because of the presence of multiple churches, crosses, and other markings of Christian presence—for any of these reasons and more, I am reminded time and again that European Christianity was imposed on indigenous lands and has transited and continues to transit through indigenous and black bodies. We cannot deny that Christianity took root through the processes of European settlement, invasion, and conquest. We also cannot deny that indigenous and Afro-descendant peoples have incorporated Christianity into their being, their personhood, their communities, and their ways of life.

Many LGBTQ people are Christian; they are people of faith and, oftentimes, of deep faith. As a non-Christian scholar and author, therefore, there exists an ethical imperative to interrogate my own positionality and its limitations (my biases). That said, I am confounded, personally, by what it could look like to imagine Christianity as a faith that is not implicated in ongoing imperial expansion and the racist, homophobic, misogynistic violences that accompany these political, economic, and social processes. To imagine that, for me, requires imagining and attending to conversations with Christians who seek to unsettle the violence of Christianity's past in the process of shaping decolonized futures as well as with those Christians who advocate for women and LGBTQ peoples' human and civil rights at the intersections of faith. Even then, the question still remains for me: When so many other spiritual and religious traditions exist, why do LGBTQ people continue to practice and have faith in Christianity at all?

J. Lorand Matory reminds me that Christianity has deep (temporal, cultural, and spiritual) roots throughout Africa. Speaking specifically about Oyo-Yoruba

39

cultures, Matory posits that "interaction among [Christian, Islamic, and *orisa*] religions is a constituting dynamic [of *orisa* worship] . . . which resists being classified as fixed and bounded" (2005, 67). To speak, therefore, of African and Afro-diasporic religious and spiritual traditions is to also speak of foundational Christian and Islamic beliefs as central to those practices. If we are to take this claim at face value and pair it with Matory's simultaneous proposition that gender in the Oyo-Yoruba cultures signifies completely distinct relationships of power than those produced through colonialism in the Americas, we are able to trace the spaces of tension where those distinct relationships of power (say, in the figure of the *iyawo*) clash and intersect with Christian colonial biblical binaries and presumed heterocomplimentary. If, however, we take Matory's claim about the centrality of Christianity to Oyo-Yoruba cultures and pair it with Oyèrónkẹ́ Oyěwùmí's claim that "western gender categories are presented as inherent nature (of bodies) and operate on a dichotomous, binarily opposed male/female, man/woman duality in which the male is assumed to be superior and therefore the defining category" (1997, 4), then we are required to consider the drastic effects of Christianity's transit through Yoruba cultures on terms that unsettle any claims to gender as an applicable analytic category. In other words, we must consider "the ways in which 'gender' was (re)constituted in and through the practices of colonialism, colonial violence, and the racialized relation to bodies of color" (Méndez 2015, 102) in the shaping of the fundamental questions with which we attempt to approach Yoruba lives and experiences. The tension produced through the distinct viewpoints represented by Oyěwùmí and Matory is productive in expanding the terrain by which we might come to conceptualize our streetwalking experiences in the New World.

The New World was constituted explicitly through Christian *colonial* violence in ways that the Yoruba people—and African peoples more broadly speaking—were not. The dispossession and decimation of indigenous peoples in the Americas through invasion and conquest and the subsequent importation of millions of peoples from Africa and the violent ontological restructuring of personhood produced through the Middle Passage are Christian enterprises that locate Christianity within a different set of historical relationships than those that might emerge through indigenous Yoruba worlds. Whereas my biases generate personal questions about Christianity's liberatory potential in the context of streetwalking, my training has taught me to attend to the ways in which my interlocutors produce meaning, knowledge, and relationships. In that process, I must also attend to the context in which these productions of meaning, knowledge, and relationship take place. For my interlocutors, many of whom are LGBTQ persons of Christian faith, the pain, hurt, and loss produced by the homophobia, transphobia, and xenophobia of Christian institutions and leaders have produced erotic orientations rooted in alternative epistemologies of personhood. These alternative epistemologies emerge from embodied experiences, producing powerful discursive and collective strategies with which to confront the violence emerging from these institutions.

Given all this, the work of this book is not to produce a direct dialogue about what unsettling Christianity could look like. Rather, it is to share the stories of LGBTQ activists in the D.R. as a way to generate further thinking about liberation. I begin by first presenting the context in which LGBTQ activists in the D.R. operate. The conversations presented in this section, "Street Smarts," highlight the ways in which Christian coloniality and Christian fundamentalisms are interwoven with colonial and contemporary nation-state apparatuses in the production of what I call *sexual terror*. Applying Foucault's archaeological approach to change and transformation (2010, 166–177), this text brings to light some of the presumptions that presuppose Christian salvation as a component of incremental rationalized Enlightenment and the instantiation of the liberal individualized subject and as markers of progress. This interweaving between religious philosophy and political thought and institutionalization has produced conditions that directly diminish and threaten the lives of LGBTQ peoples. These are the epistemic grounds on which racial, gender, and sexual hierarchies; binaries; categories; and identities came into being. They are our collective inheritance and what my interlocutors grapple with—and in turn what we must grapple with—on the path to transforming silence into power.

I have divided this section into two chapters. The first chapter, "Christian Coloniality," provides a discussion and theorization of Christian coloniality. I locate Christian coloniality within the slow, centuries-long processes of colonialism's reformulations of meaning. While it is important to consider that Hispaniola was a marginalized colony within the broader Spanish Empire, it is also important to consider that it was a significant rehearsal ground for the implementation of colonization, settlement, encomienda, sugar cane plantations, cattle ranches, *cimarronaje*, revolution, nation-state building, authoritarianism, U.S. imperial expansion, and neoliberalism. Today, LGBTQ people suffer under the accumulated weight and palimpsestic force of Christian coloniality as it manifests through the Catholic Hispanic nation-state of the Dominican Republic. This chapter describes the structures of power that shape the backdrop for streetwalking.

The second chapter, "Sexual Terror," illustrates the myriad ways in which Christian coloniality sustains and produces homophobic and transphobic violence. Definitions of sexual violence are often constrained to violence produced through sexual acts: for example, sexual assault, sexual abuse, rape, and incest. Here I discuss sexual terror as the completely encompassing modes of violence that permeate the social body, striking against those whose desires, feelings, and erotic dispositions do not conform to Christian colonial morality—in particular, Christian colonial ideas of biblical manhood and womanhood. By theorizing sexual terror, I draw attention to the structural ways in which LGBTQ personhood is restricted and produced.

CHAPTER 1

Christian Coloniality

In her essay "My Worlds Will Be There," published as part of the collection *I Am Your Sister*, Audre Lorde writes,

> I see protest as a genuine means of encouraging someone to feel the inconsistencies, the horror, of the lives we are living. Social protest is to say that we do not have to live this way. If we feel deeply, as we encourage ourselves and others to feel deeply, we will, within that feeling, once we recognize we can feel deeply, we can love deeply, we can feel joy, then we will demand that all parts of our lives produce that kind of joy. And when they do not, we will ask, "Why don't they?" And it is the asking that will lead us inevitably toward change. (Byrd, Betsch Cole, and Guy-Sheftall 2009, 162)

There is a horror to knowing that my life is at risk simply for being who I am. There is a horror to knowing that my lesbian, gay, bisexual, trans*, queer, and intersex friends' and loved ones' lives are at risk simply because they are who they are. There is a horror in knowing that there are families, communities, institutions, and nation-states that don't care whether we live or die, and in some cases, they participate in perpetuating the very violence that leads to our premature and often terrifying deaths. There is a horror, there is a horror, there is a horror.

And so I am moved—as a scholar, an artist, an activist, a healer—to attempt to grasp the root causes of this horror. I feel deeply that my life and the lives of other LGBTQ people have inherent value. I feel this way in a world that does not reflect that sentiment back to me. Therefore daily I must draw from the deep fountains of joy, of love, and of my capacity to question in order to articulate my inherent sense of self-worth and of value for myself and others. I must know this. Actor and director Laurie Carlos once said to me, "You just have to know you are brilliant." I said back to her (yes, I did), "But how do we know we are brilliant if no one told us so?" She said, "Well you just know. You've just got to know." I responded, "But what if we've never been told that?" And she closed the issue by stating simply, directly, "Well I'm telling you now, aren't I?" What does it mean to walk in the world *knowing we are brilliant*? And what are the forces that prevent us from knowing this?

Attempting to find the root causes of my horror and to take up Laurie Carlos's call to know our brilliance as who we are in the world are the two clashing emotional sources informing my theorization of Christian coloniality as presented in this chapter. I will first locate Christian coloniality within the slow, centuries-long processes of colonialism's reformulations of meaning, first by focusing on the idea of "gay marriage." This conversation about gay marriage in the twenty-first century leads us to unearth the various formulations of morality in the context of producing the human, which I then follow up by theorizing the Catholic Hispanic nation-state and its historical applications of Christian colonial morality in the management of public spaces and the production of specific kinds of human citizen subjects.

What's Gay Marriage Got to Do with It?

It was June 2013, and I was in the D.R. when the U.S. Supreme Court's decision to strike down the Defense of Marriage Act (DOMA) was announced. The Supreme Court's decision effectively made it illegal to deny marriage to same-sex couples, opening the way for what is commonly referred to as "gay marriage." I heard about the decision first from my Dominican LGBTQ activist friends and interlocutors. In that moment, they were preparing for that year's Caravana del orgullo. They were paying attention to what was happening in the U.S. because President Obama had just appointed an openly gay ambassador to serve in the D.R. Much of the political content of the Caravana that year was in support of the appointment. In addition, some Dominican LGBTQ activists were considering gearing up for their own campaign for gay marriage. By 2013, there had been several successful court rulings on gay marriage throughout Latin America. In 2010, the Inter-American Human Rights Commission had ruled on a case in Chile and "urged the Chilean state to adopt legislation, policies, and programs to prohibit and eradicate discrimination based on sexual orientation" (Díez 2015, 1). A year before in Argentina, a judge had expanded marriage to include LGBTQ couples. And also in 2009, Mexico City's assembly approved "reforms to the city's civil code allowing for same-sex marriage" (2). These successful cases and the U.S. Supreme Court decision could potentially serve as a model for local activists to propose and fight for legislation even as it became fodder for Dominican Catholic-Evangelical protests. Dominican LGBTQ activists argued that if large democratic governments like Argentina, Mexico, Chile, and the U.S.—which for so long had opposed gay civil rights—were suddenly allowing gay marriage, then anything was possible.

But Dominican LGBTQ activists were not only paying attention to what was happening in the secular courts of Latin America and the imperial courts of the north. They were also paying attention to the Vatican's response. Just earlier that year, Pope Benedict XVI had stepped down, and Pope Francis had taken his place. LGBTQ activists across Catholic countries everywhere were watching to see how this new pope would respond to the abuse of children by priests; they were also looking to see what Pope Francis would say about homosexuality and gender identity. His track record as archbishop of Buenos Aires, Argentina, demonstrated that he was both religiously and politically adamant about his opposition to gay marriage and ambivalent about the place of homosexuals in God's plan. A letter leaked to the Argentinian press in July 2010 stated, "This [battle for gay marriage] is not just a simple political battle; its *aim is to destroy God's plan* ... it is not a mere legislative project (this is only its instrument), but rather a strategic *move by the father of all lies, who aims to confuse and trick God's children....* Here we also see *the Devil's envy,* by which all sins entered the world, which aims to destroy God's image: man and woman who have a mandate to grow, to multiply and have dominion over the earth" (TN.com.ar 2010; emphasis in the original). The letter circulated not only within the Argentine press. It spread across networks of feminist and LGBTQ activists throughout Latin America. If this was the archbishop's position in Argentina, what would be his position as a religious and political leader of the international Catholic Church?

On March 13, Cardinal Jorge Mario Bergoglio was selected as the new pope of the Catholic Church under the religious name of Pope Francis. Pope Benedict XVI's (Ratzinger's) resignation in February was surprising to most of the world and came at the tail end of a range of Vatican financial scandals and over a decade of pedophilia scandals (Horowitz and Goldstein 2018). I was with Marivi, a Catholic woman and highly esteemed educator in the D.R., when the news of Benedict's resignation was announced. When I asked her about the state of Catholic life in the D.R. and about rumors that the church was losing followers, she responded, "Yes, it's true. In my lifetime, the majority of my friends have left the Catholic Church. Many of them are in Evangelical churches."

For many Dominican Catholics and former Catholics with whom I spoke, Pope Benedict's resignation represented their own *pena* (sadness, shame) at the state of the church: their own self-understanding as belonging to a church in crisis—a church that has shaped them in fundamental ways but no longer corresponds to their own or others' lived realities, values, or expectations. This *pena* was mediated by arguments that positioned Ratzinger as an intellectual—someone who could have potentially engaged with the world as a modern rational thinker. From this perspective, his downfall resulted from insufficient flexibility before a theological position within an institution that was being challenged by shifting social norms. But this argument sometimes undergirds a desire for a more fundamentalist Catholic presence in the face of the shame and problems within the priests' ranks.[1]

The homosexual was a central preoccupation of Pope Francis's leadership as archbishop.[2] As demonstrated by numerous articles and protests in Argentina, he was one of the primary *political* opponents to gay marriage. His efforts in 2010 to use the moral authority of the church to pressure the Senate's political decisions on gay marriage were made visible through leaks to the media. Rather than recede into the church, his public attacks against LGBTQ activists became even more visible and open. Despite the pressure placed by the church on the Argentine Senate, they approved legalizing gay marriage in July 2010.

After he was ordained as pope, he led the rites of Holy Thursday—what I learned is a reproduction of the biblical story of Jesus's washing of the apostles' feet. I was with my friend Gerardo, a former priest who was now openly gay and out of the priesthood. We were watching the rites on television. He commented to me his shock at Pope Francis's actions, and we discussed the contradictions symbolized by the pope's actions on this day:

> GERARDO: He went to the jails to wash the feet of the young men. I get goose bumps. That is a very powerful statement that he's making. He says that the Church has to go to the margins.
>
> ANA: He talks about margins, but he's a huge homophobe.
>
> GERARDO: Yeah? Well, the church will never accept gays.
>
> ANA: But how can he defend the margins and not those who are marginalized, like gays? As a cardinal in Argentina, he really showed himself, you know?
>
> GERARDO: He's Francis—his flock is among the poor. And besides, he can't do or say what he did or said when he was cardinal. He's a pope now. We have to wait and see what he does with the issue of gays.[3]

I had offended my friend's sensibilities. He was deeply moved, as a former priest, by the pope's humility as demonstrated by his actions on Holy Thursday. For him, this represented a radical shift from Benedict XVI's theology and overall approach to human suffering. He commented to me that it confirmed his deep faith in the church as an instrument of Christ's love and Paul's teachings. That I would question the pope's integrity on the basis of his stance on homosexuality was offensive and beside the point for him. The church would never accept gays, and this issue did not rest on the leadership of one person. My question and concern were irrelevant. But also, from the perspective of a person of faith—his and others—religion and sexuality are personal. As personal matters, they are supposed to exist outside the realm of public debate. The incursion of the church and state into the personal space of religion and sexuality, therefore, lies at the root of the offense against human dignity and rights. Gerardo's perspective was not unlike the perspective of many of the LGBTQ activists I worked with. This perspective underscores the contradictions and motivations of the Dominican LGBTQ movement, where for many activists, the goal of their work is to get the Catholic Hispanic nation-state out of their personal lives, even as they fight for the rights of liberal citizenship. The means by which they hope to achieve this is by hitting the streets: creating education campaigns for students, educating the

Dominican public through media campaigns and public protests calling for the assurance and application of Dominican laws and universal human rights, and refusing to stay silent in the face of violence.

But much of the crisis of the Catholic Church is the reality of homosexuality. Unlike in Afro-diasporic religions, which make room for the negotiation and inclusion of differently gendered peoples and multidimensional sexualities—thus creating the possibility of expansion and ethical reconciliation[4]—the colonial church built its house on the eradication of sodomy, polygamy, and concubinage as a condition of its modern existence. And today, homosexuals and trans* people emerge as the objects of its battle. As objects, we elucidate a powerful tension between Christian morality and Christian corruption both within religious institutions and in relationship to civil jurisprudence. LGBTQ activists seek to end the positioning of homosexuality as sinful in particular because of how this moral position perpetuates the production of repressive laws and cultural norms.

When DOMA was struck down, Archbishop Allen H. Vigneron (Abbey-Lambertz 2013) of Detroit, Michigan, stated, "The well-being of our society, our nation, and our families is intimately linked to the institution of marriage. These decisions by the United States Supreme Court will make significantly more difficult our work of upholding the truth that marriage is a lifelong covenant between one man and one woman. Such decisions, made by any civic authority, do not serve the common good. Catholics and millions of our fellow citizens will continue to make the case, respectfully yet vigorously, that marriage cannot be redefined, and that attempts to do so hurt us all." Edward Peters, legal adviser to the Vatican, not only supported Vigneron's statement but also constructed numerous legal arguments about the destructive relationship between the legalization of gay marriage and evil as proscribed by canonical law. Months earlier, he had publicly articulated an argument in support of restricting communion for those advocating for gay marriage. In his argument, he drew on canonical law to articulate a definition of marriage as *only* between a man and a woman and to articulate why the Catholic Church will recognize neither gay marriage nor anyone cooperating with gay marriage. Peters argues that based on canonical law, those who support gay marriage are subject to moral assessment "in accord with the usual principles applicable to cooperation with evil and . . . applying to cooperation in crime . . . and/or scandal" (Peters 2013).

Archbishop Vigneron and Peters's positions are representative of the Vatican's position on homosexuality more broadly. Whereas with Pope Francis, there has been a turn to "love the sinner but not the sin," much of the discourse emerging from the Vatican turns on the condemnation of gay marriage as both evil and anathema to church doctrine and law. A month after the DOMA decision, Pope Francis stated, "If someone is gay and seeks the Lord with good will, who am I to judge?" (Brydum 2013). Simultaneously, he made it clear that he considers homosexuality and trans* identities "a moral problem. A human problem. And it must be resolved the best one can—always with the mercy of God, with the truth and always with an open heart" (Grindley 2016). His position as pope mirrors broader Vatican debates, which condemn violence against LGBTQ people, condone acceptance of the person while condemning the "sin of homosexuality," and actively condemn and punish the support or enactment of gay marriage. The church's concern with gay marriage is critical to the shaping of marriage debates in families, schools, communities, and national and international publics. The Catholic Church's global political power positions the institution as a moral authority on civil law and sociopolitical personhood. This political power is an outgrowth of what I call Christian coloniality.

A CHRISTIAN COLONIAL CHRONICLE

After changes in U.S. marriage laws in 2013, I could no longer ignore the centrality of debates about gay marriage in the Catholic Church's arguments about the nature of homosexuality and trans* identities. What, I wondered, was this focus on marriage (and the family) really signaling? How had marriage (and monogamy) become embedded within social measures of morality and the capacity to embody national belonging? Had marriage always been the measure of moral personhood within the Christian world? What is it about homosexuality and gender nonconformity that seems to confound the philosophical and moral positions of Christian churches? Why do Christian leaders care about who sleeps with whom and about peoples' gender? Sodomy (the *acto nefasto*), tribadism, concubinage, and polygamy/polyandry are still alive and well and enjoyed by many—despite centuries of religious persecution. How is it that Christian concerns about sexuality and gender "discipline both Native people and non-Native people through sexuality?" (Finley 2011, 34). Is this really about saving our souls?

   Streetwalking is an inquiry driven by my horror at the violence produced through Christian coloniality. In this section, I discuss the deep relationship between Christian ideas of morality and the formation of the human, moral personhood and citizenship. I start with the idea that the role of Christianity—in processes of colonization and in the reorganization of knowledge, power, and being—continues to inform our contemporary experiences and understandings of modernity. Renderings of modernity and, by extension, coloniality that fail to account for the centrality of Christian discourses and mechanisms fall short. Centering an analysis of the role of Christianity (its discourses, material practices, and institutions) in processes of colonization and Spanish colonial expansion allows us to examine the continuous and discontinuous processes of the moral regulation of gender and sexuality as central to the project of modernity. It is not sufficient to denote how the crucifix accompanied the sword; the crucifix was attached to the sword, and sometimes it was and continues to be the sword (Goodpasture 2000) that cuts through the lives of LGBTQ persons.

Anibal Quijano (2000) argues that coloniality—that is, the practices, legacies, forms, and modes of knowledge that developed through European colonialism in the Western hemisphere—stems from the control of labor, race, and sex. Maria Lugones (2010) adds to Quijano's argument by suggesting that the concepts of gender and sexuality were produced through coloniality as the primary mode for the distribution of power. Jumping off from these claims, I posit that these processes of coloniality—the formation of gender and sexual categories, as well as the management of labor, race, and sex—emerge from Christian concepts of moral personhood. Within Christian colonial structurings of power and being, gender was developed as a binary structure that mirrored biblical binaries—Adam and Eve, Abraham and Sara, Joseph and Mary, and so on. This binary was (is) best embodied through monogamous heterosexual complementarity. By heterosexual complementarity, I refer to the ways in which men and women became defined as separate, distinct, and essentially different subjects, whereby each "needs the other to supply the missing traits and behavior that when joined signify human wholeness" (Gudorf 2014, 232). Human wholeness is rooted in the idea of the "biblical man" and the "biblical woman." The biblical man and woman have been inscribed as essential to the moral fiber of humanness (and citizenship), including the attendant heterocomplimentarity that is assumed within them. Biblical manhood continues to be reified as one in which man "constituted a continuous process of creation, for it is in him, in his seed, in his semen, that the potential for new and future beings is harbored" (Garza Carvajal 2010, 17). Similarly, biblical womanhood has required that women be purely passive receptacles within procreative processes.

The construction of gender and sexual difference—imagined as a fixed set of qualities, behaviors, and identities—position heterosexuality and heteropatriarchy as the representations of order and the transcendence of the spirit over flesh, while homosexuality and gender nonconformity are configured as the embodiment of sin and deviance. Furthermore, these differentiations result in a moral context in which homosexuality and gender transgressions become that which must be contained or excised from the Christian corpus, *terra*, and *gens*. Christian coloniality seeks to foster the continual perpetuation of procreative sexuality and the subject capable of reproducing Christian personhood and the colony. This inscription of personhood required the discursive demonization of a vast range of nonbiblical sexual desires and the material punishment of biblically condemned or nonbiblical sexual gender practices.

The church's focus on sexuality and gender differences as sin, illness, and crime served as important sites for the consolidation of the church's political authority within governance structures in the colonies. As Pedro Garza Carvajal outlines, "Over the course of the early modern period in New Spain, colonial officials, jurists, theologians, and other writers associated signifiers like the diabolic, anthropophagy, inebriation, and effeminacy with perceptions of the *pecado*

nefando. By insisting on an inherent link between these multiple cultural constructs, historians, chroniclers, and theologians devised one more 'just cause'
for the permanence of colonial rule in the Indias" (2010, 132). From the earliest
colonial periods through the rise of the modern nation-states in the nineteenth
century, Christian policies of conversion and marriage served as measures of the
successes of both Christian evangelization and Spanish rule (Schwaller 2011).

In the earliest colonial chronicles, the clearest measures of the success of
the Evangelical mission was in the visible re-formation of families. The mission to reform families and intimate relations created a continuously charged
context for the formation of colonial/modern notions of gender, sexuality, and
significantly, racial hierarchies (Lugones 2007). The management of sexuality was deeply co-constitutive of the racialized hierarchies established through
the Christian colonial settlement of the Americas and its attendant processes.
These processes include three distinct elements: the management of sexuality
and gender, the operationalization of the logics of blood, and the production
of the human.

The sexuality and sexual desire of Indigenous and Afro-diasporic peoples
was a central Christian preoccupation, as evidenced by confessional practices
and capital punishments and other "technolog[ies] of the flesh" (Foucault 1978,
113) aimed at curbing masturbation, concubinage, sodomy, and adultery among
many other sexual desires and behaviors of subjugated colonial subjects. Theological legal debate had succeeded in defending the divine nature of human existence and the place of *indios* and *indias* within divine nature.[5] In the colonial
past, Catholic priests sought remediation of vices against natural law—sodomy,
polygamy, adultery, and concubinage—through Catholic rites and conversion.
Successful conversion to Christianity was explicitly measured in indigenous
American and African peoples' ability to conform to both correct gender expression and monogamous heterosexual complementarity.

The Christian colonial desire to manage sin among *indios* equally justified
Christian colonial occupation, expansion, and rule. Laura Catelli writes, "Effectively, marriage between 'indios' seemed to represent to the Crown—judging by
its insistence on the propagation of that institution—an avenue for conversion,
acceptable sexual practices like monogamy, the patriarchal family, and other
morally acceptable behaviors" (2011, 228). But the Christian colonists of Hispaniola not only propagated marriage between *indios* and *indias* directly; they also
forced the sexual submission of *indias* to Christian colonists—including through
rape, sexual slavery, and marriage. The birth of children resulting from these
sexual encounters enabled *mestizaje* to emerge as a tool of Christian conquest.
Catelli argues that *mestizaje* was a tool of the Christian colonial project used
to subjugate indigenous women (and peoples more broadly) to Spanish rule.
Through *mestizaje*, it was possible to construct new categories of personhood
(e.g., the *mestiza*) but also to change kinship structures through the vehicle of

marriage and reproduction. These changes in kinship structure, which now included Christian Spanish men, opened up the possibility for the appropriation of lands and the further subjugation of indigenous communities.

Whereas Christian colonial practices regulating indigenous peoples, bodies, and lands enabled genocide and increased expansion across American lands and territories, the introduction of African chattel slavery and non-Christianized Africans into the New World economies required the increased control over bodies and their reproductive capacities. This need for increased control fomented the further development and entrenchment of Christian colonial discourses of race and blood mixture rooted in the logics of blood purity (*pureza de sangre*). The development of the elaborate racial schema of *castas* and the accompanying Christian colonial policing of them also demonstrate the overlaps between the Catholic Church's moral concerns and the colonial governments' concerns about population management.[6] Christian colonial ideologies were deployed to develop and maintain gender binaries and, through those binaries, to measure and constrain blood mixtures. Blood mixture, *mestizaje*, and all the regulations of blood mixture and *mestizaje* point to the regulation of sexuality. Put in plain words, Christian coloniality indexes the role of Christian institutions and discourses in the regulation and management of sex as an attempt to maintain and develop a racial hierarchy that would substantiate the continual expansion of Christian rule over territory and subsequently over the bodies necessary for the ever-increasing accumulation of wealth produced through slave labor.

The Christian colonial regulations of gender and sexuality were central to figurations of the human. Through baptism and conquest, indigenous American and African concepts of gender, gender relations, and ideologies were subsumed and suppressed—through numerous discursive, material, and institutional mechanisms—into the biblical binary of men and women. Biblical gender binaries and their resulting racial hierarchies were part and parcel of the reformulation of Christian doctrines necessary to justify the violent processes of colonization. Through Christian debates over the fate of indigenous peoples and the management of black bodies in these devastated and conquered territories, the universalized figure of the human took on both impulse and form. Human nature, Sylvia Wynter argues, emerged in the context of the New World as a subjective ordering principle that undergirded the organization of distinct human groups into a presumed "naturally ordered distribution of degrees of reason" (1984, 34)—a hierarchy of reason and imagined human potentiality. The same logic that enabled the differentiation of the divine from the secular, of the spirit from the flesh, was now used to differentiate a "Self" from an "Other" and to "domesticate the representations of the Other, whose mode of difference alone enable[d] the mode of Sameness" (34). The creation and sustainment of a natural hierarchy was explicitly possible not only through the construction of new modes of being but also through the knowledges created, validated, and consummated in service to these new orderings. In this view, the *encomienda*, plantations, and chattel slavery were justified for, to use Wynter's words, "the purpose of rationalizing [*indios* and *negros*] as an inferior mode of being in need of rational human baptism" (35), while conversion and the processes of "converting human beings," following Talal Asad, "expressed a desire to bring outsiders within the fold of a universe in which eventually individual autonomy and secular reason became the source of morality as well as of truth for all human beings" (2015, 399). The presence of desires or expressions outside of biblical manhood and womanhood contributed to the construction of racialized difference that marked some beings as human and others as incapable of humanity. The same humanist logics that undergird the bifurcation of flesh from spirit order bodies and relations in ways that produce streetwalking as a site for the perpetuation of Christian colonial violence.

Streetwalking challenges the idea that "the West, over the last five hundred years, has brought the whole human species into its *hegemonic*, now purely secular…model for being *human*" (Wynter and McKittrick 2015, 21). Streetwalking makes manifest the ways in which the Christian colonial logics that developed through the management of being, knowledge, and power in processes of colonization were extended into the formation of modern nation-states. The idea of the secular, in fact, has served to obscure the Christian colonial structuring of power and knowledge in the West (Asad 2003). Christianity's discursive and material powers in Latin America, specifically, were no less diminished by the modernizing processes of secularization. First, Christianity "is the only religion which has organized itself as a church" (Foucault 1982, 783). Second, while modern nation-states were formed as potentially secular structures of governance, the majority of modern nation-states in the Americas retained relationships with the church—as a separate but fundamentally essential institution—or with church ideologies and discourses. The latter is what Foucault conceptualizes as "pastoral power"—that is, the extension of Christian ideology and doctrine through the vehicle of the nation-state.

In the late eighteenth and early nineteenth centuries, as independent nation-states emerged throughout the Caribbean and Latin America, ecclesiastic institutions lost material function and influence. Pastoral power "spread and multiplied outside the ecclesiastical institution" (Foucault 1982, 783), thereby enabling the development of nation-state institutions aimed at formulating new subjectivities grounded in Christian moral notions of personhood and citizenship. In Latin America, these ecclesiastic foundations were grounded in the institutions, imperatives, discourses, and practices of the Catholic Church. Staking a claim in Foucault's arguments about the subject and power, I argue here that the extension of pastoral power through the mechanisms of modern nation-states reconfigured relationships between institutions and ideologies to extend Christian coloniality into the present.

Christian churches—as institutions with moral and, in many cases, political authority—continue to operate alongside and within the structures of modern nation-states. Together, these relationships and modes of power are expressed in the ongoing regulation of moral personhood, explicitly through the management of gender and sexuality. Christian colonial fixations on gender and sexuality are organized around underlying moral questions about souls and salvation, specifically the reconciliation between flesh and spirit, as prerequisites for upstanding personhood and citizenship. Disciplinary power is carried out toward, against, and through the bodies of those who do not fit or exercise biblical manhood or womanhood, including those of us streetwalking. I think this is why "marriage" and "family" are so important to Christian institutions and leadership—because they represent two sites where Christian coloniality can continue to regulate personhood and maintain legitimacy vis-à-vis the nation-state.

As universal indices of Christian colonial structures of power and being were established—and now continue to be perpetuated—those who challenged (and continue to challenge) those categories of being became both a threat to Christian morality and a target of violence. Streetwalking ruptures biblical gender binaries and racial hierarchies. The contemporary, universal category of LGBTQ exists outside of the framework of universal Christian colonial gender binaries. As a subject category, *LGBTQ* draws attention to the existence of desires, behaviors, and persons who do not conform to biblical gender binaries or expectations of monogamous heterosexual complementarity. For these reasons, sexual and gender difference is often marked as deviant, and LGBTQ political identities are in turn constructed as a threat to both the institutions of "family" and "marriage" and, by extension, the nation-state. In streetwalking, our personhood is always already configured as inviolable because our human being-ness is always already in question. Being configured as already outside the purview of Christian colonial personhood, our suffering is rendered both illegitimate and illegible. Our suffering is configured as a result of our refusal to conform to the imperatives of Christian coloniality. Our suffering is configured as something that is a result of our violations of Christian colonial imperatives and our refusal to embody Christian colonial moral personhood. Therefore, we can also propose that ours is a suffering produced explicitly through the production of the universal human as always already gender-conforming, biblically man or woman, and heterosexual.

Tracing the rise of humanist discourse in the development of secular law (Hobbes and Locke, in particular), Talal Asad discusses how "the essence of the human comes to be circumscribed by [nineteenth-century/Enlightenment] legal discourse: the human being is a sovereign, self-owning agent—essentially suspicious of others—and not merely a subject conscious of his or her own identity." This definition of the human is how "the right to freedom of belief and expression was crafted" (Asad 2015, 135). The question remains, however, as to why certain humans are deemed worthy of not just human rights but human being.

In this, I invoke Asad's reflection on the inhuman, which, he argues, "presupposes that there are human ways of killing and dying as well as inhuman ones" (135). The bifurcation of human being-ness from human rights is also a primary condition of a presumed secular modernity. In his discussion of secularism, Asad traces how contemporary structures of international law and citizenship divorce human rights from human being. He states, "Nothing essential to a person's human essence is violated if he or she suffers a consequence of military action . . . when that is permitted by international law. . . . The suffering that the individual sustains as a citizen—as the national of a particular state—is distinguished from the suffering he undergoes as a human being" (129). Similarly, the suffering of LGBTQ persons in the context of the New World is a suffering that is justified through Christian moral authority as distinct from secular law. Nation-state and international political processes mirror this bifurcation of the human and maintain the Christian colonial logics that perpetuate the naturalized orders of personhood.

Christian coloniality has directly contributed to our understandings of universalized subjects such as the human (as always already racialized, sexualized, and gendered). This configuration of the human has particular relevance in global discussions about human rights. The concepts and tenets of human rights are rooted in Christian colonial concepts of morality that serve as a parallel, universally applicable measure of development and modernity. The development, enactment, and enforcement of human rights doctrines have become central to contemporary negotiations of citizenship within nation-states and in the international arena. I turn now to a discussion of the relationships among Christianity, the global Catholic Church (the Roman Catholic Church, the Vatican, the Holy See, and the local Catholic *jerarquías*), Christian Evangelical movements, and national and international political institutions.

What Christian institutions and the Catholic Church say matters in the realm of human and civil rights (Fleishman 2000; Radford Ruether 2008; Ryall 2001). Evangelical Christian leadership has entered the realm of national and international politics throughout the world, specifically in the areas of reproductive health and human rights. U.S.-based Evangelical leadership has directly impacted international funding and service structures throughout the Global South (Freston 2008; Hofer 2003). Through its "global transnational character, its elaborate bureaucracy, and its enduring ideology" (Heger Boyle, Golden, and Liao 2017, 396), the global Catholic Church has managed to shape political relations and law for centuries. Today, the Vatican's position on homosexuality, cleric marriage, and reproductive rights affects the laws and policies for contemporary struggles in many countries. But as the Vatican continues its opposition to homosexuality and reproductive rights, radical Catholics, LGBTQ Catholics, and their allies all over the world are challenging the disciplinary effects of Christian coloniality.[7]

Political processes rooted in Christian coloniality become manifest through what are currently some of the most contentious international debates about the rights of women and LGBTQ persons and indigenous peoples and on topics like xenophobia and racism. The United Nations (U.N.) is one international body designated to manage "political and economic cooperation among member countries [through] economic and social development programs improving human rights and reducing global conflicts" (U.N. 2015). The UN has become a critical site for the consolidation of global capital and power among countries of the Global North, even as it serves as an important site for the negotiation of new protections and rights for those dispossessed by the Global North's globalized, neoliberal economic policies.

While not an official member state of the United Nations, the Holy See, which serves as the central administration of the Roman Catholic Church, does have a privileged position as a permanent observer, a position established by Pope Paul VI in 1964. It is the only religious body in the world to have this status within the UN governance structure, thus "linking universal global principles to Catholic religious tradition . . . and ultimately privileg[ing] one religious ideology" (Heger Boyle, Golden, and Liao 2017, 399) above others. The Roman Catholic Church has also been an active participant in international conferences on human rights, including the 1993 Vienna Conference on Human Rights and the 1994 International Conference on Population and Development. As such, the Roman Catholic Church is one of the most powerful global organizations in the world and serves as an important "counterpart to the contemporary system of nation-states and international governmental organizations" (Heger Boyle, Golden, and Liao 2017, 396). Many debates around whether the Holy See and Vatican City qualify as either state or nation have taken place since the designation as permanent observer (Holy See, n.d.; Center for Research on Population and Security, n.d.). These debates emerge most contentiously in relation to the role of the Holy See in the ratification of international resolutions, agreements, and treaties.

While the Roman Catholic Church benefits from its institutional structures and political reach, other Christian denominations manage power in quite a different fashion. In contradistinction to the Catholic Church, most other Christian denominations function through on-the-ground, decentralized authority. Evangelical Protestantism is one of the fastest-growing religious communities in the Americas. Between the 1950s and the 1990s, "over 50 million Latin Americans converted to Evangelical Protestantism" (Betances 2007, 210). Protestant groups differ significantly from their Catholic counterparts: they are decentralized, ministers are chosen by their communities and ministries are sustained by their membership, and missions are carried out in the poorest sectors of society rather than among the elites. Evangelical Protestantism also allows for a high degree of adaptation and acculturation, permitting it to be absorbed within multiple social and cultural contexts. Many scholars attribute these factors to the fast spread of Evangelical Protestantism throughout the region and the globe (Kalyvas and van Kersbergen 2010; Meyer 2004; Robbins 2004). The impact of Evangelical Protestantism and its fundamentalist Christian Right strains can be felt around the world—from Taiwan to Uganda to the Caribbean.

Fundamentalist Evangelical groups draw our attention to an important current within Christian colonial logics. On the one hand, they lack the kinds of institutional and political validation of the Catholic Church on a global scale and sometimes even on national scales. On the other hand, they reify the regulatory mechanisms of Christian colonial power in the everyday. For example, in the D.R. in the last ten years, I have noticed that a common response to greeting someone in the street is "Amen." As I pick up my groceries or leave a vehicle, it is common for someone to tell me, "Que Dios te bendiga" (May God bless you). Walking through the streets, Evangelical men and women are highly visible because of their modes of dress. Evangelical Christian men wear dress pants, dress shirts, and ties; their hair is trimmed with neat edges. Evangelical Christian women wear ankle-length skirts and blouses with sleeves down to their wrists. They do not straighten their hair but rather wear it "natural," in a single bun tied to the back of the head. These visible distinctions make Christian personhood an element within the streets as part and parcel of the everyday. In contrast, when we are streetwalking, we may show skin, cleavage, or the contours of our curves/edges; we may wear clothes that disrupt biblical binary gender norms; we may wear our hair or brighten our faces in ways that are considered unnatural; we may call attention to ourselves through jewelry, or the flip of a hand, or a strut. Evangelicals, who are socially authorized moral arbiters, are empowered to publicly surveil and comment on streetwalking. In this way, the distinctions in dress become an opening to potential violence. The logics of Christian coloniality and the regulation of biblical gender binaries and sexual norms, as well as disruptions to these norms, are written on the body.

Christian coloniality is the ideological and material framework for the development and perpetuation of the Catholic Hispanic nation-state, as exemplified by states such as the D.R. As Sara Pérez writes, "In the Dominican Republic, the Catholic Church is the axis, the oldest patriarchal promoter; it is the most arrogant, the most efficient, the most solid, the most coherent and the most implacable [institution]. More so than the military, who as organized 'Armed Forces' are a parasitic incorporation that is relatively recent in Dominican society and more so than economically privileged groups. . . . Only the Catholic Church has [such a] strange fossil nature[:] it remains the same church that [it] was 500 years ago" (2004, 269).

Streetwalking emerges as a challenge to the presumed moral and political wholeness of the modern nation-state. It is in this context that LGBTQ activists rupture Christian colonial logics *and* the moral and social limits of the Catholic Hispanic state. What does the Catholic Hispanic state look like, then, *en la calle*?

The Catholic Hispanic State

The history of Dominican heterodoxy remains unwritten; but experience
demonstrates that our nationality ends where the [Protestant] "Churches" and
"voodoo" begin.

—Luis Martínez Fernández, "The Sword and the Crucifix: Church-State Relations
and Nationality in the Nineteenth-Century Dominican Republic"[8]

My use of the term *Catholic Hispanic nation-state* references the explicit, long-
term relationship between the Spanish colonial / Dominican nation-state and
the Roman Catholic Church. This relationship was complicated by the interplay
of colonial and postcolonial power struggles during the long period of hemispheric modern nation-state stabilization taking place during and following the
Haitian Revolution, Colombian Independence, and the U.S. Civil War. Why,
people ask, do I single out Catholicism, especially given both the development of
decolonial and liberation theologies within the Catholic Church and the rapid
rise in Evangelical Christianity throughout Latin America, including the D.R.?
Whereas in other Caribbean countries, different modes of Protestantism
(Anglican, Methodist, and Baptist traditions) took hold, the Christian logics
that shaped early modes of Christian colonization on the island of Hispaniola
were Catholic, and they were negotiated, incorporated, contested, transformed,
and absorbed through modern nation-state processes (Martínez Fernández
1995, 70). Current decolonial scholarship both presumes and subsumes the role
of Christian theological debates about the human in favor of a historical mate-
rialist analysis of power. Rather than subsume a discussion about the role of
Christian institutions, discourses, and debates to the background of a seemingly
broader conversation about colonization or coloniality, and rather than relegate
this same discussion to the sphere of historical analysis, here I argue that Christian coloniality continues to impact our contemporary understandings of personhood and subjectivity.

During the nineteenth century—at the same time that other emerging Latin
American nations such as Mexico were fighting for *estados laicos* ("layperson's"
states)—the D.R. was establishing itself as an independent nation-state aligned
with Catholic Hispanic ideologies: a Catholic nation-state rooted in Eurocen-
tric and Hispanophilic ideals of personhood and governance (1844 Constitution, Art. 38; Martínez Fernández 1995). This was achieved both through the
discourses of independence and through laws, policies, and mandates—such as
those stated in the 1844 national constitution and in the thirty-six constitutions
that followed (Sáez 1987).[9] In this way, the D.R. proved to be quite the opposite
from other Latin American countries. Not only was the nation-state, through its
various iterations (independence, annexation, war), consistently Catholic, but at
times Catholic clergy exercised greater power than the nation-state. For example,

during the period of Spanish annexation (1861–1865), Spanish clergy, empowered by new Spanish legal codes, "prescribed banishment and prison terms for those practicing, promoting, or publishing doctrines contrary to the Roman Catholic Church" (Martínez Fernández 1995, 83). The Catholic Church and Catholicism were critical sites for the articulation of a national Dominican identity and provided a contrasting power to U.S. Protestant imperialism at a time when national leaders were divided between annexation and independence.

Another key historical moment was during the period of authoritarian rule that began with Rafael Leonidas Trujillo and that continued through Joaquín Balaguer's presidencies (Fortunato 1991). These iterations of the Catholic Hispanic nation-state proved to be significant for the relations between the nation-state and the Catholic Church, relations that were fortified and manipulated in nationalist discourses and processes. Trujillo proposed and then signed a concordat (political agreement) with the Vatican in 1954, concretizing the political relationship between the Dominican government and the religious body of the Roman Catholic Church. The Concordat continues as an official agreement that influences every aspect of Dominican political, social, and cultural institutions. The Catholic *jerarquía* in the contemporary Dominican context has continued in its repressive role of sanctifying elite interests. Alongside them, other religious orders (Jesuits, Dominicans, Salesians, Geronymites, etc.) continue to play an active part in shaping popular social movements. All branches continue to uphold three basic moral values: (1) that homosexuality is a sin, (2) that life is defined from the moment of conception (recently concretized in the Dominican Constitution), and (3) that abortion is morally wrong. Most importantly, when the Catholic Church acts locally, it is also acting as part of a global religious organization that has a documented history of active involvement in defining and ratifying conventions internationally.

Within the Catholic Hispanic nation-state, Evangelical Protestants have also taken hold; even so Evangelical Protestants are still a minority. According to a 2006 population survey, 40 percent of Dominicans identify as practicing Roman Catholic, 29 percent nonpracticing Catholic, and 18 percent Evangelical Protestants—including Baptists, Pentecostals, and Assemblies of God (Ministerio de Economía, Planificación y Desarrollo 2010; Bureau of Democracy, Human Rights and Labor 2010). Evangelical Christianity has grown exponentially in the past twenty years, reflecting a larger trend throughout Latin America (Betances 2007). This growth has caused shifts in the social fabric and in the negotiation of political power both in local communities and on the national level.

In the D.R., the first Protestants arrived in 1824 with the freed blacks and runaways from Philadelphia and North Carolina. They were invited by the president of Haiti, Jean-Pierre Boyer, to settle in Samaná. Throughout the earlier half of the twentieth century, various Evangelical ministers from Puerto Rico, Cuba, the Bahamas, and Haiti established Pentecostal and other missions in the

smaller towns and rural areas. During the U.S. occupation, Protestant mission-
aries arrived as part of the United States' civilizing efforts. Afro-Antillean Black
Protestant ministers also accompanied the many Anglo-Antillean laborers who
came to work on sugar cane plantations in the first few decades of the twentieth
century (Mayes 2014). But it was not until 1979, when the writer and revolutionary President Juan Bosch accorded Evangelical groups political recognition, that
Evangelical Protestants in the D.R. began to gain political power. Under Bosch,
and all the subsequent administrations, Protestant groups began to receive allo-
cated funds from the Dominican government, though not to the degree afforded
to the Catholic Church (Betances 2007).

Another significant shift took place in 1994, when the Dominican government
invited Evangelical leaders to witness the signing of the Pact for Democracy. Since
then, they have participated alongside the Catholic Church in national political mediations and policy. And in 2004, President Hipólito Mejía Domínguez
signed a second social pact that broadened the scope of Evangelical Protestant
participation throughout the state. This pact "included broad participation in
education, recognition of Evangelical institutions in the administration of public health programs, integration into state-sponsored patronage in health and
education programs, provision for the assimilation of Evangelical chaplaincy in
the armed forces and national police, acceptance of civil marriage performed by
Evangelical pastors, creation of the legal framework for Evangelical media, and
allowance of tax exemption status to religious items and vehicles deemed necessary for church use" (Betances 2007, 238). The pact was signed into law in 2010
under the presidency of Leonel Fernández Reyna. In 2011, the Confederación
Dominicana de Unidad Evangelica (CODUE) was accorded the power and role
to shape educational curricula for primary, secondary, and tertiary education.

The church, as a fourth pillar of the government, has a say in what is approved
as law and policy, what is encompassed in "the national," the management of
bodies and populations, and the management of what is morally (and by impli-
cation, legally) right. While protective laws are often ignored or not enforced,
repressive laws are enforced quite heavily against and through those deemed
undesirable: homosexuals, trans* people, Haitians, dark-skinned people, women,
and the poor. Proof of this resides in the redefinition of life in the Dominican
Constitution, the ongoing criminalization of abortion, the cardinal-sanctioned
deportation of thousands of Haitian people, the denationalization of Dominicans of Haitian descent, and the tactics of sexual terror used to intimidate LGBTQ
people, whose presence is not illegal, but is configured as an affront to *la moralidad pública* (public morality). In this way, the D.R. provides an ideal context
for thinking through theories of Christian coloniality because Santo Domingo,
the Spanish colony, was always already Catholic. The nation-state of the D.R.
has always been articulated as a Roman Catholic nation-state.[10] The political
insistence on Catholic Hispanic nationalism generates richly detailed contours

through which to trace the Christian colonial effects and ongoing processes on contemporary subjects.

In the colonial-imperial wound (Mignolo 2007) created through Christian colonial processes, one is witness to the friction between people and peoples' historiographies/histories and battles over the dispossession of land and bodies. *Streetwalking* adds to the already existing rich literature on dispossession by focusing on the ways in which contemporary streetwalking requires us to navigate the material and discursive results of sexual terror, a mode of violence that strikes against those whose erotic orientations do not conform to Christian colonial morality—in particular, Christian colonial ideas of biblical manhood and womanhood. The disciplinary effects of Christian coloniality through the social and political body of the nation replicate the same humanist logics that undergird the bifurcation of flesh from spirit that orders bodies and relations. They produce violence, and they produce streetwalking as a site for the radical articulation of freedom.

Given the moral values accorded by Catholic and Protestant institutions and the degree to which they are incorporated into the Catholic Hispanic nation-state's institutions, LGBTQ people cannot rely on the church—in any of its incarnations—for a just and morally justified alternative to social and political condemnation. Dominican LGBTQ struggles make the Catholic Hispanic nationalist moral and spiritual battle grounds apparent and affectively immediate. In countries like the D.R., where the church also plays a key political role within the state government, LGBTQ activists actively question the church's investment in nation-state governance. LGBTQ activists have identified the church's relationship with the Dominican government as a primary obstacle for the full exercise of human rights. LGBTQ activists challenge Christian coloniality by streetwalking, hanging out, and making noise. In this context, the concept of *moralidad pública* becomes a tool and a weapon for the Christian colonial management of those streetwalking within the streets of the Catholic Hispanic nation-state.

MORALIDAD PÚBLICA

The transition from being subjects of the Spanish Crown to becoming subjects of a liberal modern nation-state was mirrored in the nineteenth- and early twentieth-century public debates about the role of religion versus secularism in the formation of a civilized modernity. These debates were taking place across Europe and the formerly colonized, newly emerged nation-states of Latin America. At stake were the continuing authority of the church as well as the protection of its properties and persons. The debates included questions about the role of religion in relationship to the sovereign and the role of the church in relationship to the nineteenth-century postcolonial state. Chaotic nation-state building processes generated shifts in the role of religious institutions within new national societies. In most instances, the church was forced to operate under the new nation-state governments, and in this way, "church leaders became acolytes of the State as the religion of the State replaced that of the Church, or more accurately, the very concept of religion as separable from the Church was invented" (Cavanaugh 1995, 408).

On the island of Hispaniola, the Catholic Church that had been operating in alongside (and not always in agreement with) the Spanish Crown under the Real Patronato scrambled to define its place within the body of the postannexation Dominican nation-state. The formation of new national institutions generated a civil public sphere in which the role of religious authority within modern Dominican society was likewise contested. With the establishment of the D.R. as a Catholic apostolic nation-state, the question of morality—and specifically, Catholic morality—would exist as a matter of internal conscience within the new state's citizenship. In this sense, Dominican citizenship was construed as an inherently Catholic citizenship whereby the enactment of national character would be explicitly construed as an expression of religious faith and moral personhood.

As the state sought to confer its own legitimacy, it drew on Christian colonial notions of morality, and the concept of *moralidad pública* emerged as a state-fomented framework for the management of public space, people, and citizenship. Julio Luis Martínez Martínez defines *moralidad pública* as the ideology in which "the behaviors of any citizen have social repercussions and can be evaluated based on assumed and accepted ethical criteria established by civil society and publics" (2002, 271). In the case of the D.R., these ethical criteria were established through the incorporation of Catholic moral values and Catholic religious leadership within the body of the Dominican nation-state and through the intellectual mechanisms that would be mobilized in the definition of Dominican personhood. Whether we look at President Archbishop Meriño's influence or the influence of the Catholic Church on Dominicans in the face of U.S. occupation, one factor is clear: the Dominican Catholic Church, once established, maintained a significant role in the management of Dominican national institutions, including in the propagation of discourse and policies regulating moral citizenship.

Simultaneously, the deployment of intellectual agendas and police authorities in the service of the *moralidad pública* contributed to the construction of morally marginalized populations, such as prostitutes, the "loud" urban poor, and the dark-skinned and those associated with them—those who were streetwalking through the early twentieth century. As in Cuba, "an analogy [was] established between the sexualized human body and the sexualized social body; that is, we can see the construction and design of the project of the (sexually determined) nation emerging" (Sierra Madero 2004). This sexually determined nation-state and citizenry was proscribed as biblically male or female, biblically patriarchal, and biblically heteronormative.

The articulation of the domestic space as private space and the street as public space was key to the management of moral citizenship. Teresita Martínez-Vergne writes, "For the government, public (in the sense of not private) space signaled permission to interfere" (2005, 80). Key to the investiture of the patriarch was the formation of the private family space over which the presumed heteropatriarchal father could exercise his rule and impart either secular or religious moral education. Key to the investiture of the Catholic Hispanic nation-state was the formation of a public space over which the heteropatriarchal state, and its actors, could exercise rule of law and order in the enforcement of moral citizenship. In both education and the moralization of public spaces, the process of forming elite citizen subjects was carried out through and against the policing of a racialized populous by Dominican state-builders and nationalists. At the onset of nation-statehood, race, gender, and deviant sexuality were also constructed through ongoing historical disruptions of streetwalking, of those with desires and orientations that fell outside the narrow prescriptions of Catholic Hispanic moral citizenship. Despite all this architecture, streetwalking disrupted the totalizing Christian colonial desires of the Catholic Hispanic nation-state.

Those who were streetwalking through the early twentieth century included the working poor—many of them women who moved through the city streets as vendors, domestic laborers, or sex workers. As they moved through the city's streets, they created their own public hangouts. These hangouts were under their control, even as they functioned within geographic limits and heavy surveillance. Unique to the hangouts created through streetwalking was the characterization of these spaces as "everybody's space, the zone of sociability, composed of stores, cafés, pubs, market stands, plazas, and street corners, where people conversed, exchanged money or goods, kissed, argued, played, or worked" (Martínez-Vergne 2005, 80). Streetwalking prevented the totalization of a moral citizenship. In the cities' public spaces, movement and celebration undermined the control of private acts; notions of *moralidad pública* failed to be sustained. In other words, even with the intellectual and official (church and state) mobilization of discourses of *moralidad pública* and mechanisms of population control, streetwalking enabled dissidence through the intentional occupation of public spaces through acts such as hanging out.

Marriage was another key site for the formation of moral citizenship. It enabled the consolidation of state and intimate Christian colonial heteropatriarchal power. Through the establishment of the Catholic Hispanic nation-state, the institution of marriage shifted from being exclusively religious to becoming a secular practice of civil government that conferred the progressing nation-state with its future: presumably heterosexual male or female children produced in the bosom of a monogamous, nuclear, heterosexual family.[11] Marriage was the vehicle by which sexuality (and, by extension, Catholic Hispanic purity) could be contained within the new nation-state, even the occupied nation, for the purposes of a civilized, Catholic Hispanic, heteropatriarchal, modern nation-hood (Reyes-Santos 2015). Simultaneously, the secular practice of marriage enabled the Dominican nation-state to legitimize itself both within the broader context of Enlightenment liberal thought about progress and modernity and also in the context of U.S. occupation. Maintaining a population that was heterosexual and with clearly defined genders flew in the face of U.S. occupation discourse that structured Dominican personhood as perverse and dysfunctional. The end result, however, was that those who could not participate in the structure of the marriage and of the heteropatriarchal Christian family—"sexual workers, single mothers, economically independent women—fell per force outside the pale of Dominicanness. In order to maintain nationality within male elite boundaries, then, worthy men situated bourgeois women under their guardianship and dismissed working-class women as unimportant to nation-building" (Martínez-Vergne 2005, 125).

Teresita Martínez-Vergne, April Mayes, and Elizabeth Manley (among others) all identify and discuss the ways in which the protection and elevation of bourgeois womanhood was central to the construction of the Dominican nation-state and moral citizenship, from the period of the emerging state up into the Balaguer era of the late twentieth century. All three of these scholars also discuss how the surveillance and policing of women in public spaces, especially those who failed to conform to bourgeois womanhood, was key to both safeguarding bourgeois womanhood and the image of the nation-state as legitimate. But these discourses and mechanisms were not just about secular citizenship; they were also about the maintenance and subsequent solidification of the Catholic Hispanic nation-state. Just as the nation wrote itself with the ideals of who should belong—*blancos de la tierra*; heterosexual, bourgeoisie men; and the masses who could aspire to those positions—it also wrote out of itself and its historiography the lives and possibilities of those who were anything but Catholic Hispanic.[12] Streetwalking disrupts hegemonic racial narratives, and those who enact sex work, gender play, *mal vivir*, *mariconeria*, and *locura* were and continue to be a constant threat to the social order. The threat to the Catholic Hispanic nation-state lies in the potential among all those who walk the streets to cross over into aberrant behavior that could compromise the *moralidad pública*. This *moralidad pública* is required by the Catholic Hispanic nation-state to preserve its image as modern, progressive, and moral. Where morality fails, public health takes over.

During the U.S. occupation, the management of prostitutes and people living in zones of prostitution was framed as a preoccupation with the contamination and the spread of disease—specifically venereal diseases—among U.S. troops (Mayes 2014). Dominican participation in hygiene measures also draws from Christian colonial ideas of sexual morality, in which venereal diseases signal an immoral soul (as made explicit in the *Confesionarios* of the nineteenth century). Sex workers, as those who ruptured the strictly policed boundaries between

Dominican society and U.S. soldiers, became the primary subjects of public health management. The management of their persons, their bodies, their labor, their families, and their movement through public spaces was both a technology of the Catholic Hispanic nation-state and a technology of U.S. empire.

Streetwalking, sex workers threatened the boundaries of private/public life. As a result, they were configured in nation-state discourse as threats to health and safety, as well as to *moralidad pública*. In this instance, the management of streetwalking and the discursive control of ideas of moral citizenship and U.S. imperial desires were projected onto the bodies of poor women, black women, and those who did not conform to biblical gender binaries or Christian colonial sexual norms. In the conflicting spaces (streets, brothels, barracks, fields, homes) between U.S. Protestant ideas of hygiene and Dominican ideas of *moralidad pública* was the looming vision of the Catholic Hispanic nation-state. *Moralidad pública* is a primary mechanism for mobilizing state-sanctioned and extrajudicial violence, or sexual terror.

Conclusion

In this chapter, I have traced some of the ways in which Christian coloniality preconfigures LGBTQ life and death as excess, as morally justified, as outside of the prescriptions of *moralidad pública*. I have also discussed the ways in which Christian preoccupations with sin and salvation continue to inform contemporary preoccupations with moral personhood. The battles over gay marriage signal a much deeper epistemological struggle over moral personhood and citizenship. To engage Christian coloniality is to be able to identify the mechanisms by which Christian constructions of being, knowledge, and power limit and redefine LGBTQ lives and protest. Our primary site for theoretically engaging the concept of Christian coloniality is the D.R., a Catholic Hispanic nation-state.

But it is insufficient to just consider the imbrication of Christian discourses, ideologies, and institutions with nation-state formations. In the next chapter, I present various examples that deepen the discussion of Christian coloniality by focusing on its attendant sexual terror, or the modes of violence that permeate the social body, striking against those whose desires, feelings, and erotic dispositions do not conform to Christian colonial morality—in particular, Christian colonial ideas of biblical manhood and womanhood. I argue that sexual terror does not just encompass the daily lived experiences of Christian coloniality; it indexes the intentional structural and institutional regulation of gender and sexuality through the vehicle of the Catholic Hispanic nation-state.

CHAPTER 2

Sexual Terror

It was a hot May afternoon. Chantal, a trans* activist, and I sat in the interview room as the sound of traffic ricocheted off the walls. We were wrapping up our conversation. I had just asked her what she thought about the relationship between the Catholic Church hierarchy and the Dominican government. She responded that Cardinal López Rodríguez was at the heart of the church's problems and that his position on homosexuality and migrants made him an awful representative of the church. I then asked her if she had a message for him. Chantal directed her curse into the audio recorder. She leaned down and slowly enunciated,

> That damned man—I say it with intention—he should have a heart attack and die. That idiot bastard. That man does not allow us to exercise our power, to have a disco where we can enjoy ourselves, to have a park. He sends the Politur to remove us from the park as though we are immigrants from another country . . . because he is homophobic. . . . When I see someone who wants a state where all of us free and independent people can't have a place, we who don't harm anyone, that person should retire because he does not deserve to live. People like that cause a lot of damage to peoples' sovereignty. . . . I am not someone to judge, because God does not want anybody to die, but God has to make an example of him so that he can see we are human beings and we shouldn't suffer discrimination, because we feel and we suffer—just like him. . . . We, too, are human beings. (interview, Chantal, May 15, 2013)

Chantal's curse was mirrored by Yeisha, who stated, "There are Christians who really don't like to discriminate. When I pass in front of their church, they'll say, 'Little brother, little sister—we have a door open for you. We offer a lot of love. You can come when you want, as you are, as you feel good.' The church I don't like is the one that has that cardinal, the one who should die" (interview, Yeisha, May 17, 2013).

Trans* activists are deeply aware of the sexual terror that shapes their lives. They are also clear about its roots in Christian coloniality. And they are not alone. At an antinuke (nuclear war) rally on March 16, 1982, at Grace Cathedral in San Francisco, Alice Walker stood before the gathered crowd and read aloud a curse she had culled from Zora Neale Hurston's notes. The curse begins by invoking "the Man God: O Great One" and lists the wrongs that have occurred. It then calls in the four winds from the four directions, mobilizing them to bring destruction to the curse-prayer's enemies. The curse calls down extinction, disease, paralysis, death, starvation, thirst, destruction, desolation, pestilence, and the loss of the mind, of power, of wealth, of mercy, of language. It is by all means a radical attempt by the curse-prayer to ensure survival. The irony, of course, is that the curse-prayer's survival is ensconced in a prayer meant to destroy everything that has been built through colonialism and slavery. Walker follows up her reading of the curse by attempting to theorize the personhood of this curse-prayer. She identifies them as a woman, a person of color, or aboriginal and as someone who has been trying for a long, long time to "tell the white man of the destruction that would inevitably come" (1995, 41). Walker leads us through her own troubled preoccupations and her own hopes in delivering this speech as a treatise on ecological disaster at the intersections of centuries of racist and heteropatriarchal violence. From the articulation of this curse as a desire for revenge, Walker restitutes its message as a call to protect earth. As she says, "Earth is my home—though for centuries white people have tried to convince me I have not right to exist, except in the dirtiest, darkest corners of the globe." She ends her speech by stating, "But if by some miracle, and all our struggle, the earth is spared, only justice to every living thing (and everything alive) will save humankind. And we are not yet saved. Only justice can stop a curse" (42). As Walker reminds us, our planet is tied together by ecological suffering. And it is also united through the production of categories of personhood whereby some are deemed worthier of life than others.

I understood Chantal's and Yeisha's anger in relation to the anger of other people who had expressed their disgust with the cardinal and his continuing disregard for the lives of poor, black, and gay people. But I also understood it as a curse, a mobilization of unseen forces with the hopes of achieving particular material ends. The curse was directed to the cardinal's person, a person that Yeisha and Chantal hoped to injure in accordance with the social and psychic injury they had received by way of the cardinal's homophobic, racist ideologies. But these curses were mobilized with the full understanding that I would likely publish them. These were curses meant to extend across space and time in ever-reverberating echoes bouncing off the walls of the cathedral and the surrounding colonial walls. They are a mobilization of unseen forces in the face of sexual terror. They, like the curse unearthed in Walker's examination of Hurston's papers, are curses that project an unmitigated desire for justice.

In *Scenes of Subjection*, Saidiya Hartman reminds us that terror is inscribed in present notions of that which is *black*. She writes, "It [the sheer force of the utterance *black*] acts as a reminder of the material effects of power on bodies and as an injunction to remember that the performance of blackness is inseparable from the brute force that brands, rapes, and tears open the flesh in the racial inscription of the body. In other words, the seeming obstinacy or the 'given-ness' of 'blackness' registers the 'fixing' of the body by terror and dominance and the way in which that fixing has been constitutive" (1997, 58) of particular kinds of human and nonhuman subjects. For Hartman, the words *black* and *blackness* contain within them the terror of subjugated bodies and subjugated desires, and the impossibility of freedom in a racialized world.[1] In this world, *black* is always already an object of terror and slavery. In the process of performing, expanding and recuperating blackness, racial meaning and subjectivity are both produced and challenged. Enactments of (white) power and the reiteration of "the conditions of enslavement" come together to attempt to constrict black life while providing the fungible terrain for the production of meaning.[2] Hartman's description of racial terror captures notions of terror embedded in the U.S. Southern colonial project and the ways in which the productions of blackness have relied on terror as a mode of control for the production of new kinds of subjectivities. I expand on this theorization of racial terror through an elaboration of the concept of sexual terror as it took root in the Spanish colony of Hispaniola. It is important to note that as bodies were broken within spaces of labor, racialization occurred through all the discursive and material apparatuses of Christian coloniality—in particular, through the management of sexuality, sexual relations, and ideas of blood purity and mixture. The monogamous heterosexual family was the greatest measure of Christian colonial success as far back as 1496.[3] In the sexual management of enslaved bodies, *indias* and *indios*, *negras* and *negros*—and all the various racialized iterations of these—became containers for the exercises of Christian moral authority over the souls and bodies of the enslaved through explicit and continuously evolving acts of sexual terror.

Sexual terror refers to the modes of violence that permeate the social body, striking against those whose desires, feelings, and erotic dispositions do not conform to Christian colonial morality—in particular, Christian colonial ideas of biblical manhood and womanhood. The seeming arbitrariness of sexual terror "negates human freedom more efficiently than any tyranny ever could" (Arendt [1968] 2007, 430). Sexual terror as an element of Christian coloniality gives rise to the possibility of racial terror, and has sustained itself over the last five hundred years through the bodies of gender and sexually nonconforming people—for example, when sexuality is used as a way to define race and to mark racial transgression. Sexual terror allows us to elaborate on ideas about racial terror by reframing how the control of the soul was mitigated through sexual subjugation and the control of bodies and desires. Sexual terror is rooted in the control of sexuality as central to the construction of race as an organizing framework. Concerns about *pureza/limpieza de sangre* (and in Aragonia, the sodomite) became the vehicles for achieving the Christian goals of reproduction, evangelization, and capitalist accumulation. Through the control of sexuality, discourses on racial and gendered difference continue to be perpetuated through the continual reinscription of sin/criminality/illness on bodies and desires that are constructed as *different*. As Hortense Spillers reminds us, "Sexuality is the locus of great drama—perhaps the fundamental one—and, as we know, wherever there are actors, there are scripts, scenes, gestures, and reenactments, both enunciated and tacit" (1987, 66). In this drama, streetwalking always leads to the inevitable failure of becoming.

As with racial terror, sexual terror is an all-encompassing experience of violence that permeates Christian coloniality and the structures of knowing and being produced through it. Sexual terror signals the construction of otherness or nonhumanness through sexuality. Sexual terror then marks the shifting interstices and intersections in which personhood is defined, to the exclusion of those who are already configured as nonhuman. Understanding how sexual terror shifts and moves across different kinds of bodies also helps us understand how anyone at any time can suddenly become something other than human, something other than a person.

In turn, streetwalking allows us to navigate both the nonhuman and human realms of being; it is sexual terror that ruptures our personhood. Streetwalking reside not within an individual subject but rather in the relations of power that must be negotiated in response to sexual terror. Streetwalking can emerge through an intentional choice (such as pulling on a leather jacket or sexy lingerie) or by the sudden, unexpected experience of sexual terror—such as being verbally or physically assaulted.[4]

Sexual terror is not something that is limited to the streets or that occurs only as a result of abuses of state authority. For many LGBTQ people, terror can begin in the home, at school, and in the everyday. The fact that the boundaries between public and private domains are often rendered nonexistent is one aspect of Christian colonial power that is made visible through streetwalking. Families and the discourses around families are one such site that brings this aspect to the fore. But so are state, national, and international policies. In the next sections of this chapter, I will discuss how national and international debates and policies contribute to the production of sexual terror. I will first focus on the production of LGBTQ identities and refutations against laws within international fora. I then turn to a discussion of how homophobic and transphobic violence transits through the institutions and discourses of the Catholic Hispanic nation-state and into broader publics, as demonstrated by the actions surrounding the appointment of James "Wally" Brewster to serve as ambassador to the D.R. This chapter ends with an analysis of universalized concepts of LGBTQ identities and the various ways in which LGBTQ activists both appropriate and subvert homogenized concepts of personhood.

God and Gays

On January 28, 2011, a broad range of Caribbean LGBTQ organizations and affiliated groups, including those in the Dominican Republic, issued a statement to the international online media about Ugandan activist David Kato's murder (Gettleman 2011). The statement signaled the mobilization of the universalized categories of LGBTQ in the service of local struggles. It states, "Were it not for advocacy late last year, thirteen Caribbean countries would have allowed 'sexual orientation' to be removed from an international statement of commitment [UN Resolution A/HRC/14/24] to protect persons from unlawful killing because of who they are. David's death, following threats against his life, is a gripping reminder of the importance of those protections, and a sobering one of how much more work needs to be done to give people the right to freedom over their bodies in places like Africa and the Caribbean" (SASOD-Guyana 2011). At the time, Kato's murder was part of a larger wave of media exposure about homophobia-related violence in the Global South. In 2010 alone, international media reported numerous extrajudicial killings of gay men in Jamaica as well as a series of death threats against and assassinations of gay, lesbian, and transgender activists in Honduras. In the Dominican Republic, just a month before Kato's murder, a Dominican trans* organization posted a report on their web page detailing violence against trans* women. In 2010, there were eleven documented (known) murders of trans* women and gay men in the capital city of Santo Domingo. For many Dominican LGBTQ activists, David Kato's murder was an international reflection of a crisis that many were experiencing locally.

At the time of his murder, Kato was at the forefront of a Ugandan national effort to overturn a parliamentary bill proposing the death sentence for homosexuality. The bill had been put before Uganda's parliament following the March 2009 visit of three U.S. Evangelical ministers "who held rallies and workshops in Uganda discussing how to turn gay people straight, how gay men sodomized teenage boys and how 'the gay movement is an evil institution' intended to 'defeat the marriage-based society'" (Gettleman 2011). These ministers were critiqued in the international media for the role they played in promoting the bill.

In spring 2010—mere months before Kato's murder—the United Nations General Assembly was in a debate that focused on the question of protection for homosexuals and other sexual minorities from extrajudicial, summary, or arbitrary executions. This debate—the first of its kind on the General Assembly floor—was an outgrowth of over eleven years of advocacy by LGBTQ international human rights organizations and groups as well as local and regional efforts throughout the world. Among those opposed to the resolution was the Holy See's permanent observer to the United Nations, Archbishop Celestino Migliore, who stated,

In particular, the categories "sexual orientation" and "gender identity," used in the text, find no recognition or clear and agreed definition in international law. If they had to be taken into consideration in the proclaiming and implementing of fundamental rights, these would create serious uncertainty in the law as well as undermine the ability of states to enter into and enforce new and existing human rights conventions and standards. Despite the *statement*'s rightful condemnation of and protection from all forms of violence against homosexual persons, the document, when considered in its entirety, goes beyond this goal and instead gives rise to uncertainty in the law and challenges existing human rights norms. (Vatican 2008)

Archbishop Migliore signaled the development of a legal category of gays, lesbians, bisexuals, and trans* persons as the primary reason for opposing UN Resolution A/HRC/14/24. By creating a legal category of "those protected from discrimination" (Pullella 2008), he argued, these resolutions, toolkits, and initiatives would create the ground for legitimizing gay marriage—something the Catholic Church would unequivocally oppose (Catholic League 2009). In addition, Archbishop Migliore expressed concerns that this resolution would create a situation in which states that were opposed to gay marriage would be unduly reprimanded. On May 26, 2010, a majority of countries signed Resolution A/HRC/14/24, which included sexual minorities and homosexuals as a protected category (UNHRC Report 2010; United Nations News Service 2011). Among countries in Africa, the Caribbean, and Latin America, there were a total of thirty-two signatories—far from a majority.[5]

The resolution also preceded the adoption of a document developed by the European Union (EU) Working Party on Human Rights on June 8, 2010: the "Toolkit to Promote and Protect the Enjoyment of All Human Rights by Lesbian, Gay, Bisexual and Transgender (LGBTQ) People." The toolkit aims to provide employees of the EU working with developing nations (in embassies, in delegations, and as representatives) and "international civil society organizations" with the tools necessary to "promote and protect the human rights of lesbian, gay, bisexual and transgender (LGBTQ) people" and "to enhance the EU's capacity to proactively address cases of human rights violations against LGBTQ people and structural causes behind these violations" (EU Council 2010, 6). I learned about the toolkit from Dominican LGBTQ activists who posted the announcement through various online forums in autumn 2010. Dominican LGBTQ activists, who have historically received financial and logistical support from numerous international foundations and groups (including the EU, U.S.-based foundations, the Centro Cultural de España, and the Centre Cultural Française), were excited to see the document because several of them were adamant that this toolkit would benefit local advocacy efforts for LGBTQ rights in the Dominican Republic (interviews in December 2010 with D.C.M., N.H.M., R.R., and V.S.D.). The toolkit includes

EU Human Rights Toolkit [handwritten annotation]

language now standardized and universalized within international human rights work and scholarship on LGBTQ persons. It reads, "Lesbian women and gay men are homosexuals: people whose sexual orientation is towards someone of the same sex. Bisexuals are people whose sexual orientation is towards both sexes. Transgender is the state of one's 'gender identity' (self-identification as male, female, both or neither) not matching one's 'assigned gender' (identification by others as male or female based on physical gender). 'Transgender' does not imply any specific form of sexual orientation. Sexual orientation (attraction towards others that may or may not involve sexual activity) is distinct from sexual activity" (EU Council 2010, 4). Shortly after the publication of the toolkit and following the Amnesty International (2011) report, U.S. and EU representatives began to extensively document human rights abuses against LGBTQ persons in the D.R. Simultaneously, the Cardinal López Rodríguez increased his discursive attacks against streetwalking, focusing on Dominicans of Haitian descent, sex workers, LGBTQ people, and others socializing in gay clubs and public spaces. His attacks included pressuring local neighborhood groups to shut down gay clubs, encouraging police round-ups of LGBTQ people socializing in public spaces, and continuing his public outcries about foreigners who had come to poison the country's youth with their aberrant sexual behavior.

The ongoing persecution of streetwalking in Dominican society makes this a difficult subject to consider, given that Dominican LGBTQ activists are caught between the Global North's imperial interests and the struggle against the sexual terror produced by Christian coloniality. To date, the U.S. and the EU governments, as well as international human rights groups based in the Global North, have documented human rights abuses against LGBTQ subjects in the Dominican Republic. And just as new attention to human rights abuses by the U.S. is complicated by imperial relations, the EU toolkit is not necessarily an immediate cause for celebration. It did not prevent David Kato's murder, nor did it foment accountability from governmental and police institutions in Uganda. In the larger context of Uganda's execution bill, Kato's murder prompted EU pressure on President Museveni. With the threat of losing foreign aid, the Ugandan execution bill was subsequently scrapped.

This use of pressure by the EU is part of a longer history and larger trend of the policing of postcolonial bodies and spaces by former colonial imperial powers. The former colonial empires of Europe established the terms for the persecution of subjects who did not / could not conform to biblical gender binaries and heteronormative imperatives. Today, these former colonial empires, now allied within the rubric of the Global North, continue to exert their power through the continued management of gender and sexuality. The same states that once persecuted sodomy and buggery in the colonies now exert pressure on former colonies to uphold LGBTQ human rights. This is despite their dismal track records that include numerous LGBTQ civil and human rights abuses within their imperial

Discipline

home spaces. We then have to consider how LGBTQ subjects and questions of LGBTQ human rights have become central to colonial-imperial initiatives aimed at disciplining nations of the Global South. Foreclosed by nationalist discourses that position them as the "other's other"—as a subject inherent to European/U.S. imperial dominance—those same LGBTQ subjects are not necessarily welcome within the borders of the states of the Global North that so promptly defend them in the international arena (Puar 2007; Reddy 2011; Stoler 1995). LGBTQ activists in the D.R. are fully aware of this dynamic; recall Thalia's story of the protest against the cardinal in 2004, when LGBTQ activists took to the streets ironically singing to the cardinal, "Send me to Europe, or to New York . . . ," knowing that Europe and New York did not necessarily want them there either.

In the D.R., a 2006 public-opinion survey demonstrated that 56 percent of the population was opposed to granting equal civil rights to LGBTQ people. That same year, the Dominican government legalized prostitution (Artiles Gill and Ortega Espinal 2008). In 2009, Dominican subjects and the Dominican Congress were engaged in a battle over citizenship and the constitutionalization of protections for women *and* LGBTQ Dominicans. Though there is no explicit antisodomy law, an April 2011 human rights report released by the U.S. embassy in the Dominican Republic cited extensive police brutality and social discrimination against LGBTQ people (U.S. Embassy 2010): LGBTQ youth are kicked out of public schools and people are arrested without charges, are fired from their jobs, are denied housing, and experience physical attacks, intimidation, assaults, and threats of violence. The D.R.'s social, political, and economic landscapes are undergoing rapid neoliberal transformations that include (for example) the signing of the Dominican-Central American Free Trade Agreement (D.R.-CAFTA) in 2005, a new constitution in 2010, and the presidential elections of May 2012. As the D.R. becomes further embedded within globalized neoliberal economic structures, it is also further consolidating its Catholic Hispanic territorial and ethno-racial claims. As a result, those who challenge Catholic Hispanic racial, gender, and sexual ideologies become increasingly vulnerable. In 2009, two trans* sex workers were murdered by police, who have yet to be prosecuted (Sosa 2010); at the June 2010 Pride parade, as I will recount in chapter 3 (Confrontación), a police officer assaulted a prominent lesbian activist in a car full of trans* and gender nonconforming people. All the conditions and public experiences of violence resulted in an upsurge of social and political engagement by LGBTQ activists, the development of new social and political groups, the establishment of a LGBTQ legal aid society, and a Metropolitan Community Church (ICM). It also produced the conditions by which the LGBTQ framework made the violences of the Catholic Hispanic nation-state legible and parallel to those violences that had produced Kato's murder.

international orgs. eroding family

Family Values

On January 27, 2012—two years after the Dominican government ratified a new constitution (and two years after the first international report on LGBTQ human rights in the D.R.)—Cardinal López Rodríguez and then first lady (and vice president since May 2012) Margarita Fernández stood on a stage for the opening of the new Center for the Integral Formation of Youth and Family. There, they spoke to the serious threats made on families "at this time." These threats, according to the cardinal, emerged from the "fraudulent politicians and international organizations" (Jiménez 2012) working on behalf of "liberal governments" who support homosexuals and, more explicitly, gay and lesbian marriage. The cardinal stated, "Not only is it general understanding that has turned against the family. Now, all types of perversions have spread everywhere. [Including in] irresponsible legislation" (Jiménez 2012). The cardinal and the first lady made it clear that family and human values come from the home—literally, the "breast" of the home (Jiménez 2012; Hoy Digital 2012; "El Cardenal" 2012). Immediately following the event, the first lady went on camera declaring, "Families are made up of a man and a woman. Men and women, we have the responsibility to raise our children, to shape them. . . . Families have to understand that it is families which are the center of development in all societies" (Jiménez 2012). *bio determinism* ✦

In this political crèche, the church and state apparatus was made evident via the figure of the paternal voice of God (the cardinal) speaking before and to the mother/wife figure of the nation (Vice President Fernández). This apparatus holds a logic of divine right over and above secular law and human or civil rights. This has implications not only for contemporary Dominican society but also for the forging of an imagined future state toward which contemporary society must work. Patriarchal authority, derived from divine authority, is inscribed in political doctrine in such a way that "the evolution of the monogamous family is the best guarantee within evolutionary time for political authority to be securely grounded in fatherly authority" (Das 2007a, 96).

In 2009, Dominicans and the Dominican Congress (with support from the Catholic Church hierarchy) were engaged in a very public and brutal battle centered on citizenship and women's rights. These debates resulted in the 2010 constitution—subsequently referred to as the new constitution—that passed on January 26, 2010. Provoked by the platform on which President Fernández was elected in 2008, the new constitution is unequivocal in its assertion of citizenship as a status reserved only for Dominican (*jus sanguinis*) adults "18 years of age and/or for those who are or have been married, even if younger than 18 years of age" (article 21). Citizenship debates have been entrenched in Dominican public policy debates even farther back than 1942 (Mayes 2008; Zeller 2010), when Trujillo granted suffrage to women. The new constitution takes up these inheritances and inscribes them with Christian colonial logics that center neoliberal rhetorics of inclusion, equality, progress, and democracy while simultaneously codifying specific kinds of racial, gendered, and sexual belonging within the fabric of the Catholic Hispanic nation-state.

The repression of the Catholic Hispanic nation-state became extremely evident with the constitutional reform process, which continued the denial of constitutional protections for LGBTQ citizens at the same time that it fostered the criminalization of abortion in 2016 (Camara de Diputados 2016). Contradictions embedded within the language of the constitution generate a context for increasingly repressive measures as well as potentially unresolvable constitutional conflicts (Paiewonsky 2009; So 2011). The repressive nature of the conflicts generated by the new constitution most explicitly demonstrates itself in four forms: the inconsistent use of gender-inclusive language throughout the text, the development of amendments that explicitly nullify women's rights, the implicit exclusion of protections that specifically affect LGBTQ subjects and ethnic minorities, and the continual, purposeful replication of a Christian colonial biblical binary gender ideology.

Prior to the new constitution, the D.R. was the only nation-state in Latin America and the Caribbean to lack a statement of equal rights based on gender (Molyneux 2000). That this changed with the new constitution represented potential constitutional advances in key areas relevant to women and gender equality (Ministerio de la mujer 2010), including "the principle of equality, women's right to a life free of violence, the recognition of domestic labor, the recognition of common law marriage, the right to equal pay for equal labor, . . . and the presence of the language of gender throughout the Constitutional text" (CLADEM 2011). But there are many problematic assumptions in these areas of advancement. For example, the recognition of domestic labor refers to the recognition of bourgeoisie—middle- and owning-class—women's roles as *amas de casa* (housewives); it does not consider the thousands of women who work as domestic laborers *for* the *amas de casa*. Similarly, equal pay for equal work does not address gendered divisions of labor. For example, in banks, only women *de buena presencia* ("of good appearance"—a racialized, gendered, and age-specific term) are hired, and they are hired to occupy specific positions. Women, in general, are not promoted as bank managers and are not hired for many professional positions; dark-skinned women generally do not occupy positions in public. While effeminate men *de buena presencia* may have public positions, they, too, will not generally be promoted to positions of authority, and *macha* women and trans* folks won't even get a foot in the door. In this case, the problem is less so access to equal pay than it is access to equal labor positions or even opportunities to work.

The reality of trans* Dominican subjects' lives highlights yet other shortcomings of the new constitution. For one, the gendering of Spanish language replicates ideas of biblical manhood and womanhood as mutually exclusive and

opposite degrees of being that specifically exclude gender nonbinary and trans*
possibilities. Spanish language extends gender all the way to inanimate objects,
but conflicts about the gendering of animate beings have generated new gender
language forms that are not yet in use in the Academia Real de la Lengua Española or the new constitution. Most importantly, and most complicatedly, the
elaboration of gender specificity within the new constitution signals a success
for the feminist movement while obfuscating the realities of trans* Dominicans'
lives. The feminist movement's urging to include gender binary language as a
way to specify women's place within civil, economic, political, and social worlds
also deeply undermines the existence and realities of third-gender or multigendered persons. Lastly, centering LGBTQ subjects in this discussion highlights
how fights for marriage equality continue to replicate the ideology of biblical
manhood and womanhood as cisnormative standards for civil freedom.

The union of divine and secular authority within the new constitution is
most clearly articulated in article 37, which states that "the right to life is inviolable from conception to death" (Asamblea Nacional de la República Dominicana 2010). Only one of a handful of constitutions in the world to define life
from the moment of conception, the new constitution created the parameters
for the criminalization of abortion in all circumstances. Juridically distinct from
the protection of "unborn children," defining life from the moment of conception draws from two key preceding documents. The first is the 1983 Holy See's
Charter of the Rights of the Family, in which article 4 states, "Human life must
be respected and protected absolutely from the moment of conception" (Holy
See 1983). The second is the American Convention on Human Rights, article 4.1,
which states, "Every person has the right to have his life respected. This right
shall be protected by law and, in general, from the moment of conception. No
one shall be arbitrarily deprived of his life" (IACHR 1969). Recent legal analyses
of constitutional shifts throughout Latin America demonstrate that a narrow
interpretation of defending life from the moment of conception is mutable (Bergallo and Ramón Michel 2016). However, in the D.R., the codification of defining
life "from the moment of conception" was mobilized for increasingly repressive
measures.

The new constitution, however much it served as a landmark for a more open
democracy, has not resulted in greater gender equality or the furtherance of
rights among the most vulnerable in Dominican society (Tejada Yangüela 2012).
Rather, it has fomented potentially unresolvable constitutional and legal conflicts
between the national constitutional mandate "to protect the right to life from
the moment of conception" (Asamblea Nacional de la República Dominicana
2010, Art. 37) and the international mandate to protect women's rights, including
reproductive freedom as outlined by the Convention on the Elimination of All
Forms of Discrimination against Women (CEDAW; U.N. 1979).[6] The redefinition
of life from the moment of conception created the constitutional basis on which,

in 2016, the Dominican legislature criminalized abortion under all circumstances (Pérez Reyes 2016). Seemingly, the Dominican legislature's decision is perhaps a reflection of the fundamentalist forces at play within the nation-state more so than a reflection of the fundamentalist potential of the idea of life from the moment of conception.

Veena Das has argued that the regulation of birth and reproduction is a site through which "the idea of God as author of nature and time is displaced and the political body is seen as subject to death and decay" (2007a, 94). But in the Catholic Hispanic nation-state, a Christian colonial concept of nature and time reformulates the political body as the grounds through which the Catholic Hispanic nation-state intervenes to ensure the survival of both state and God. This is carried out through the lives of its subjects. The processes of the Catholic Hispanic nation-state reflect a deep and willing integration of Christian moral values into the secular structure of constitutional and civil law.[7] Within this context, women who seek abortion are guilty of not only immorality (Why were they pregnant in the first place, and by whom?) and murder (life is from conception) but potentially also treason (an attack on the life of the fetus is an attack against the nation) and abomination (an attack on the life of the fetus is an attack against the Christian God). The sovereign must not only (re)produce himself, but he must do so in perpetuity. The state, holding rights over death and life, thereby relies on the idea of both "nature" and God in the project of its own reproduction (Agamben 2005; Foucault 1978). In this framework, the death of women in childbirth or because of childbearing is only one other duty that assures that women, like men, are "ready to die for the continuity of the political [sovereign] body" (Das 2007a, 100) and Christian redemption.

This logic is also extended to LGBTQ persons. As beings lacking moral personhood vis-à-vis the Catholic Hispanic state, LGBTQ persons' deaths are reconceptualized as a necessary sacrifice in the larger project of the nation-state's perpetuation. These same forces that seek the nation-state's *and* Christianity's perpetuation also espouse liberal discourses of equality. Article 39 of the new constitution is yet another example of the new constitution's embedded contradictions; it guarantees the right to equality, with several important exclusions. It states that "persons are born free and equal before the law, they receive the same protection and treatment from the institutions, authorities and other persons and enjoy the same rights, freedoms and opportunities, without any discrimination for reasons of gender, color, age, disability, nationality, family ties, language, religion, political or philosophical opinion, and social or personal condition" (Asamblea Nacional de la República Dominicana 2010). Gender, the first of the protected classes, in a strict interpretation only refers to biblical manhood and womanhood, as clarified in clause 4, which states that "woman and man are equal before the law." The implicit exclusion of third- or multigender categories creates a context of inequality. LGBTQ activists in the Dominican Republic have mobilized for the inclusion of sexual orientation and gender identity as two additional protected classes. In many cases, they have proposed the idea of "social or personal condition" as an entrée into the expansion and articulation of protections within this article.

Though there are no ratified international laws in relation to sexual orientation and gender identity, the Yogyakarta Principles, developed in 2006, make a set of recommendations for the development of international standards. International bodies have shown continual reticence toward the idea of ratifying any sort of human rights document or protections on the basis of sexual orientation or gender identity (O'Flaherty and Fisher 2008). However, a few states have commended the principles and have adapted language from the principles in national discourse. This, of course, does not imply an equal application of laws or true political, economic or social change. Equally problematic are the moves by countries from the Global North to use another nation-state's standing on the rights of sexual minorities to enact racist national and immigration policies (Puar 2007). Given that the new constitution "gives constitutional status to international human rights laws that have been signed and ratified by the Dominican Republic" (So 2011, 730), international conventions do have a role to play in challenging irresolvable constitutional dilemmas. They present strategically universal opportunities for the negotiation of locally repressive policies.

As in other Caribbean nations, in the D.R., "sexual agency and erotic autonomy ... pose a challenge to the ideology of an original nuclear heterosexual family that perpetuates the fiction that the family is the cornerstone of society" (Alexander 2005, 22). The new constitution is a document that establishes racist, xenophobic, heteropatriarchal, and religiously fundamentalist ideologies. A constitution that focuses on a narrative of progress vis-à-vis gender without questioning the fundamental "conviction that women must be governed by men [as a belief that has become] interwoven social and political forces ... at the heart of structures of power and subordination" (Pateman and Mills 2007, 135) or that gender itself is not a mutable category undermines its own authority even as it seeks to legitimate democratic principles of equality. It fails to encompass the wide range of gendered and sexual experiences of those at home and abroad. It also effectively reflects tensions central to the negotiations among Christian institutions' moral authority, the nation-state's responsibility to its citizens, and the lived realities presented by all of us streetwalking through the nation's *calles*.

MR. BREWSTER GOES TO GAZCUE

In June 2013, U.S. president Barack Obama nominated James "Wally" Brewster, an openly gay man, as U.S. ambassador to the Dominican Republic. Cardinal López Rodríguez and other Catholic Church representatives immediately voiced their disapproval of the nomination, claiming that the values and laws of the U.S.

gay ambassador [handwritten margin note]

and the D.R. were inherently different, and on that basis, Dominican national values had to be respected. While not directly opposing to the nomination, the cardinal sought to diminish it by critiquing the U.S. government. He stated, "We can never predict what the U.S. will do." The bishop of Santo Domingo, Pablo Cedano, took a stronger position, stating that Brewster's reality "is far from our cultural reality" and that Brewster would "suffer [if he came here] and [would] have to leave" (*RB News* 2013). He went on to critique President Obama's decision as a "lack of tact and respect by the United States" (Listindiario.com 2013).

The Evangelical church coalition convened large public demonstrations in front of the U.S. embassy in Santo Domingo and called on their members to boycott the nominations (Leclerc 2013). Pastor Sauford Medrano "call[ed] on President Danilo Medina to adhere to the Christian values that sustain the Dominican nation" and stated that Medina "[should] act with free and independent will within his role as the dignified representative of the sovereign Dominican state, to protect the values of the nation." In conclusion, he said, "We [Evangelical Dominicans] do not accept this nomination" (El Día 2013). The Christian demonstrators demanded that the Dominican president intervene in the nomination, stating that the ambassador's presence would be "an insult to good Dominican customs [and] would be a great inconvenience to society" (El Día 2013). Articles in Christian newsletters made claims that this kind of appalling act would never occur in "countries like Afghanistan or Yemen—or other nations with Muslim customs and beliefs—by virtue that [homosexuality] clashes with the legal, moral, and religious tenets" (Cristianodigital.net 2013) of Islam. By extension, the argument went, in a Christian-Catholic society such as the D.R., this logic should also apply.

The Brewster nomination was no small matter. It came in the aftermath of major changes in the Dominican Constitution, a process in which representatives of the church had active roles. The Christian ministers' demands to the Dominican government were also an attempt by Christian (non-Catholic) leaders to mirror the church's exercise of social and political authority over Dominican society. The reactions of religious leaders staved off Brewster's approval until November 2013, though through a complex interplay of U.S. political and economic power, they did not stop it. In the meantime, while Christian activists mobilized anti-LGBTQ campaigns, LGBTQ activists mobilized commercial boycotts, public conferences, and the Caravana del orgullo and drew on international attention. But the issue continued even after Brewster's appointment. In 2015, when Brewster elicited attention to widespread corruption in the Dominican government and to the issue of denationalization of Dominicans of Haitian descent, the cardinal stated, "This man [Brewster] needs to be inside his embassy, and as the wife of a man, like all wives who take care of their homes, he should also just stick to his housework" (Lavers 2015; J. Thomas 2015). These heteropatriarchal ideas about masculinity and, indeed, heteropatriarchy itself—the idea

Called out on / Discrim + corrupt [handwritten margin note]

that a gay man is not a real man and that a woman as a wife only has her place in the home—demonstrate biblical manhood and womanhood as two operative constructs within Christian coloniality. Christian coloniality itself, in turn, has contributed to the binary and racialized construction of contemporary gender ideologies that contribute to heteropatriarchy.

Through Christian coloniality, biblical manhood—in addition to being conceptualized in relationship to God—positions a man as protector of and provider for his wife and children. Masculinity itself is constituted through these vectors of relationship: subordination to the Christian God and Jesus and dominance (protective and provisionary) over women and children. Similarly, biblical womanhood positions women as having an equal duty to God, Jesus, and service. Implicit within biblical woman's service is her constitution as wife to biblical man. This gender ideology has contributed to the gender binary directly (Hird 2000). The biblical gender binary is also made apparent when representatives from the institutions of the church—in this case, the cardinal, a representative of the Dominican Catholic and the international Catholic Church—call into question a person's gender and gender roles because of their sexuality, perceived weaknesses, and/or failure to embody biblical manhood.

Cardinal López Rodríguez's critique fostered an international response that eventually led to his replacement in June 2016. But the cardinal's downfall was not due exclusively or even possibly to his homophobia. In September 2013, the Dominican Supreme Court upheld a resolution that effectively denationalized two hundred thousand Dominicans, the majority of whom were of Haitian descent (Cote-Muñoz and Rosario 2015; Gonçalves Margerin, Varma, and Sarmiento 2014; Hannam 2014; C. Pérez 2015). The ruling was declared a gross abuse of human rights by the international media, human rights activists, and other Caribbean nation states. Peruvian novelist and Nobel Prize winner Mario Vargas Llosa made an open declaration at the Mexican International Book Fair. He called on Pope Francis to modernize the Catholic Church. Within his critiques, he specifically named the Dominican cardinal, stating, "I have been actively critiquing [López Rodríguez] because, incredibly, he is supporting racist laws that deprive close to 200,000 Dominicans of their Dominican nationality—solely because they are children or descendants of Haitians. This seems totally incompatible with what it means to represent the Catholic Church" (7dias.com.do 2013). Following on the heels of this statement, the Dominican ambassador to the Vatican, Victor Manuel Grimaldi Céspedes, refuted Vargas Llosa's statements in an unauthorized letter to the pope. In his letter, he defended the cardinal and made an open critique of Brewster for having received a group of LGBTQ activists at the embassy. Claiming that the cardinal was being unjustly attacked, he explicitly articulated that "in the Dominican Republic, the State's Constitution establishes marriage as between man and woman, and the U.S. ambassador (who is 'married' with a man) has met with members of the Gay and Transsexual collective, which is attacking the Catholic Church and makes assertions that the Dominican state is not *laico* (a lay state)" (Listindiario.com 2014). By making this statement, Grimaldi indirectly named Brewster and the LGBTQ community as the instigators of a defamation campaign. He also side-stepped the immoral nature of xenophobic state policies. Immediately following his unauthorized letter, the Dominican government deauthorized Grimaldi from speaking on official terms. Grimaldi responded with a second open letter in which he defended himself by stating, "We have fundamental values that have forged us as a *pueblo*, nation and state, and these have to be respected by large and small states. With the 2010 Constitution, the Dominican state is *laico* . . . but it respects the Dominican cultural traditions that have deep roots in Christianity. And though it seems paradoxical, we are not a confessional state, we are *laico*. But, as Ambassador, I swore to defend the Constitution. And as a Christian, I will defend the values of Christian culture, independently of my personal faith" (Rosario Adames 2014).

Grimaldi's conflation of the U.S. ambassador's reception of LGBTQ activists at the U.S. embassy (El Caribe 2014) with his defense of the cardinal's well-documented racism against Dominicans of Haitian descent is emblematic of how Christian coloniality is imbricated with ultranationalism within the Dominican sociopolitical landscape. Making recourse to a very limited and fundamentalist interpretation of Catholic morality, Grimaldi minimizes the actual moral, social, and political authority of the cardinal—and the implications of his discourses—and instead attempts to locate the onus of Dominican social problems in the body and presence of the gay U.S. ambassador and LGBTQ Dominicans more broadly. Grimaldi's assertions highlight how ultranationalist calls for sovereignty derive from Christian colonial discourses that continue to replicate gendered, racialized hierarchies of power.

Like in Uganda and elsewhere, the U.S. call for the recognition of LGBTQ rights has been critiqued as a disciplinary imperial exercise. By refuting the significant role that the church plays in Dominican politics, Grimaldi attempts to invalidate the context in which Dominican human and civil rights struggles are embedded and, in its stead, articulate Dominican sovereignty as a Catholic Hispanic struggle for Christian morality—in particular biblical manhood and womanhood.

By naming marriage between a man and a woman as the site of Christian morality, Grimaldi—as in Margarita Ferndández's evocation of family—draws on a colonially constructed ideology of biblical manhood and womanhood. This ideology is challenged by LGBTQ activists. But it is not just biblical manhood and womanhood or even Dominican sovereignty that are at stake. That a Dominican ambassador brought an issue about a U.S. ambassador to the pope also conveys an understanding of canonical law and a religious political system as resting above state jurisdiction. With this series of events, we are witness to how the universal church, the Vatican, and most explicitly, the Holy See and Pope Francis are in the throes of a global negotiation over the existence of their ecclesiastical polity.

These strategies—the diminishment of political authority by critiquing a moral failure to embody biblical manhood or womanhood, the assertion of Christian sovereignty as ultranationalist sovereignty, and the manipulation of Christian morality for the delegitimization of human and civil rights struggles—are but some examples of the ways in which Christian coloniality produces sexual terror. Christian coloniality is manifest in the long history of Christian conversion; national laws defining gendered, racialized identities; national laws regulating marriage as a monogamous union between biblical men and biblical women; and our ideas about what gender and sexuality even are. But Dominican LGBTQ activists weren't having it.

A week after the Christian demonstrations, Dominican LGBTQ activists participating in that year's Caravana del orgullo incorporated both critiques of the Catholic Church's position and symbols and signs of support for "Wally," the name local activists employ in reference to Brewster. Drag queens employed Carnival-like methods: donning the garbs of Catholic authority, they paraded as the cardinal and as priests, absolving parade goers of sins and presiding over the moral temperature of the Caravana. They held Gay Pride flags, and without breaking character, they spoke to the media to proclaim Christian love for all God's children. Other Caravana participants made and posted signs in support of "Wally." Leaders of the LGBTQ activist community held a press conference and spoke to the Dominican public about Brewster coming to the country "as a diplomat and not as a gay activist" (Colectivos LGBT 2013). Some activists attempted to demonstrate how Brewster mirrored Dominican concepts of masculine heteronormative respectability and aimed to frame his position within the logics of Dominican cultural values and human rights. Arguing that the D.R. has diplomatic relations with many countries that support the human rights of LGBTQ persons, the LGBTQ community stated that they rejected the ways in which the religious sectors threatened, ridiculed, and incited hate in the Dominican population. They also questioned the same religious sector's silence "in cases of corruption, and the rape of children and adolescents, as well as the abuses of power perpetrated by religious leaders who are sustained by the Concordato and other policies" (Colectivos LGBT 2013).

In a published public statement, LGBTQ activists articulated that "democracies cannot give themselves the luxury of tolerating the constant interjections of religious functionaries in political matters as though they are *ayatolas*, demanding that the state assume and impose the religious precepts of their churches" (Colectivos LGBT 2013).[8] Lastly, leaders of the LGBTQ movement argued, "One of the primary obstacles to the development of democratic institutions in the country is the lack of an effective separation of Church and State" (Colectivos

LGBT 2013), which they cited as violations of articles 45 and 39 of the 2010 constitution. Dominican LGBTQ activists called attention to what is at stake: Christianity's moral authority within the democratic governance structures of the Catholic Hispanic nation-state.

BEING STREET SMART

In streetwalking, the gender-nonconforming bodies of trans* people are hypervisible against the deserted nighttime landscapes. Streetwalking—by sex workers, activists, entertainers, and LGBTQ activists—reminds us that "the earth is also skin and that [in streetwalking we] can legitimately take possession of a street, or an entire city, albeit on different terms than we may be familiar with" (McKittrick 2006, ix). The potential of death lingers in the night air, behind every car door. The policing of trans* bodies is another chapter in the legacy of Christian coloniality that marks streets as spaces of hypersurveillance. The trans* activist Christian Dumont (who uses multiple gender pronouns) tells us,

> Being trans*, walking through the street at night to take a *carro publico* [share cabs] or a taxi, they load you into their cars for nothing—to round you up. When that happens to me, I know that if you have your *cédula* [national identity card], they can't arrest you because they could easily say they were taking you in for being undocumented. Instead, I fight and I tell the police they have to let me go. But if I am with a *compañero*, to intimidate him, they say to him, "You come with us, not you [meaning me]." I get in the middle and say, "No. You aren't taking either of us in. There are other people here. You have to take everyone on this street if you are taking us in." (interview, Dumont, April 2013)

During the Trujillo dictatorship, there existed extreme and visible modes of surveillance and discipline—including public torture, haphazard disappearances, and the ever-present black *cepillos* (Volkswagen buggies) that patrolled the city streets on the lookout for dissidents. The *cepillos* held both material and symbolic value, embedding the power of the Trujillato in the time-space of the streets. They came to signify political terror through their increasing presence and the repeated association of their presence with the increasing disappearance of loved ones. They were, in effect and in action, an extrajudicial, semiprivate space that moved throughout the veins of the city. People were swallowed up by the *cepillos*, usually alive, and they could disappear altogether or reemerge dead. The silhouettes of those inside were only visible as shadows, masking the very real torture being enacted through both speech and physical acts. Today, the use of cars to carry off those who are streetwalking—including sex workers, trans* people, undocumented people, and Dominicans of Haitian descent—in the middle of the night is a direct replication of a Trujillo-era state tactic, and one that is used regularly to instill sexual terror.

For Dumont, there was nothing exceptional about getting picked up by police. In fact, it was so commonplace that Dumont knew how to defend their self. As a person with a *cédula*,[9] Dumont also had the tools necessary to defend their rights as a citizen, despite the fact that the context of defense is already a violent, unjust circumstance. Their ability to use deflection tactics also emerges from an understanding that if they draw attention to the police officers' actions in a voice loud enough to draw attention to the scene, the likelihood of something happening (abduction or harm) is greatly reduced. A loud, witness-drawing *confrontación* draws attention to the matter at hand. By calling others who are streetwalking to attention, the police are outnumbered, surrounded. Dumont makes it clear that there is a collectivity when they state, "There are other people here. You have to take everyone on this street if you are taking us in." Though it might not work every time, the possibility that Dumont will disappear is lessened because of the act of collective witnessing. Choosing to speak rather than remaining silent enables Dumont to mobilize that collectivity in a way that weakens, and even stops, the police's abuse of power. Dumont's experiences are but one example of the ways in which sexual terror permeates Dominican society.

Being street smart is about knowing what is going on around you. In this section, I have aimed to bring our collective attention to what's going on in the streets. Specifically, I have discussed the case of the D.R. as a Catholic Hispanic nation-state. As a Catholic Hispanic nation-state, the D.R. provides a rich context for thinking through the long and palimpsestic weight of Christian coloniality. We can look to fifteenth- and sixteenth-century debates about the nature of the human and understand that these debates had real material implications for the lives and deaths of Indigenous and African peoples for over three hundred years. We can look to the impact of U.S. occupation and homegrown authoritarian rule in relationship to Christian colonial ideals in order to understand the ways in which sexual terror permeates all aspects of contemporary society. The Catholic Hispanic state brings these dynamics and stories into sharp relief, but they are stories that teach us to think about similar processes taking place across the Americas, the Global South, and the world.

Christianity is far from homogenous or singular. The history of Christianity is deeply structured by local, regional, and global struggles over the discursive meanings of the divine and the divine's relationship to the human. This is of particular importance in the realm of human rights as they affect LGBTQ people.

Within the Spanish colonial processes of the fifteenth and sixteenth centuries, Christian theologians grappled with the discursive justification for genocide, enslavement, and dispossession. For example, in the trials of Valladolid in 1550–1551, Bartolome de las Casas and Juan Gines de Sepúlveda debated notions of the human and whether these notions could be universal and thus applicable to the indigenous peoples of the Americas. In the end, both theologians came to distinctly different conclusions. While Sepúlveda advocated that natural law (drawn from Aristotle) could be universally applied, he suggested that within the premises of natural law, a natural hierarchy existed in which indigenous peoples—and other non-Christian "barbarians"—were squarely at the bottom. Las Casas, on the other hand, drew on concepts of natural law to conclude that all persons—especially those who were not heretics (such as Muslims and Jews)—were capable of embodying Christian virtue and Christianity (Adorno 2007). From Las Casas's point of view, Christianity and its successful embodiment could become the measures of universal personhood. In this way, Christianity was taken up by colonial governors such as Nicolás de Ovando to establish universal Christian measures of human being. The goal of Christian colonial policies was to assist indigenous peoples in that process of entering into "humanness." Those who failed to meet the standards could be (and were) enslaved, killed, and discursively reconfigured as belonging to a primitive past. In other words, by failing to meet the requirements of personhood as determined by a Christian framework, indigenous people inadvertently and unknowingly abdicated their rights to their lands, their belongings, and their persons. It was never a just war.

Our contemporary concepts of human rights emerge from these same Christian colonial preoccupations with the nature of human being among America's indigenous and Africa's sub-Saharan peoples. The possibility that all beings could be human but might not be was deeply interconnected with Christian theological preoccupations with salvation intertwined with Spanish colonial preoccupations with just war and expansion. Las Casas, in particular, is named as the Christo-patriarchal source of human rights law. Drawing on Spanish juridical texts, canonical law, and the Bible, Las Casas argued that natural law made potential Christian subjects of all persons. He did not argue against Spanish conquest but rather against the violence of the conquest, positing that Christian love and its universal messages were more just motivations for expansion across indigenous territories—territories that he argued needed to be protected against savage tyranny. Las Casas effectively constructed universalist arguments of common nature while at the same time making recourse to the necessity to respect the sovereignty of indigenous kingdoms.

Today, human rights and civil rights as applied to liberal notions of citizenship within modern nation-states seemingly represent the broadest and most inclusive modes of personhood and belonging. But is this really the case?

Dominican LGBTQ activists purposely use lesbian, gay, bisexual, and trans* political identities even when tacit subjectivity (Decena 2011) is an option, even when other affective sexual dispositions exist. In this way, LGBTQ personhood serves as a strategic universalism that connects Dominican LGBTQ activists with others facing similar struggles transnationally. The mobilization of LGBTQ personhood as a strategic universalism allows for the possibility of claiming a universal moral personhood that is both human and gay/lesbian/bisexual/ trans*—epistemic categories that are mutually exclusive within the parameters of Christian coloniality. In contrast to strategic essentialism, which collapses distinct enunciations of personhood into essentialist categories for rights struggles, strategic universalism enables us to conceptualize the mobilization of identities like LGBTQ, feminist, and *Afro-descendiente* to "make redemptive personal and ethical sense of the human depth of [our] experience of sexuality [and spirituality] ... [thereby] reclaiming our sexuality and our moral powers of love and transcendence on terms of equal justice" (Richards 1999, 96).

Universalism is an empty signifier "whose very emptiness and lack creates a pluralized, difference-based competition on the part of various particularisms in a democratic social-symbolic field to assume the position of the universal organization" (Lott 2000, 670). Dominican LGBTQ activists transcend the particularities and specificities of their ontological locations to enact and mobilize internationalized, universalized concepts of identities and rights with the full knowledge that these identities do not begin to reflect or encompass the complete range of local, ontological understandings of humanness or personhood. In contrast to Paul Gilroy's use of strategic universalism as a cosmopolitan "planetary humanism" (2000, 327) that transcends but does not transit through the national, in which the particularities of black or LGBTQ struggles are subsumed or erased as viable political concepts (Robotham 2005, 564), the way that Dominican LGBTQ activists enact strategic universalism is through the operationalization of universalized categories like LGBTQ personhood in the struggle against Christian colonial sexual terror. The use of identity categories such as LGBTQ serves to index the *resistencia* mobilized through streetwalking. By taking recourse to international and, in some cases, cosmopolitan LGBTQ identities, Dominican LGBTQ activists draw attention to the shortcomings and breaches of Catholic Hispanic nationalist ideologies while also revealing nationalist anxieties about modernity, progress, and global citizenship. By engaging in these universalisms, Dominican LGBTQ activists are able to access the spaces, resources, and tools necessary for realizing a local struggle against sexual terror, including those persons who may identify as lesbian, gay, bisexual, or trans*. This political orientation is also informed by the principles of *guatiao* and *ubuntu*, concepts distinct from the liberal renderings of personhood that demarcate LGBTQ categorizations.

Attending to erotic orientations undermines totalizing liberal (and neoliberal) narratives of subjectivity. For those who exercise an LGBTQ politics in the realm of social struggle, the issue is not the viability of a public queer life or the radical realization of a Christian spiritual-religious life. The recourse to the language of human and civil rights, however, allows them to navigate both without sacrificing either. For Dominican LGBTQ activists, the promises of liberal human rights activism lie in the realization of LGBTQ *resistencia* to universalized concepts of the human that exclude their very existence—that is, the highest purpose of human and civil rights is the possibility of freedom from church-state oppression as people who fail to conform to biblical notions of personhood. Even as LGBTQ activists fight for civil and human rights, what lies at the heart of the struggle eschews liberal notions of the individual and provides an alternate road map for what it means to be both liberated and a citizen. LGBTQ activists have drawn from the cultural concepts of *guatiao* and *ubuntu*. Building on Allen's (2011) discussion of friendship as a space for freedom that elides liberal notions of citizenship, *guatiao* and *ubuntu*—as fundamental aspects of LGBTQ activist struggles for liberation—recenter notions of friendship and love as strategies and possibilities inherent to *resistencia*. They reveal how erotic orientations are grounded in shared experiences and in a subjectivity that is always already in relation to others.

As Deivis Ventura, an outspoken and well-known gay activist, explained to me, *guatiao* is an Aboriginal word that means "I am you, you are me" (Whitehead 2011). Deivis also equated it with the Xhosa term *ubuntu* in the same conversation. He clarified that both *ubuntu* and *guatiao* mirror the same basic principle: a sense of self as a sense of community. Sitting in a small office at an HIV advocacy organization, I asked Deivis what he understands LGBTQ activism to be about:

ME: Why fight for the rights of LGBTQ people?

DEIVIS: We are not fighting for exceptional rights or special benefits. We are fighting for the rights that are ours to begin with—human rights, rights that we have as Dominican citizens.

ME: I've also noticed that many Dominican LGBTQ activists are involved in other struggles—like the 4 percent education struggle and the *lucha* for the rights of Dominicans of Haitian descent.

DEIVIS: That's right. It is related to the concept *guatiao*, or *ubuntu*. *Guatiao* comes from the Taino and *ubuntu* from Africa. Both concepts mean "I am you, you are me. We are."

ME: Why is this concept so important to Dominican LGBTQ activists? I have heard others use it too.

DEIVIS: First of all, people say we deny our *negritud*. That is not true. Then they say we all want to be *indios*. That is also not true. But to say we are not *indio* and then to deny the way we live our *negritud* is very violent. So in instances when we have met with other Caribbean LGBTQ activists, it has become important for us to clarify our values, our understandings of our identities and histories, and the values that shape our approach to our activism. *Guatiao, ubuntu,* allow us to do just that.

ME: So would you say that these concepts are part of what it means to be Dominican?

DEIVIS: I wouldn't say that people have this as part of their general consciousness, no. But in the LGBTQ community, we know that when we fight for
ourselves, we fight for everyone.

As I wrapped up our interview, I asked Deivis where he first heard the term
ubuntu. He laughed and scolded me: "From Mandela! You don't know Mandela?!" I laughed but admitted that though I knew of Nelson Mandela, I did
not know the history of the word *ubuntu* outside of its presence in the African
American holiday Kwanzaa, which had been acknowledged and celebrated in
my high school. *Ubuntu* is a term from the Nguni language of the Xhosa/Zulu
people. Mandela discussed the term in a 2006 interview and described it as "an
innate duty to support one's fellow man" (Oppenheim 2012, 370). As presented by
Claire E. Oppenheim in her cross-cultural comparison of the concept, "ubuntu
is a spiritual ideal, a way of life that is conceptually represented in a wide range
of sub-Saharan African societies" (2012, 370) and carries within its definition a
"moral directive to create community," "to become more fully, genuinely human,
in unity with one's fellow man" (371). It is also a conceptual framework for how
to carry out the development of this ideal: ubuntu "requires that [ones' harmo-
nious integration into one's community of fellow man] be largely comprised of
direct, face-to-face, positive interaction with one's community members" (371).

As a value and a practice, the concept of *ubuntu* provides Dominican LGBTQ
activists with the necessary framework for grounding their work in the overall
spiritual development of Dominican personhood. Similarly, within the precepts
of LGBTQ activism, *guatiao*, aside from being a social practice, is also a *political*
practice for the establishment of relationships between different communities,
reframing the terms on which solidarities are constructed. In historical literature,
guatiao has been articulated as similar to the Spanish process of *compadrazgo*
(godparenting), in which, "through the sacrament of baptism, parents and god-
parents are united in an indissoluble union" (Arrom 1973, 16). This metaphor is
only problematic in that it is based on unequal relationships between two individuals and mobilizes Christian colonial logics that presume these hierarchies.
Guatiao has also been defined is the practice of establishing mutual alliances
through intentional relationships and the exchange of names (Guitar 2013) and
as the actual name that indigenous people used to describe themselves in the
Caribbean (Whitehead 2011). From these definitions, as well as usage practices
among the Kalinago today, we can surmise that *guatiao* could be construed as
an indigenous Caribbean naming practice that confers alliances, inscribes communal histories onto interpersonal relationships, and redefines communities. As
a concept, it is marked by endemic understandings of interdependence, often
extending beyond the individual to the family and the nation and beyond the
nation to international relationships (personal conversation, José Barreira, October 2012).

In this sense, *guatiao* and *ubuntu* were articulated to me as part of the under-lying cultural logic that informs the Dominican radical politics of belonging among LGBTQ activists in the D.R. *Guatiao* is a concept that has generated a "sense of recognition"—a self-identification that helps things fall into place. As Deivis elaborated to me in our interview, "If you can understand that the strug-gle for human rights is one aspect of what *guatiao* is, then you can understand why we LGBTQ activists don't struggle simply for our rights—*we fight for every-body's rights*" (Deivis's's emphasis). Time and time again, with a diverse range of LGBTQ activists, I heard the same sentiment. Chris, a trans* activist, stated, "What makes us *quír* is that we fight for everybody." Or Monica, another trans* activist, said, "I'm not interested in being free simply to be free. If I am free, it is because we all are." Or Mirla, a lesbian activist, told me early on in my research, "A lesbian politics has to do with the fact that all of us are able to have the same rights—without being part of an institution."

Although these sentiments could be read as expressions of liberal notions of equality, the underlying contextual meaning, and the place of articulation, speaks volumes. When Chris made their statement, we were at a protest organized by a group of people fighting for *justicia fiscal* (economic justice). Chris was not responding to any sort of question; I had not asked Chris why they were there or made any comment about why I was there. Chris was articulating a political position in a group context in which several people were standing around and talking about government corruption. Chris was, most specifically, articulating a *quír* presence—a presence informed by ideas and understandings of community interdependence. It was also a specific location, within *quír*-ness itself, of a politics that extends beyond HIV advocacy or simply belonging. Monica and I, though in the context of a one-on-one interview, were discussing what it means for her to be trans*. Monica's sense of freedom was most importantly about being free in relationship with and to others' freedom. *Guatiao* and *ubuntu*, as Deivis explicitly articulated, offer political possibilities that enable LGBTQ activists to establish alliances with other marginalized groups and with Dominican society as a whole. In this sense, *guatiao* and *ubuntu* signal an erotic orientation toward streetwalk-ing. They enable LGBTQ activists to express their strategic goals in their struggle for civil and human rights as encompassing the exercise of one's power to make decisions for one's personal and collective life without harm to others while also demanding the transformation of the Catholic Hispanic nation-state.

The *guatiao* and *ubuntu* frameworks operate alongside an explicit mobiliza-tion of a strategic universalism that consists of framing local struggles in the language of international movements. This purposefully brings attention to the juridical dimensions of the discrimination Dominican LGBTQ activists face. And despite the potential for instilling the exclusionary logics of neoliberal-ism, the local use of a universal, political notion of *LGBTQ* does not obscure or diminish other self-articulations of LGBTQ relationality. As yet another lesbian activist, Jennifer, stated, "I consider myself a lesbian because it is the classification that society has given a woman who loves another woman." When Mirla stated, in the context of a one-on-one interview, that "a lesbian politics has to do with the fact that all of us are able to have the same rights—without being part of an institution," she was very consciously aware of her own political location and was being clear to me that she is an autonomous, radical lesbian. The entire interview, in fact, was about her personal trajectory in the Dominican lesbian feminist movement and the many instances in which she had been excluded from different circles of activists *because* of her insistence on not belonging to a feminist institution invested in the Catholic Hispanic nation-state. For her, lesbian politics is about the transformation of our idea about what rights are or could be—beyond the institutions or structures that confer them. It is also about rights that extend beyond the personal experiences of lesbians and includes others adversely affected by the policies and actions of a Catholic Hispanic nation-state.

When Dominican LGBTQ activists confront the church (rather than the Dominican government) in protests demanding the recognition of gay marriage, their demand takes on an equally significant moral imperative: the protection of the lives and souls of LGBTQ persons. In the D.R., the grounds for political possibilities shift beyond the mere structures of secular democratic principles, extending into a struggle over the epistemic and ontological realization of human life.

Conclusion

In this chapter, I have traced the ways in which the logics of Christian coloniality produce the conditions of sexual terror. Sexual terror is not just an intimate kind of violence; it also includes the structures and institutions that uphold the ideologies central to the perpetuation of violence. I focus on the multiple layers of structural and institutional Christian coloniality—from how LGBTQ persons are configured through power struggles between the Global North and South to how the state configures personhood as rooted in the heteropatriarchal family. By discussing the social response by Christian leaders in the D.R. to Ambassador Brewster's appointment, I also bring to light the very material, concrete ways in which Christian fundamentalism shapes public conversations about who belongs and who does not. I bring us back to a conversation about universalisms and ask us to consider how universalisms like human rights provide tools for LGBTQ activists to articulate political strategies. But LGBTQ activists in the D.R. are also well aware and make manifest other articulations of personhood.

By drawing out an analysis of Christian coloniality and its attendant sexual terror, I conclude my discussion of the context in which LGBTQ activists live their lives and formulate protests. In the next section of this book, "Streetwalking," we will turn to a discussion of the multiple and overlapping strategies utilized by LGBTQ activists in the realization of their vision for a more just world.

PART II

Streetwalking

Whereas in the previous section I focused on the context in which streetwalking occurs, in this section I focus on the strategies of *resistencia* rooted in erotic orientations toward justice and the transformation of silence—what I call streetwalking.

Streetwalking is a malleable disposition rooted in a range of erotic orientations that simultaneously "valorize the logics of resistance" (Lugones 2003, 175) while reconfiguring relations of power. Streetwalking also enables us to mobilize universalized political identities, discourses, and structures in order to rupture the infrapolitical, producing new fields for the mobilization of acts of *resistencia*. Here I present an exploration of how the habitation of LGBTQ political identities at times expands on the liberatory potential present within streetwalking while at other times it constrains the definitional scope of *resistencia*.

As a conscious and intentional strategy to protest national doctrines and laws, LGBTQ activists consistently point out the collusion between fundamentalist Christian colonial ideologies and Dominican nation-state policies. In a powerful letter published in the months preceding the 2016 Dominican elections, LGBTQ activists stated,

> The Coalition of Lesbian, Gay, Transsexual, Transgender and Bisexual activists and organizations in the Dominican Republic calls to the Dominican *pueblo* to not be confused by pseudo-religious leaders in the upcoming elections, scheduled for May 2016. . . . The religious Catholic and Evangelical leaders who have entered the political game standing in alliance with the extreme [political] right, disqualify themselves as potential mediators of the national body. They have abused faith-based organizations, negotiating with detractors of human dignity, and motivating votes for groups that incite hatred, violence, and discrimination against those who go out onto the streets to work for a better country every day. The freedom of religion is a human right; it is also a right protected by our Constitution, which applies to all. Human rights are for all of us. Freedom of expression is for all of us—but not to incite hatred, racism,

and violence. Church leaders have shown us that they have lost their horizon, by acting like conventional political parties, attacking the common worker, and not attacking the true ills that affect us all: corruption, *delincuencia*, sexual violence against children and adolescents, drug trafficking, murder for money, etc. We ask our *pueblo* to think, to question; calling for discrimination, violence, and xenophobia is not patriotic. (*ElDesahogoDominicano* 2016)

With this open letter, LGBTQ activists drew on universal discourses of human rights—as they apply to LGBTQ *and* faith communities—to articulate a clear agentive response to both local homophobic/transphobic violence and global Christian colonial gender ideologies. When the state is both in collusion with the fundamentalist elements of the church *and* unwilling to respond to homophobic and transphobic violence, calling attention to globalized Christian colonial concepts while making recourse to universalized concepts such as the term LGBTQ enables a multifaceted and engaged strategy toward justice.

In the context of the D.R., the definition of LGBTQ identities signals the mobilization of a political logic that connects Dominican LGBTQ activists with others facing similar struggles regionally, hemispherically, and globally. The acronym/ term LGBTQ has served to make local collective efforts legible to neoliberal international funding structures, human rights organizations, and networks. It also enables the articulation of a political category that can be made juridically legible in both national civic courts and international human rights platforms. Dominican LGBTQ activists first and foremost mobilize LGBTQ political identities to draw national attention to the ways in which the church and nation-state collude to repress people and communities that fall outside of the framework of Catholic Hispanic personhood. LGBTQ political identities open up space for marking social difference even as they mobilize a homogenized, universalized liberal subject. By marking social difference and universalized identities in this way, streetwalking mobilizes a plethora of economic, political, and social resources in the struggle for existence.

When Dominican LGBTQ activists streetwalk, they are bringing attention to instances of unregulated Christian colonial moral and political power that produce and maintain the conditions of sexual terror that feed into the loss of street-walking life. By using a range of strategies—including the mobilization of the universalized term LGBTQ—Dominican LGBTQ activists also bring attention to how their local struggle is directly informed and impacted by the global, universalized LGBTQ human rights framework.

While Gayatri Spivak's concept of "strategic uses of essentialism" (1988, 291) has proven useful, here I choose instead to reimagine the central debates underlying the construction of strategic essentialism by theorizing a countervailing dynamic I call *strategic universalisms*. Central to Spivak's concerns about identity and essentialisms are questions about the ways in which power structured representations and actions by subaltern subjects—specifically, poor, postcolonial, third-world women and women of color. Spivak critiques how the production of knowledge itself extended European and U.S. colonial-imperial desires over and through the bodies of those deemed Other to produce subjects (e.g., women) while also making it impossible for these subjects to exist outside of the limits of Western discourse.

In this sense, we can understand LGBTQ identities as strategically essentialist: the Western construction of nonheteronormative sexualities and genders has been homogenized into the construct of a category of personhood indexed by the acronym LGBTQ. Similar to the subject category of women, the concept and construct of LGBTQ sexual identities emerged explicitly within the context of the Global North, and they emerged as already unstable and mutable. In the Global North, sexual identities have been "provisional, ever precarious, dependent upon, and constantly challenged by, an unstable relation of unconscious forces, changing social and personal meanings, and historical contingencies" (Weeks 2002, 186). The theories and activisms that have emerged from sexual and gender justice struggles and scholarship in this context have existed at the boundaries between essentialist desires and constructivist critiques, producing queerness and all other derivations within an ever-broadening display of sexual and gender variance (Duggan 1994, 5). Ironically, it was the process of colonial-imperial conquest that instituted the conditions by which sexuality was first suppressed and then expressed as a distinct subject and political location within the Global South (Garza Carvajal 2010). But now that we are here, and after decades of arguments within the Global North about the usefulness, valency, and applicability of sexual and gender identities, the acronym LGBTQ has developed as a political category that circulates in national and international social, political, and juridical contexts. In other words, streetwalking does not passively assume LGBTQ identities. Streetwalking activists are savvy about the ways in which the Global North's discourses can be appropriated to forward their own complex local and national sociopolitical agendas.

As an identity category, LGBTQ indexes specific kinds of sexual and gender differences and desires in ways that eschew one of the primary political goals of sexual and gender justice activism—which is often to undo the categories of sexuality and gender altogether. This political contradiction is central to the active, self-aware appropriation of LGBTQ identity as a political choice that enables a particular kind of work in relationship with the Global North while also transparently signaling who and how those positioned outside of the Global North are subject to its disciplinary mechanisms. In this sense, the interpretive shift between strategic essentialism to strategic universalism aims to highlight how in streetwalking, our capacity to act is predicated on the capacity to conceptualize the self as always already in relation. While LGBTQ has functioned as a strategic essentialism in the Global North, in the context of those *subject to* the Global

North, the same identity serves to enter universal governance institutions and mobilize international resources and mechanisms in service to local and national movements. The mobilization of LGBTQ political identities is much less about subjectivity and much more about the mobilization of strategically universalized identities as a strategy from which to assert broader understandings of Dominican personhood.

In the chapters that follow, I will talk about additional elements of streetwalking, specifically the strategies used by LGBTQ activists in their *resistencia* to the sexual terror produced by Christian coloniality within the Catholic Hispanic nation-state. In the first chapter of this section, "Confrontación," I tell three stories. In each story, I demonstrate how LGBTQ activists grapple with violence and how they use their experiences of violence as a launching pad for *resistencia*. I share stories about trans* activists' intimate histories, gay activists' encounters with the police, and lesbian activists' responses to verbal and physical violence. In streetwalking, erotic orientations are at times moving toward (Ahmed 2006, 115) a sense of survival and at others toward a sense of *supervivencia*, and they are usually always toward justice. In streetwalking, LGBTQ activists transform silence into power through *confrontación*, where they bring the truth of their lives front and center. In the second chapter of this section, "Flipping the Script," I discuss moments when streetwalking transforms silence into action. I share the stories of how streetwalking is interpellated through Christian colonial violence and the violence of the Catholic Hispanic state. LGBTQ activists subvert the conditions under which they are called into question, repositioning themselves as worthy of respect. They transform accusations and violence into gestures and practices of *resistencia* that—like my own *tigueraje* with the immigration officer—challenge the assumptions of Christian colonial violence and power. And in the last chapter of this section, "Cuentos," I discuss the creation of queer archives through the sharing of *cuentos* (stories) that draw on what is both possible and impossible, what is spoken and unspoken—revealing how the contours of silence are shaped and revealed through *cuentos*. Existing at the intersections of what can and cannot be said, what can and cannot be proven, *cuentos* generate spaces of meaning where streetwalking becomes more than death and instead produces life.

CHAPTER 3

Confrontación

Streetwalking enacts *resistencia* along various registers of *confrontación. Confrontación* translates into English as "confrontation." But *confrontación* in Spanish implies a wrestling with internal subjective states and of ideas of oneself and others alongside a wrestling and struggle with others. This struggle with others may include speech acts or physical confrontation, usually originating with the affirmation and acceptance of oneself as capable of *confrontación.* Dominican LGBTQ activists use *confrontación* as one strategy within a Christian colonial social context marked by a long history of public political protest against authoritarianism and imperialism; other political protest strategies have included guerilla warfare, armed resistance, clandestine resistance, and the development of extensive social mechanisms to deal with authoritarian police forces. These other modes of resisting repression are not usually inscribed within global LGBTQ rights frameworks.[1] However, they deeply inform streetwalking dispositions toward repression—to fight against it, to confront it.

Since the signing of the Concordat, the Dominican Catholic Church *jerarquía* has received undisclosed amounts of money from the government and the president's discretionary funds for its parishes, buildings (churches, cathedrals), educational centers (seminaries, primary and secondary schools and universities), and health centers (hospitals, dispensaries). The church also directs all matters related to education; its bishops, archbishops, and cardinals are appointed as colonels and generals in the national army; and its members actively participate in national politics and bestow legitimacy to private enterprises. In addition, its "religious, educational and welfare work with the population allowed the church to emerge as a power to be reckoned with when examining Dominican social and political realities" (Betances 2007, 157).

It is within this broader context that Cardinal López Rodríguez wielded his power to make proclamations detrimental to the lives, livelihoods, and well-being of LGBTQ persons. From calling gay people in the colonial city *lacras sociales* (Weber 2014), to using his pulpit to make vitriolic assertions about homosexuals as foreign invaders, to insulting international ambassadors, to

aligning with Dominican government representatives to delimit the boundaries of family structures, Cardinal López Rodríguez consistently and constantly
preached about the moral danger of homosexuality to the Dominican social
fiber. He staged a discursive war against LGBTQ persons for well over a decade
(Associated Press 2013; Jiménez Polanco 2013; Religión Digital 2013). He was
not alone, however. The national Consejo Dominicano de Unidad Evangélica
proposed a constitutional reform in 2007, attempting to prescribe the criminalization of "homosexuality and lesbianism" (Abreu 2007, 2) as well as abortion.
While the conservative religious forces within the Dominican government did
manage to criminalize abortion—first redefining life from the moment of conception in the 2010 constitution and then making it a crime within the Dominican penal code in 2016—they did not succeed in making LGBTQ identities and
persons criminal subjects.

But the religious battle against streetwalking does not stop at the level of discourse or legislative petitions. Since the early 2000s, the Dominican police have
raided gay bars, arresting those inside (including employees) and publishing
their names in newspapers as a method of social shaming. Oftentimes, the publication of names has resulted in loss of employment and blackballing. The church
and the military conducted purges, both eliminating LGBTQ persons from these
institutions and generating anxiety among the general population. As noted by
Padilla and Castellanos, "There has been a close moral and rhetorical relationship between the church and the military high command on the issue of sexual
perversion for some time, such that the cardinal's vehement attacks on LGBTQ
populations . . . are often echoed by pronouncements or repressive actions by
the military or the police" (2008, 38). Increasingly, and especially following the
recognition of non-Catholic Christian denominations by the Dominican government in 2006, the relationship between religious institutions and the Catholic Hispanic state has fomented an increase in the exercise of Christian colonial
moral authority as a key element of Dominican governance.

In the stories that follow, I trace the ways in which streetwalking enables LGBTQ
activists to confront the extreme forms of violence that they experience within the
confines of the Catholic Hispanic nation-state, especially as this nation-state continues to uphold Christian colonial ideas about moral personhood. I engage with the
opinions and stories provided by LGBTQ activists in their *confrontación* with state
and religious authorities and the Dominican public as they attempt to create spaces
for their continued existence and the expansion of personhood: at home with their
families, on the streets, and during Pride celebrations.

EL IMPULSO

Confrontación is an impulse toward self-preservation and self-defense and a val-
uation of the self in the face of a society and a political system that gives no value

to LGBTQ lives. To *confrontar* all the injustices that LGBTQ activists face, there is also a need to articulate a shared understanding of the problems one is engaging with. Across the board, LGBTQ activists (and feminist activists among them) told me[2] that they believe a formal separation should exist between the Catholic Church (*la Iglesia*) and the Dominican government (the *estado*). During my fieldwork period, the feminist movement was actively working to promote *un estado laico* (Blancarte 2011; Gutiérrez, n.d.). This feminist work included holding public conferences to discuss the idea of the *estado laico*; public protests at government, embassy, and church offices; articles in national newspapers; and eventually confronting the church in court over the right to sex education (as discussed in the introduction to this book). Feminist LGBTQ activists were part of these efforts to theorize and develop a popular response to the repression enabled by the relationship between the church and the Dominican government. And the LGBTQ activists I interviewed repeatedly pointed out problems with both the cardinal and the relationship between the church hierarchy and the state. Here are some of their responses to my questions about their thoughts on the relationship between church and state:

> RITA: What's so intense is that the cardinal, if he wants to . . . he sends everyone to take a bath, and the politicians accept it because he is the cardinal.
>
> ERICA: The cardinal in this country doesn't care about poor people; he doesn't care about black people [*los negros*].
>
> ROBERTO: If the cardinal focused on the children who are sleeping in the street rather than on gay marriage, we would be a better country.

For Rita and Erica, both lesbian activists, and for Roberto, a gay activist, the cardinal's role in mobilizing church power had a direct impact not only on politics but also on the personal and intimate lives of the people—specifically poor, black, and gay people. They articulated their critique of him not just on the basis of his personal attitudes but explicitly on his misuse of power in the mobilization of political leaders and the diffusion of his personal opinions under the guise of Catholic moral and institutional authority. Patricia, a lesbian journalist and activist, critiqued the relationship between the church and the state because it doesn't allow for religious diversity—a diversity she articulates as necessary for the full exercise of "liberty and sovereignty" as Dominican citizens:

> PATRICIA: It's about time that we Dominicans realize that we are free and sovereign and that we respect the church—but everyone on their side. [And] let's allow for those who are Evangelical or Pentecostal to have their space. There is no need to exclude them.

Here, Patricia mobilizes an articulation of "liberty and sovereignty" as capaciousness rather than something predicated on exclusion or disrespect. Wendy, a lesbian activist, though not as open as Patricia, is equally inclusive in her understanding of the right to religion. However, in her analysis of the relationship between Evangelical Christian institutions and the church, the problem—as she sees it—lies in their attitudes about homosexuality:

> WENDY: The church that is most in charge is the Catholic Church. But I also see that the *Evangélicos* also hold political office and that they try to incorporate their beliefs and their ethics to improve the government. They combine religion and government to make—as they say—a government in Christ. I don't think it's going to help a great deal that those two powers are combined, because the church discriminates against homosexuals.

Others saw a separation of church and state as an imperative:

> DANNY: The church shouldn't get involved in things that are not their business.

Or as a mark of progress and/or development:

> VICTOR: It's sad that all over the world, states have separated themselves from religion, but in the Dominican Republic, it's the opposite. And you can see that in the last reforms—that the church has been granted greater power.

Others articulated a direct link between the church's involvement with the state and the repression of civil and human rights:

> DORA: The church needs to be separate from our public offices, from the state. If that happens, we will be able to achieve many more things. An anti-discrimination law, for example. Or friendly health services.
> JORDAN: It's unfair that we have to be subjected to state affairs because the church imposes them. Why can't we have sex education in school? Why does the church oppose this?

For a small group of those interviewed, the church's involvement with the state was more of a moral problem than a problem of rights:

> JOSÉ: The church is not focusing on what it should be focusing on—on what its Catholic laws guide it to do.
> BETTY: The church should not have anything to do with affairs of the state. The church has a higher authority, and then there is the state authority.
> SHAKIRA: That's where you see that the church is dirtying, contaminating itself, [in its relationship with the Dominican *estado*].

For Eugenio, the current relationship between the church and state is secondary to the historical problems of the church's errors, in which its participation in oppressive institution-building or doctrines has a long history. From his perspective, it is this history of oppression that produces the possibility for unified struggle for black people, women, and gays:

> EUGENIO: The church is an institution that—regardless of how much it says it's about faith—is an Inquisitorial organization. The church has made so many mistakes, and it's stood against human rights. That it's changed at all, that is recent. Now the problem is the gays, but first it was the *negros*, and women—well, that's still a problem. If there is one institution that excludes, it is the Catholic Church—and it's the one closest to the state.

These various insights into church-state relations undergird a shared understanding of some of the root causes behind the homo/trans*phobic violences that LGBTQ activists encounter. The circulation of Christian colonial values through the institution of the Catholic Hispanic nation-state impacts ideas of citizenship and proper moral personhood, the family, institutional authority, and presence in public spaces. With this shared understanding—including all of its complexities—LGBTQ activists mobilize *confrontación* across multiple spaces and in various forms.

"HAY QUE TENER UNA FORTALEZA FUERTE"

Families—in particular, mothers—and schools are two Dominican social institutions charged with the moral education of the Dominican nation's future adults, a legacy of late nineteenth-century *normalista* policies (Martínez-Vergne 2005). The impossibility of existing as gender-nonconforming beings at home and at school generates a series of choices in which survival is pitted against belonging. As Junior put it, "I love being within my family, to spend time with my family. But when I had to decide either my life or my family, I decided on my life. They were enslaving me to their desires and did not allow for mine. I had to deny myself many things."

Faced with the impossibility of being or belonging, the gender suppression that trans* people experience is a secondary form of violence that builds on the presumption of murder and death as the only legitimate futures for those who fail to perform biblical manhood or womanhood. This impossibility of being is a mode of sexual terror that is about ontology. Rather than accept death, trans* people—in their courage and protest—instead settle into "being trans*." Up until this moment of acquiescence, trans* activists often describe actively hiding their bodily dispositions and/or practices from their families and peers until reaching an age of psychic rupture (being unable to tolerate violence) or economic independence. They tend to leave their homes and schools at an early age, which often leads them to sustaining themselves through informal economies (including sex work) until they develop relationships and enter spaces where they can assert their visible presence through bodily dispositions, practices, and associations. Assertion in this context then helps them gain the strength necessary to do assert themselves in general society, often with varying social and economic consequences. Collectively, this is one type of *confrontación* enacted by trans* activists: one in which self-acceptance, social assertion, and day-to-day visibility are embodied. When asked about how they came to accept themselves as trans*, despite how their families treated them, interviewees responded as follows:

> SHAKIRA: I had to confront my family because I am *transvesti*, because I am gay, because I am trans*. *One has to confront their family, like society in general*. At fourteen years old, I decided not to go back to school, ever. I learned cosmetology, how to work in a kitchen—and because of limitations [not being able to get work], I was a sex worker between the ages of seventeen and twenty-eight. (emphasis mine)

> TANIA: I always put on makeup at friends' houses. It was a double life. At home, or on the street, I was a boy. But at the disco and at the gay bar, I was a woman. My friends were the only ones who knew me as a woman; at home they didn't know me like that.

> PALOMA: I am not going to give up on life. I find a way to maintain myself and to keep studying. That's why I started doing sex work, where I have to expose myself to danger, to hate crimes, to police violence and violence from clients—a lot of things that one is aware of but, because of fear, does not speak of.

> DUMONT: To reinsert myself into society, I had to stop dressing that way [with long hair, women's clothes, makeup, and long nails]. I don't dress hypermasculine, but I do have my hair short.

These narratives are examples of what trans* activists term *supervivencia*. This is a complex concept that encompasses various layers of meaning. To speak of it in English requires touching on multiple references and translations. By moving out of the performance of biblical gender scripts into "being trans*," Dominican trans* activists enter into the ontology of *supervivencia*. Directly defined, *supervivencia* is to live after the death of another or to live after an event of great danger, to overcome a test or difficult situation. *Supervivencia* as it is used by trans* activists, includes both *supervivencia*, or the ability to live with little means and in adverse conditions, and *pervivencia*, or the ability to keep on living despite difficulties.

Supervivencia is explicitly about living after, above, over, and through difficult circumstances, death, or events of great danger. It is the practice of survival, exposing oneself to danger, to the "things that one is aware of but, because of fear, does not speak of," as Paloma explained. It is about "keeping on keeping on," as it is most well known in African American vernacular English, in which the "keeping on" is the praxis of living as oneself, without literal or metaphoric restraints on the full expression of the gender-nonconforming body. It is not about entering a gay-topia—or trans*-topia, as the case may be—but rather about being able to make active choices about maintaining oneself, confronting one's family (truth-telling), and making strategic choices about self-presentation. To become a full member of society is not to be above it but to be of it. In this sense, *supervivencia* counters the temporality of liberal notions of LGBTQ liberation as a utopia or the radical queer ideal of queerness as a "thing that is present but not actually existing in the present tense" (Muñoz 2009, 9). *Supervivencia* helps us understand how trans* activists enact streetwalking in the here and now, despite all the factors constraining their personhood. Streetwalking, we don't wait for someone to realize that we have always already been here, especially since "here" is always shifting depending on the ways in which power articulates itself through and against real bodies in space and time.

In the case of Dominican trans* activists, conceptualizing life beyond and in rejection of inevitable violent death is an ongoing commitment to a personal autonomy grounded in the strength garnered from being a valued member of one's specific community and the larger society. Trans* liberation, as articulated by numerous activists, is about achieving that kind of autonomy. For Dominican LGBTQ activists, within LGBTQ lives and struggles lie the seeds of a collective memory in which trans* lives are fully possible.

All trans* interviewees were adamant in assuring me that they are proud to be trans*. Several stated that "if they were reborn," they would want to be reborn as trans* and that though the struggles with their families had been difficult, they had managed to transform these relationships to their best advantage. Despite the violence they grew up with, their families are still an important aspect of who they understand themselves to be. Thalia, who has a national LGBTQ following and is famous in the *colmado*[3] performance circuits, shared a family narrative that challenges a one-dimensional reading of family and belonging:

> In the beginning, my mother knew I was a little *rarito* [strange]. And I began to perform. She didn't want me to dress as a woman when I was around the house, but it was OK if I was at a friend's house. I could come back home in the mornings, dressed up, because the neighbors weren't awake. Until I went to a trans* friend's house, and I was amazed because she dressed as a woman all the time and her family lived right next to her. I wanted to be like that. I didn't want to hide from my family. [One day] I waited until my mother was downstairs drinking a beer with some friends, and I put makeup on. I stood by the window thinking, Do I go down or not? Until I went down. When she saw me, she was surprised. And I said to her, "Look, beautiful, prepare yourself, because I am going to dress like this." I left and came back later and she didn't say anything to me. So then I decided to put in hair extensions—the very next day—and I started using makeup from that day forward. I was finishing high

school then. I would help my mother clean the house, and by 6 a.m. I was
ready: with makeup and all. That performance with my mother was symbolic,
because she never scolded me or anything. I lived with my mother, my two
sisters, and my grandmother, and there were never any problems.

Thalia's narrative locates family as a site for the small drama of *confrontación*.
If Thalia was the only one who had found acceptance from her family, then perhaps I would claim that she is exceptional. However, all but two of the trans*
activists I interviewed live with a family member. And several of them made references to other trans* friends who live with family. Despite the initial ruptures and
experiences of violence within their own families, the majority of the interviewees are deeply embedded within their families' lives, and their families—usually
women (sisters, mothers, aunts) or nephews and/or nieces—play a continuing role in their self-making and being once they have reached adulthood and
self-acceptance. Despite the sexual terror many of them grew up with, the family becomes a site of self-actualization, of a small drama of *confrontación* that
enables *confrontación* with the larger society. The dynamics of family space, and
what happens when streetwalking takes place within it, further problematize the
public-private divide that is so central to Christian colonial concepts of gender.
Being trans* and gender nonconforming renders those divisions futile.

Emerging from the space of family and school, trans* activists also described
violence in their lives as *discriminación*, manifested as physical and verbal violence. When asked, all the activists responded that they had experienced *discriminación*. For the majority, this included being yelled at or having objects (eggs,
oranges, trash) thrown at them while on the streets—both in the context of their
daily lives and, in some instances, when some trans* activists were engaged in
sex work:

MICHELLE: Yes, I have experienced violence. I have been discriminated
against. I am not respected. I am yelled at. I have been physically and verbally assaulted. I have had objects thrown at me, and that is a form of psychic and mental assault. It could happen moving through the street. They
look at you, they assault you, they yell at you.

JEISHA: A lot of *discriminación*. A lot of violence. In the street they shout
"*maricón*" at me. Sometimes when I am walking the street, or working.

THALIA: We are very discriminated against. Girls have told me how they've
been just standing on the street corner and PAH!—someone throws a cup
or a rock at them.

JUNIOR: Sometimes, they bring out sticks to hit me with, and they want to hit
me, and sometimes I ended up yelling and fighting back [verbally]. People
laugh. In this country, you fall in a hole and people laugh, so imagine when
there is a man hitting a gay person. That's the day's amusement.

Everyone I interviewed explained that they feared seeking medical services at hospitals because of the potential for *discriminación*[4] in the form of denied services, ridicule, and spectacular objectification (being made an object of spectacle). I also knew, from conversations with LGBTQ human rights lawyers, that one of the trans* women who had died in 2011 was left to bleed to death in the hospital emergency room (IURA, personal communication, June 2011). The majority of those interviewed were unable to gain employment—either because their identity records did not match their gender presentation or because of early educational experiences that prevented them from completing their schooling. In a country with 35 percent of the population in the informal employment sector, trans* activists are further limited by Christian colonial sexual terror. All but one of the activists interviewed is or has been a sex worker, regardless of education level or degree of gender conformity. Emphasizing their own *supervivencia*, Freddy states, "I am not gay; I'm trans*. It's that. I do sex work; I get dressed up at night and go out into the street to do sex work. I survive even though I don't have formal employment. I take care of myself."

Confrontación, the act of facing one's own and others' discomfort, is a necessary aspect of *supervivencia* in the context of ongoing sexual terror. When individual strategies no longer suffice, trans* activists turn to collective action as a way to seek redress. When asked what being trans* meant for him, Junior responded,

> God gave me many things, and one of the things he gave me was to be *transvesti*. Because I can experiment with this male body, changing it in a matter of minutes—like creation itself, like a work of art. To see a body that is so rigid, so strong, so masculine become something so feminine. To play with makeup, heels, wigs, the way I dress and walk. These are things in which you condition yourself. At first it looks like a game, but it's a condition (a way of being) because you have to not only be in the role of being a woman; you have to feel that you are a woman. But when you are in the world as a man, it is not the same. The patterns change. Trans[vestism] for me is a work of art. It is not about a definition. I can have double roles: I can be as much of a man as a woman at the same time.

Paloma, in turn, responded, "When I realized and discovered that I am trans*, it is because I felt an attraction to those of my same sex at the same time that I started to explore my body and to feel something different. I liked girls' toys and accessories. I felt something different. I am transgender because I began to change physically. I wax my eyebrows. I have my ears pierced. I do more feminine things than masculine, and I use clothes with finer details. I like all things feminine, and I feel feminine physically and spiritually."

Junior identifies himself as a transvestite, someone who lives in the world as a man but enters the world of trans* life through the crafting of a feminine self: a particular kind of self-fashioning (Allen 2011) that includes and centers on artistic expression. Paloma sees herself as transgender because of the process of (self) realization and discovery that occurred through her affective development, a sense of feeling attraction to someone such as herself that accompanied the physical changes she experienced as an adolescent. The shifting of Paloma's sense of being from gay to trans* transcended the implicit rules of homoerotic orientations and homosexual being and entered into a different ontology: streetwalking ruptures the stasis of categorical belonging. And yet trans* identity is not an evacuated, meaningless site for Paloma or Junior. Their erotic orientations produce the affective fields in which they articulate their political and personal desires to live free from sexual terror and violence. This is a shared, collective desire.

One Monday afternoon in 2013, I was in the offices of the national trans* advocacy organization TRANSSA (Trans Siempre Amigas) in Santo Domingo, interviewing trans* activists, including Shakira. I had asked her how it is for her in the D.R. In response, she smiled the acquiescent smile of an all-knowing aunt, her right hand in a fist, indicating gathered strength, as she leaned slightly forward to utter the words "Hay que tener una fortaleza fuerte." Her statement translates to "You have to have fortitude," and it struck me not only because of how Shakira said it to me—with a quiet conviction and firmness—but also because of the resilience and determination it implies.

As we sat in a small meeting room overlooking the busy street, one of the other trans* activists poked their head in through the door, interrupting us with only a murmur. Shakira stopped midsentence to listen. She nodded and turned back to me.

"We just found out that one of our *compañeras* was murdered this weekend."

I paused, wanting to gauge whether it was appropriate to continue speaking, given this disturbing news.

"Do you need to go?" I asked.

"No, let's continue. Let's finish."

"Was she a friend of yours?"

"We knew each other, but [with a big sigh] these things happen."

Shakira was the first in a series of interviews. That afternoon, and in the days following, nobody cried or expressed sadness. Shakira had sighed. Another spoke to me almost under her breath, "You have to know how to take care of yourself." The director of the trans* organization took the occasion to speak to me about the high number of murders with the formality of recounting a yearly report. Throughout the week, as I returned to the space to continue interviews and to attend meetings, I heard different narrative versions of the murder:

"They followed her home and murdered her there. They say she knew the guy."

"No one is saying anything because she—well, you know: she comes from a family."

"She leaned into the guy's car and he shot her point-blank."

"She was working, and she got in the guy's car, and then he shot her."

When I asked if they were going to memorialize her, one of the activists told me, "Maybe. Her family doesn't want anybody to know. And, well, I'm not sure how many people here really knew her. But we always try to do something when they murder one of our girls." I did not inquire directly about why people seemed so disinterested in mobilizing around this murder, but there were clues in the responses to my questions about who she was and the circumstances of her death. For one, the "murdering of our girls" was a frequent occurrence—something I know from what activists have told me but also from my own observations. Second, there was a palpable sense of frustration about how the victim's family was making the circumstances of the murder invisible. Nobody could publicly bring attention to the case because *the family* was powerful enough to cause problems for the organization should the victim's name/gender/work be revealed.

Because the *compañera* was potentially from a wealthy or politically visible family (implied in the expression "she comes from *a family*"), her death marked various registers of silencing. The family would want to silence the fact, first, that their child was trans*; second, that their child was a sex worker; and third, that their child was killed in the act of sex work as a trans* sex worker. The death, in this case, would be marked as anonymously and silently as possible so as to not draw attention to the circumstances of the person's death—or life.

As several interviewees informed me, because she was a sex worker, the *compañera*'s death brought judgment from not only her family but also the trans* community, which has been seeking to legitimize its struggle within the broader context of the fight for trans* human rights. Within the trans* community, there is significant discrimination against those *chicas* who choose sex work as a primary means of sustenance, even though all those interviewed spoke about how sex work is often "the only option." But given that the murder did not even appear in the newspapers, on blog pages, or in social networks—in comparison to the sixteen trans* murders that had taken place in the four years prior—I gathered that the family had more to do with its silencing than anything else. This murder would, in fact, be relegated to the space of *cuentos* (see chapter 5).

The narration of this murder by trans* activists told me a great deal about their social anxieties more broadly. The murder of one of their *compañeras* was a reminder of the fragility of their own lives and the undignified ways in which many trans* people die. It also increased the urgency of focusing on the struggle for trans* human rights and dignity. What could be sorrow was channeled into *supervivencia* and into the impetus necessary to continue in their struggle as activists. One interviewee, Chantal, expressed to me, her eyes turned downward as she spoke,

There is a lot of mental, physical, and verbal *discriminación*. Killing one of us is like killing a *ciguita* [a small bird]. I'll tell you, they even killed one of my *compañeras*. They killed her because the damn jerk thought my *compañera* was a woman, and when she got in the car—they didn't even do anything—he just killed her. Just because she got in the car and he thought she was a woman. She got into the car and he shot her and threw her out like she was a bag of garbage, like something that you throw from the side of your car on the highway, and then he ran away.

The constant repetition of "she got in the car" emphasized the almost quotidian nature of murder as yet another specter haunting us as we streetwalk. Unlike other people I spoke to, who referenced the need for trans* sex workers to take care of themselves and express a sense of control over their own lives and conditions, for Chantal, this sense of control was diminished by the circumstances of her *compañera*'s murder. "They didn't even do anything," she says, not because murder would have been excused had her *compañera* done something (i.e., engaged in a sexual act or exchange), but rather because it was clear from the "not doing" that the murder was provoked as a result of her friend's trans* being.

For Chantal, her *compañera*'s murder was an insult to collective humanity. It highlighted the ubiquity of transphobic violence. When she states "They didn't even do anything" and "just because she got in the car," Chantal is pointing to her *compañera*'s innocence. Innocence is often a quality that streetwalking does not afford. Trans* collective fragility and innocence—as human beings but also as trans*—is contained in Chantal's use of the metaphor of the *ciguita* (in English, the palmchat)—a small, delicate, rare bird known for its melodic birdsong. This metaphor is not incidental. The *Cigua palmera* is also the national bird of the D.R. Chantal's use of the *ciguita* as a metaphor was meant to mark not only trans* fragility but also trans* life and national belonging.

Chantal directly expressed the anxiety generated by her *compañera*'s death, but in other cases, it reared its head when we explicitly discussed discrimination and violence against trans* people in the Dominican Republic. What constitutes exceptional forms of violence for many nontrans* people (or cisgender people) exists as everyday forms of violence for trans* people.[5] These everyday forms of violence shape the struggle and movement of trans* activists through Dominican society. When asked if they experienced discrimination, the trans* activists I interviewed generally began by telling their stories in a chronological order as a mode of oral history. They often started with their childhoods. The majority described experiencing violence from the earliest part of their lives, beginning with their families:

YEISHA: When my dad found me [wearing women's clothes], he would spank me; he would slap me. I would be punished, and it was a strong punishment.

CHANTAL: At first they would hit me [for not acting like a boy], and they would lock me inside my room. I would stay locked in for several hours when I was a child.

JUNIOR: In the beginning [after I entered the life], they rejected me. They didn't want to know anything about me. They would treat me like a contagious disease, like a cold, or the black sheep of the family.

SHAKIRA: [When I was 14] my mother told me to leave the house. It lasted three months, and then she slowly accepted me. I had to confront my family for being *transvesti*, for being gay, for being trans*. One has to confront one's family much as we do the population in general.

The kind of bodily policing allowable within the rubric of parental upbringing is one enactment of the hegemonic social forces that give definition to gender and sexuality as a biblical binary in which men and women exist as separate, natural categories of being with strict boundaries defining behavior, relationships, dress, and identity. As discussed by many feminist legal scholars in relationship to questions of marriage and abortion, the idea of family as a private sphere and hallowed institution is false (García-Del Moral and Dersnah 2014; Nikolas 1987; Romany 1993; Spillers 1987). The falsity becomes even more evident in the ways that families carry out broader social, *political*, and religious ideals in the policing of LGBTQ children and youth.

The Concordat requires the state to provide Catholic education in all public schools. Over the course of my fieldwork (2010–2015), I witnessed an increase in the number of fundamentalist Evangelical school directors and teachers in primary and secondary schools. This shift aligns with broader shifts across Latin America. Like their Catholic counterparts, Christian teachers impart biblical lessons and Bible-informed civic education. The Concordat, in addition to shaping public education, also specifies that the nation-state agrees to diffuse Christian doctrine and morals across all communication media.[6] As the Catholic Church sets the educational agenda in public schools, it also sets the public discourse around civil rights as well as the legislative priorities. This level of participation and influence is rooted in concepts of moral citizenship that emerge explicitly in contradistinction to streetwalking.

The familial experiences of violence among trans* activists result from the extension of the specific modes of sexual terror emerging from the Christian colonial nation-state. As numerous researchers have noted, gender regulation in Dominican public discourse has been a key element in the construction of national belonging within the Catholic Hispanic nation-state (de Moya 2004; Horn 2014; Krohn-Hansen 2009). In particular, the relationship between sexuality and an unquestionable masculinity "define[s] identity, individuality, and what is understood as womanhood and manhood" (Rodriguez 2010, 54). Maja Horn (2014) theorizes how particular modes of virile masculinities were established through the Trujillato and Balaguer regimes and how they continue to permeate contemporary political and social relationships, neutralizing hierarchical relationships between political elites and popular classes through masculinist discourses. Even through the specific masculinist formations that emerged during the Trujillato regime and beyond, these formations have been very much informed by how Christian moral codes delimit the boundaries of acceptable sexuality and gender (Balaguer 1993; Jiménez Polanco 2004). As Antonio E. de Moya points out, "The Christian ideology of monogamous marriage as a sacrament emphasizes values such as premarital chastity, the nuclear family, fidelity, motherhood, and care of children and elders, among others. . . . Women place their loyalties at the service of their husbands, children and households, while men can place loyalties both at home and in the street, trying to strike a viable balance between the two sets of moral ideals" (2004, 78).

The experiences of trans* activists highlight the intimate spaces in which ideas of being good Christians and patriotic Dominicans translate into experiences of gender-based policing in the everyday. As Lugones states, "Home is lived as a place inseparable from other places of violence, including the street" (2003, 209). De Moya (2004) extensively traces how the fear of children breaking from the expectation of what is construed as inherited biblical manhood and womanhood shapes child-rearing practices across classes. He lists what his subjects call God-given common practices that include teaching boys about positions they can and cannot sleep in; toys they can and cannot play with; bodily gestures they can and cannot embody; clothes they can and cannot wear; and forms of intimacy they must not have with other men but are expected to have with other women by puberty (de Moya 2004, 73–74). From my own experiences in childhood, I can speak to the many ways in which girls' bodies are disciplined: the ways girls can and cannot sit; the ways girls must constrain their bodies when walking in the streets; the numerous hygiene rituals girls must engage in; the clothes they can and cannot wear or how they can or cannot wear them; the spaces they can enter or not, and so on. A trans* child who fails to exercise an appropriate gender role could bring up questions about a family's morality and their patriotic duty. According to the trans* activists interviewed—in particular, Paloma, Shakira, and Dumont—a child who failed to act according to a prescribed biblical gender expectation was punished at home for being "diabolical," "a bad child," and "a spoiled fruit" and for shaming the family.

In addition to punishment at home, discipline and disciplinary ridicule are also carried out by peers and teachers in schools. School is also an early site of violence and gender policing, most explicitly through peer teasing and exclusion or teachers who call attention to students' differences:

> CHANTAL: In elementary school, the students would laugh at me, they would make fun of me, but there was no physical aggression. They wouldn't hit me, but they made fun of me; they talked. I felt it in adolescence too.

PALOMA: I had to make an effort to be one of the guys, to go to school in the uniform—pants, shirt, shoes, short hair—to avoid problems. I felt discrimination, and that's why I isolated myself. I was always to one side, by myself. I wouldn't hang out with anybody. That all reflected on me. The school would call my family to tell them I had psychological problems. I isolated myself out of fear, out of the fear that the boys would not let me become part of their group.

TANIA: The school was only boys. Imagine that. In being different, in having different behaviors—as a little boy I had a lot of mannerisms. I had to try to be rigid when I walked. I had to think twice before moving a hand so that I wouldn't be discovered. Since we were all boys, I didn't want to be the butt of jokes.

DUMONT: As a boy, I had no idea. They would call me Vikiana, and I would dance like her. Later, as an adolescent, the discrimination was more acute. I hid what I am and tried to imitate the boys and not be singled out as different.

SHAKIRA: I was scared to go to school. The boys would threaten me along the way. I had to hide. I was scared of the teacher who always punished me. He would call me *maricónsito* [little faggot] and would hit my head. The boys didn't respect me. The teacher, who was the authority, made fun of me and mistreated me.

Streetwalking is about refusing Christian colonial sexual terror, even at a young age. LGBTQ children are marked by an upbringing characterized by gender suppression: opting to exercise bodily control, measured bodily gestures, restraint, and constraints in order to attempt to embody Christian colonial ideas about gender. Literally silencing themselves and metaphorically binding the movements of their hands and hips, trans* children continuously fail at the act of gender performance, only to reveal their true nature at great cost. Butler points out that "intelligible genders are those which in some sense institute and maintain relations of coherence and continuity among sex, gender, sexual practice, and desire" (1990, 23). In this sense, LGBTQ children disrupt, from an early moment in their lives, the potential for the Christian colonial continuity between biblical men and women, Catholic men and women, heterosexual Christian men and women, and procreating biblical Christian men and women.

These modes of sexual terror, of the belittling and physical punishment of sexual-gender difference, in the home, at school, and on the streets delineate how some bodies are deemed more expendable and accessible to violation than others. They also call attention to the values and attitudes in society that generate the misrecognition of those who streetwalk as incapable of legitimate human being and social, political, and economic worth. The strategies of *confrontación* that trans* activists employ against these modes of sexual terror are subtle and multilayered. They include embodiment, self-acceptance, self-assertion, and visibility within the everyday. These strategies, rooted in erotic orientations toward liberation, then enable further political engagement whereby streetwalking can foment activists who are empowered to articulate the conditions of their repression as well as potential social, civil, and human rights solutions.

Violence in the aforementioned examples is most visibly expressed against people who do not conform to gender norms through their dress, bodily expression, or labor. The experiences of trans* activists are made explicit because of their ruptures with biblical manhood and womanhood. However, others in the LGBTQ community also experience related forms of sexual terror.

"¿Si No Nos Tiran Chinas, No Somos Maricones?"

Like trans* activists, Dominican gay and lesbian activists also spoke about experiencing violence at home, at school, and on the streets. But it was the experiences of extrajudicial police violence that were considered especially egregious. Lesbians spoke to me of cases where police forced them to perform oral sex or threatened them for walking down the street together. Gay men spoke to me of arbitrary arrests and verbal harassment. These experiences of violence bring up questions about the role of violence in the production of LGBTQ identities. One gay activist, Gerardo, asked a group of men, "Do we have to have oranges thrown at us to be gay?" In other words, Gerardo was asking, are there not other terms aside from violence under which gayness comes into being? Though the groups of gay men I interviewed in 2012 and 2013 left this question unanswered, it was, ironically, Gerardo who shared one of the most direct examples of the sexual terror produced through Christian coloniality and its impact on his own life.

Over the course of several meetings between 2012 and 2013, I collected narratives in the context of individual and group interviews with gay activists at the offices of the national gay men's HIV services organization. Unlike the trans* activists, gay activists asked me to use pseudonyms in the representation of their stories. This different posture regarding visibility speaks volumes about the distinctions between trans* and gay struggles. As Dumont mentioned, "We are *orgullosamente* [proudly] trans*." In turn, for several of the gay activists, privacy is not about hiding who they are. As Gerardo mentioned, "It's about respect," meaning that for him in particular, protecting his identity is about respecting his decision about how to manage knowledge of his sexuality. As I asked them what it meant for them to be Dominican and gay, the men entered into passionate debates about the nature of being gay and the relationship between being gay and being perceived or assumed to be gay, the differences between gays and trans* people, and experiencing violence.

As the debate became heated, some of the men claimed that being gay was a matter of context or dress, about people assuming you are gay versus declaring your homosexuality. But they agreed that unlike trans* folk, gay men could be respected because they are not signaled as gay unless they can be read as such through physical demeanor or dress or by breaking social norms and expectations of male behavior (in other words, they could inhabit Christian colonial modes of *respeto*). For these activists, those who conform to social ideas of masculinity can be seen as "normal men," while those who do not or cannot are most certainly subject to greater degrees of violence. Even as he spoke about the "normal man," Bisul was quick to point out that what he meant was "normal man between quotation marks"—in other words, that "normal" was a measure outside of his own gender registers and that "normal" came into question either through choices one makes about self-fashioning, through engaging in sexual acts not sanctified by Christian moral authorities, or through public participation in gay spaces. Equally for Bisul, it was this attachment to normality that made being gay a reality in which violence had come to be expected. It was in rebuttal to the idea that gayness and violence had a relationship to each other that Gerardo stated, "Arguing that violence is what shapes us is like saying that if they don't throw oranges at us, then we aren't gay." As all the men laughed, another man, Raúl, responded, "And in that, Dominican men are very particular. Because if we haven't been shot by bullets, it's like saying, 'I haven't eaten rice today.' And a Dominican who hasn't eaten rice hasn't eaten at all. And so, if they haven't thrown an orange at you, then you aren't a *maricón*." And Samuel added, "And if they don't shoot you during the day, they will certainly shoot you at night."

This debate, which formed the center of the group interview and was the point that the men returned to again and again throughout the following two hours, signals multiple tensions not only in the formation of gay identity but in the relationship between an articulated gay identity and violence. Whereas, as Raúl stated, if you have not had an orange thrown at you, you aren't a *maricón*, the laughter Gerardo's statement elicited speaks to its double entendre. On the one hand, violence and the interpellation (Althusser [1971] 2006) of violence are not the sole conditions under which gayness comes into being. And on the other hand, sexual terror is so pervasive that it is like one's daily plate of food: part and parcel of the fabric of knowing gayness. When Raúl used that metaphor, he was not only referencing a necessary act (eating); he was speaking about knowing violence like one knows hunger. Without the knowledge of that violence—knowledge of its possibility or the experience of it—one cannot completely comprehend gay identity in the context of being Dominican and vice versa.

As Samuel stated—in a final moment before we changed the topic of conversation—being gay is different from being homosexual, and the differences between being gay and being trans* are even more marked. For Samuel, "Gay is about a lifestyle, and trans* is about a marked way of being. But homosexual is what one is assumed to be regardless of one's actual orientation or desire." The other activists responded by theorizing that the kinds of violence one experiences are gradated in relationship to one's obviousness. However, at the same time, one's manner of being—such as a man of a certain age renting an apartment "without even a concubine" (Pedro) or a man wearing yellow pants during the day (Raúl)—breaks with social patterns and expectations for men. This break can be met either with respect (Gerardo) or with derision, but as Samuel points out, "It's not that you tell people you are gay. It's that they assume it." In this sense, streetwalking as a gay man is about the multiple ways one does or does not inhabit one's erotic orientation. The conversation between these gay men signaled how streetwalking mobilizes agency as a shift between sites and bodies, retreating and emerging as needed.

And it is this assumption of homosexuality by others—in particular, police authorities—distinct from an agentive sense of representing oneself as gay, or trans*, or homosexual that produces the streetwalking subject. It is in that space between gay *resistencia* and state repression where sexual terror comes into sharp, distinctive focus. Two anecdotes illustrate this juncture. The first comes from Gerardo, a police officer in his early thirties, who is by all appearances a cisgender man. Gerardo's story began in the middle of the interview, when he recounted how one night, sitting with gay and trans* friends in El Parque, he was picked up by the police. Throughout the group interview, Gerardo consistently voiced a critique of flamboyant (or what he called "obvious") gay behavior. He also made a point of telling the group that he had never spoken about being gay to his family "even though they all know." For Gerardo, it was very important to be manly in his behavior, dress, and relationships. He had asked if gays have to be hit with oranges to be gay, but he also shared this anecdote:

> There was a problem at El Parque. I was supposed to meet a friend of mine, and there were three people who had a problem with him. These three people attacked us, and I got in the middle to break up the fight. It was a problem [between people who know each other], not an attack by outsiders. One of the three was even an ex of mine. After the fight, I let the three know that they can't mess with me, and they left. But out of nowhere, the police appeared. They arrested us, not the three who started the fight. We were in the process of leaving. I was just sitting there, in El Parque, when the two police officers came up to me. They asked me what I was doing there, and I said, "Nothing, I was just hanging out." And they said no, that I was there disturbing the peace. That I was *mariconeando*. I told them I was a police officer, and they said, "What? ¡*Mariconaso!*" And they took me into the precinct.

Samuel interjected, "It's his fault for having identified himself. A *pájaro* can't be a police officer." The men laughed, and then Gerardo continued:

On my way, I explain to the police officers who were taking me in that I was simply attempting to stop a fight. I told them my mother's a high-ranking police officer, and they—trying to help me out because they know the colonel is homophobic and was going to give me problems—tell me to call her. . . . I called my mother, she arrived in a taxi, and the precinct colonel called for me. He was of a higher rank than my mother. So when he asked me what I was doing in El Parque, I was forced to lie and tell him that the people in the park were my work colleagues [from an HIV service organization] and that we were simply hanging out. He then reprimanded me, telling me that even though I worked with those people, there was no reason for me to be hanging out with *la mierda* [excrement]. And he warned me that if he found me there again, he would send me to jail for thirty days and that he would fire me. I didn't go back to El Parque for two years.

"On what basis can he send you to jail? Is that legal?" I asked him.

"Of course! He has a higher rank than me."

"He can send you to jail for thirty days for simply associating with gay people because you are a police officer?"

"Yes," he said, along with a chorus from the other men, "and he would fire me."

"Why?"

"Because supposedly one is to maintain a *buena presencia*," or respectable appearances, he explained.

Samuel added, "Because it's assumed that neither police officers nor guards should be *mariconeando*."

"No puede ser visible" (He can't be visible), Raúl affirmed.

As Gerardo shared his story, it was clear that this was an exceptional experience of violence because it signaled an abuse by official authorities despite his appearance as a "normal man" and despite his own status as a police officer. What saved him, in this case, were two allied police officers who were looking out for Gerardo and his mother, who—because of her high rank—could vouch, by association, for her son's character. But it is possible that Gerardo would not have been taken in had he been in another area of the city and had declared his status as a police officer in another context. His location at the time of his arrest was what made his status illegible and dubious. "Hanging out" is what marked him. It rendered his achieved status as a police officer moot in the face of his status as an assumed *maricón*.

The discrimination in this case was against a police officer by senior ranking officers—both the ones who took him in and the colonel who questioned him. If he had not been a police officer or had not had a mother who is a police officer, Gerardo's fate may have been quite different. In the first instance, he could have been detained for disturbing *la moralidad pública* (the public order), but his job security would not have been directly vulnerable to the colonel's whims. In the second instance, without his family connections, Gerardo would have most likely been both fired and potentially abused. It is possible that what little power Gerardo's status did give him mediated any further police violence against him.

However, what is particularly significant about Gerardo's story are the ways in which he confronted the police—his colleagues—who were rounding him up without due cause. His first maneuver was to articulate his own authority as a fellow police officer *and* to call on his personal relations to other police officers of high rank. But it was his mother's vouching for his person that enabled him to then create a reason—a lie / not lie—for why he was in the park in the first place. This second maneuver, of lying, is part of the *doble moral* that characterizes life under Christian colonial repression.

Andres L. Mateo theorizes the *doble moral* as the modes of double consciousness and double life shaped by the necessary silences of living life under authoritarian regimes of power. The *doble moral* emerged from the disintegration of the possibility of open dialogue in public spaces (Mateo 2004) and in its place produced other modes of truth. Power disciplines peoples' everyday interactions and speech acts to produce specific regimes of truth—that is, the "circular relation with systems of power that produce and sustain it, and to effects of power which it induces and which extend it" (Foucault 1982, 132). Under the Trujillato, Mateo argues, the public sphere acted as a site for the replication of authoritarian power through acts of proclamation, the suppression and channeling of dissent, and the articulation of (anti-Haitian, anti-Communist) ideals in support of the Catholic Hispanic state. This same state repression produced a powerful subterfuge that operated simultaneously. This subterfuge existed in the silences, verbal metaphors, indirect allusions, bodily gestures, and symbolic performances between people. The *doble moral* can be construed as an outgrowth of the Christian moral order, the *moralidad pública*, that was required to ensure one's continued life on earth and one's livelihood during the authoritarian regime. Those who committed the immoral act of speaking against Trujillo were just as much offending the *moralidad pública* as those whose mere existence was found offensive.

Silence is woven into the *doble moral*. It is the ellipse and the exclusion that is made apparent in the context of speech. So whereas the colonel could speak, could exclaim his opinions about who Gerardo spent his time with, Gerardo was completely silenced. His intentional use of silence enabled the colonel to produce his own version of truth. As such, the *doble moral* is an index of epistemic violence, and it serves to mark where speech is possible or not but also where it is mobilized for the purposes of unmasking and negotiating power. In Gerardo's case, the colonel's threats to Gerardo's person, his mother's person, and those who are deemed excrement produced the version of truth necessary for Gerardo to negotiate his freedom. By redirecting the colonel's attention to his professional relationships, a lie / not lie about why he was with a group of gay men, Gerardo was able to keep his job as an officer and was able to prevent the shaming of his mother, who in turn may have also lost her job as a result. For Gerardo, his allies and enemies were unmasked; *confrontación* took the form of mobilizing the *doble moral*.

Unlike in Gerardo's case, Ricky's story enables us to understand *confrontación* as a collective educational process. Ricky was a young, twenty-three-year-old, effeminate (self-described as "almost trans*") gay man who, at the time of the interviews, was fairly new to gay community activism. Ricky, therefore, had a limited set of tools to respond to *discriminación*, and throughout the group interview, he was constantly being schooled by his more experienced peers. The story he told was also fresh in his mind, as it had only occurred three days prior to our interview. Ricky was in one of the capital city's public recreational areas with two lesbian friends.

RICKY: This just happened the other night, on Sunday. It was midnight and I was walking along the *malecón* with two lesbian friends. They were visiting from the provinces. We were just minding our business, enjoying fresh air and a cigarette. As we are sitting there, a police motorcade passed us, with both Politur (tourist police) and national police. Well, they slowed down when they saw us, and I noticed that they came to where we were sitting—one on foot and the other on his motorcycle. It turns out that in the moment when they passed us, my friends were kissing. They came up to us and asked us for our documents. But instead of looking at the documents, they started asking my friends why they were kissing in public.

TOMÁS: They call that interrupting the public order (*el orden público*).

RICKY: Anyway, we were in a park. In public. Who were we bothering? It's like the police forgot about me. They cornered my friend and her girlfriend to ask them all sorts of questions. My friend's girlfriend was nervous because she is not from this country, but she lives here. So she was very nervous because of her children and stuff. And then, when the police [found out she is married], they started threatening her, telling her that they were going to call her husband to tell him she is in a park making out with a lesbian.

ROBERTO: And what did you do?

RICKY: Well, I knew what was going on because I've seen this before, but she [the friend's girlfriend] got nervous and started yelling at the police. They took her telephone and forced her to show them the photographs of her husband and her kids . . .

TOMÁS: They can't do that.

RICKY: . . . and they kept saying to her, "What if your husband realizes what you're doing? You shouldn't be doing this." . . . I mean, they were discriminating against her because she was kissing another woman. They didn't even look at her documents because what they cared about was

that they are lesbians. In the end, they didn't arrest them. They just
wanted money.

SIMON: Why didn't you say anything?

RICKY (SCREAMING): Because I felt like I couldn't say anything. I was suffering.
I had so much anger.

ROBERTO: But you didn't do anything.

RICKY: No, I didn't. Because they would have arrested me. I felt bad, knowing
what was going on and not being able to do anything. The officer didn't
even care about anything except that she was a lesbian, and he just kept
threatening that he was going to call her husband.

ME: What happened in the end?

RICKY: They kept all our phones and let us go.

Unlike Dumont and Gerardo, Ricky was not able to mobilize the necessary
tools to advocate for himself or his friends, even though he acknowledged the
injustice taking place. His lesbian friend yelled—generating a *confrontación* in
the form of an assertive speech act, which she later retreated from as the officers
increased their threats. However, Ricky stayed quiet out of an innate fear that he
would become the target and that the gender nonconformity of his female friend
and her gender-conforming girlfriend were safer than his gender nonconformity
as an effeminate gay man combined with the presumed fact of his maleness.
Despite his "obvious" gayness and his friend's "obvious" lesbianism, the target of
the police attack was the presumed heterosexual woman, who was married with
children and "kissing a lesbian." Because of her physical contact with another
woman—a kind of sexual pollution (Butler 1997)—the police directed their
violence at her. The other two, the obvious ones, were already inherently morally wrong. In the end, however, the entire episode was an elaborate setup for
extortion and, in that way, is no more exceptional than the other kinds of setups
Dominicans experience daily. The difference rested in the knowledge that the
extortion drew from the premise of "interrupting the public order" with a kiss
between two women.

In these examples, the police routine of round up, interrogation, intimidation, and reprobation was utterly unexceptional in terms of what the activists
had come to expect as part of their experiences as gay and trans* people yet still
exceptional in that they were sufficient to be remarked on. The arbitrary nature
of the harassment, its unpredictability, and the symbolic performance of Trujil-
lista terror tactics (driving people around in cars, threatening to call people, etc.)
are part and parcel of streetwalking.

Also significant in Ricky's case, however, was that given how recent the incident was, his peers used the collective space of the interview to confront Ricky
about his inaction and to also provide him with their opinions about what they
would have done. In this instance, *confrontación* became a collective learning

process meant to generate change in the person and in the person's capacity to confront everyday violences.

La Caravana del Orgullo

As an attempt to counteract the invisibilization of violence that trans* and gender-nonconforming lesbians and gays experience in the streets, the national network of volunteers associated with men's HIV service organizations arranges the Caravana del orgullo. According to the director of the national gay men's organization, the Caravana's mission is to bring visibility to the LGBTQ population in order to facilitate the struggle for LGBTQ civil and human rights. This collective *confrontación* of the Caravana acts as a gathering space for LGBTQ people to articulate their belonging to a collectivity and the nation (Acento.com 2011). As stated by Martin Manalansan, "The idea of a global lesbian and gay culture has become part of most popular discourses around queer visibility" (2003, 4). For LGBTQ Dominicans, the Caravana del orgullo serves to insert them into international, narratives of global gayness and universal human rights. The Caravana also mirrors celebrations like Dominican carnival festivals,[7] merengue festivals, and political rallies. By following the aesthetic forms of other Dominican street festivals, LGBTQ activists insert themselves into nationalist narratives. The social logics of the Caravana simultaneously evoke global articulations of gayness and nationalist imagery and local sociality.

The history of the Caravana is one of *confrontación*. The year 2001 was the first time LGBTQ activists publicly gathered in the capital city of Santo Domingo.[8] Coming on the heels of the violence and exclusion they had experienced at the Feria del Libro (a national book fair), LGBTQ activists—a group of no more than forty people—came together and sat in one of the city's many public squares. They held signs saying "Somos humanos" (We are human) as a way to draw attention to the direct and indirect forms of dehumanization many experienced within Dominican society. Within just one hour, the police quickly encircled and shut down the gathering. The group disbanded. The following year, they did the same—this time in Plaza España and surrounded by non-LGBTQ allies and friends. The tradition of gathering in public plazas continued until 2008, when musicians joined in and a small parade marched within the boundaries of La Zona. In 2010, it extended into the central corridors of the city, and I made my way to join the Caravana along with two friends who were visiting from the U.S., D'Lo and Jon.

It was a Sunday afternoon in June 2010. D'Lo had popped a *soca* CD into the car radio, and Jon was staring out the window. In the back seat, my other friends—radical lesbian activists Mirla and Maribel—were talking about trans* men and lesbian politics. As I listened to them along with Rupee's "Jump," I thought back to an incident two days earlier, when a Christian heterosexual male friend of mine had pulled me aside to ask if D'Lo and Jon were made as God intended. When I told him yes, he was still surprised to find out that they were transgender. Meanwhile, Mirla was insisting that it all comes down to a question of politics. She wanted to know, If you were a transgender man, could you still be supportive of lesbian radical politics? Maribel wanted to know if they had penises and what had happened to their breasts. She kept asking me why my friends did not like being women. As I explained what I knew about trans* struggles for integration, self-love, and self-awareness, I was grateful that D'Lo and Jon did not speak Spanish. There was no need for them to hear a group of butch lesbians grappling with these questions.

In the U.S. context, this conversation is an index of a long trajectory of epistemic, discursive, and material violence against trans* and gender-nonconforming people by *gays and lesbians*, as well as by heterosexuals. Questions such as those that Maribel asked often signal a point of danger: a sudden upsurge of unforeseen abuse or a move to delegitimize or exclude a person from lesbian/gay/queer spaces. I came to understand Mirla and Maribel's debate as a dialectic verbalization that did not carry with it the same kinds of assumptions or history. Part of what they were talking about had to do with the lack of visibility of trans* men in the Dominican LGBTQ movement. Part of it also had to do with internal negotiations of deeper Dominican understandings of gender, sex, and politics as shaped by Christian colonial ideas of biblical manhood and womanhood. As we pulled up to our meeting point, we had only begun to scratch the surface of what became a longer-term discussion about sex, sexuality, gender, politics, bodies, and nationalism. After 2010, Mirla and Maribel moved to the forefront of lesbian and trans* men's organizing, in part due to what emerged from our conversations about mutual invisibility. But in that moment, we were just trying to see each other. It was also about trying to have a good time.

D'Lo, Jon, Mirla, Maribel, and I jumped out of the car and looked around for other friends. We were in front of Club Chic, a gay club that catered mostly to Dominican men (rather than foreign clientele). Located on the *malecón*—the seaside sidewalk stretching between La Zona and the strip of sex motels at the edge of the capital—Club Chic was the official sponsor of the Reyna del Orgullo (the Pride queen). When I asked out loud why we started here, a young queen shouted out that *aquí* was always where the party started. *Aquí*—that enunciation revealed so much. Their *aquí* in this instance was not only a spatial locator; it also indexed time as ever present and a "now" marked by the collective gathering of bodies and people who mattered. It revealed some of the alliances and relationships central to the sustenance of the lives of LGBTQ people in the D.R. These included clubs, performers, gay men, trans* women, lesbian activists, Dominicans, and foreigners. The party started because we were *aquí*. *Aquí* is an important ontological articulation of being. *Aquí* signals the substantiation of body, memory, and spirit. It marks proximity to location and a time that can only be given meaning by the bodies present *aquí*. *Aquí* reinscribes the idea of streetwalking as potentiality, the potentiality of the here and now. This different locus of meaning—the *aquí* in contrast to the *allá* (there) of a horizon—is deeply reflective of other cultural logics at play. *Aquí* is not a "prison house" (Muñoz 2009), in which the possibility of another world (as evinced by the place of *aquí*) is not displaced but rather fully embodied (Ellis 2015). *Aquí* explodes with multiple meanings, as unfixed as the bodies that constitute being *aquí*. Being *aquí* signaled our collective presence "in the life" and "on the street."

As I pondered this, someone playfully threw a rainbow flag at me: that universalized marker of LGBTQ pride. Another person gave Jon a bunch of small handheld rainbow flags, Dominican flags, and a face mask—in case one of us did not want to be recognized or we wanted to be carnivalesque. We taped the rainbow flag onto the car and jumped in. I drove as D'Lo changed the music. Maribel, Mirla, and Jon sat on the edges of the windows, blowing whistles and shouting. We were behind a large truck decorated in rainbow balloons, the Reyna del Orgullo dressed in Presidente green at its helm.[9]

It was my first time directly participating in such a public LGBTQ event in the D.R. (as opposed to earlier Dominican Pride events, where I participated through the internet via stories and *relatos*). It was exhilarating to experience the crowds on the sidelines and the group of openly flamboyant Dominican LGBTQ people dancing on truck beds and along the edges of car windows. That feeling was a complicated assortment of internal negotiations between my own position as a Dominican in diaspora, as a longtime U.S.-based lesbian activist taking in the explicitly political messages around me, as a butch woman experiencing a different kind of hypervisibility, and finally as a scholar amazed at the symbolic weight of the Caravana route. We wound from Avenida George Washington, up Avenida Abraham Lincoln, across Avenida 27 de Febrero, and down Avenida [Juan Pablo] Duarte. This route traced the geography of imperial and national histories. And the gays were marching right through those histories into the laps of the national patriarch (Avenida Duarte, Parque Duarte) only to end up once again on Avenida George Washington. I was equally struck by the simultaneous use of Gay Pride and Dominican flags within the national narrative. I was struck, in other words, by the insistent insertion of sexually and gendered variant bodies, laughter, and dancing people into the heart of the nation and by their evocation of a sense of national belonging in the context of LGBTQ *orgullo*—pride.[10]

Along the way, people waved at us, smiles on their faces. Many stared at us in quiet surprise. One woman gave us the finger and told us to go to hell, and Mirla blew her kisses. The gay man sitting on the windowsill of the car in front of us bumped into a *bachata*, teasing her. The woman cursed us out some more, but we were moving, and soon she was far behind us. As we returned to the *malecón*, we crossed a string of expensive five-star hotels (reserved for foreigners), where, in front of the service entrances, small, quiet groups of men in hotel uniforms stood, waving and cheering us on. Their greetings were a way of letting us know they were *de familia*. We waved and cheered right back.

When we returned to the arbors of Club Chic, music was blaring from the terrace roof. We had taken over the entire avenue, forcing traffic to slow down as cars passed through our crowd. People partied as people do on Pride days all across the world. We could, in that moment, imagine that we were connected through this celebration to other bodies of LGBTQ people elsewhere in ways that both transcended and reinscribed the nation-state (Manalansan 2003). Amid a sea of gay nationalist flag waving, a small trio of women carried a sign protesting the 2010 constitutional amendment, article 37 (the article that defines life from the moment of conception). Another trio of women held up a banner referencing article 42 (which protects the physical, psychic, and moral integrity of persons against violation). Young people demonstrated their gender performance acumen, and trans* women strutted their queenly garbs. As I watched, Mirla told me she was going to buy beer at the corner gas station. Here, as elsewhere, alcohol was part of the party. Four of us went together, even though she was the only one buying, because it was always safer in numbers. On our walk back, an old man shouted at us, "You should all be raped!"

There are ways in which persistent sexual terror shapes your affective dispositions (Cvetkovich 2007) and seemingly thrusts you into subjective vertigo: "a dizzying sense that one is moving or spinning in an otherwise stationary world, a vertigo brought on by a clash of grossly asymmetrical forces" (Wilderson 2011, 3). The old man's "you" was clearly directed at us, as we were the only bodies within his field of vision. The leap that he made into rape is already socially prefaced by the idea and script of rape as a corrective measure to lesbianism. The vertigo was produced by the sudden sensation that in any number of circumstances, he could have been joined by others, and rape might have been possible. As the old man continued to shout slurs in our direction, I realized that this was only the second incident of the day and that I had been expecting many, many more. My vertigo receded, and I continued on my way. My assessment of the conditions of our interactions—he was alone, he was old and physically weak, I was in a group, and there were a lot of gay people around us—alleviated whatever concerns I may have had about safety and the need to respond. Though I was disgusted by his outburst, I ignored him. I did not want to call attention to myself or put my friends in any sort of danger by responding. Even as I registered the physical surroundings, I did not know if there were other men with him; my imagination of public masculine power fed into this. My unwillingness to respond to his threats also had everything to do with my status as a person of diaspora; it was a moment in which I was not sure about the social cues and how far I could go to address the situation. But the Dominican lesbians who were with me did not share my logics. They shouted back at him. They surrounded him. One of the women threw her beer on his head and threatened to beat him. He went to punch her, but two gay men appeared and restrained him. The other women restrained the one woman who had her fists curled. With the help of the gay men and our own internal negotiations, the confrontation ended, and we meandered back to Club Chic. Along the way, we all commented on the man's violence.

"He's crazy," said Tina.

"Why does he have to be here? There are plenty of other places he could be if he has such a problem with us," Rebeka commented.

I walked silently. In that moment, I realized how much I had been *affected* (i.e., how my affective dispositions had been shaped) by my years living in the U.S. I had learned a different modality for dealing with what I have been taught to recognize as hate speech and hate crimes. Having been disciplined into a different kind of civil self, I had not shouted back; I had not asserted myself against him. I had not even considered a physical response as an option. My socialization and my experiences as a gay person of color in the U.S. meant that I always assumed that in a public altercation, if the police showed up, I would be the one arrested or shot. My constant negotiation of the "Black [streetwalking] imago" (Wilderson 2011), in which black (streetwalking) death is consistently a justifiable homicide, ostensibly conditioned my response to seemingly minor threats. In that moment, that was in no way, shape, or form the concern of the Dominican lesbians I was with. For them, the man was not only wrong, but his actions demanded a swift and immediate reaction of equal or greater violence. It reminded me that "conversations in the street are not subject to the same rules of sense, nor to the same expectations" (Lugones 2003, 209), as those conversations located within sites of institutional, social, and moral power. There were other shared understandings among the group: we were no longer living within the silences provoked by authoritarian logics; this was *our* day as LGBTQ people, and he was in *our* space. As LGBTQ people engaged in a worldwide struggle for our human and civil rights, we had the right to defend ourselves. And yet our different responses to the interaction signaled an underlying specificity in enculturated affective dispositions to social violence. I meditated on this as I made my way to Club Chic's rooftop terrace.

As more and more cars wound through the crowd of protest banners and people clad in strips of sequined Lycra and feathers, police officers filtered in from all sides. By five o'clock, over fifteen police officers were dispersed through the crowd of two hundred people. I could see that two of the officers were aggressive. As I stood on the rooftop terrace, looking down, I started to sense impending danger. Years of being harassed by police in contexts around the world had taught me how to feel the shifts that were leading up to police violence. I watched as an officer pushed a young trans* person back onto the sidewalk. Someone caught them, and the young trans* person raised a fist at the officer, shouting back that the police officer had no reason to be such a jerk.

I turned to D'Lo and Jon. "Let's go."

They agreed. As two trans* men of color—legible as black or brown—they, too, knew when things were about to go sour. Also, we all felt that if violence erupted, we could be arrested. And our brown, gender-nonconforming bodies could become the sites of further violence.

I gathered everyone who had come with me, plus two people who wanted to join us. We jumped into the car and rolled through the crowd, as other cars had before us. We were looking for another friend. As I slowed down to find her, the same police officer who had pushed the trans* person walked beside me, yelling, "You have to leave!"

"Yes, yes." I pushed my palm out in a gesture that means "Calm down."

Mirla, seated in the back, shouted to him, "Why are you bothering us? Can't you see we're leaving?"

And there it was. I saw it in my rearview mirror. He reached in and punched her. I stopped the car as I tried to understand what was happening, but he took it as an opportunity to open the door. He reached for Mirla's arm, trying to drag her out of the car. She escaped through the other door. Everyone got out with her. Another officer was waiting and pushed her against the car. She pushed back, livid, screaming and shouting at the officer that he had no right. We surrounded her, two of us restraining her with our bodies. The police officers patted their guns and got closer, eyeing all of us. A circle had formed around the car. One officer called out to the other, and we overheard him saying, "They're women." I shot a glance at D'Lo and Jon. They had stepped back out of the fray. Though they did not understand specifically what was going on, they had all witnessed scenes like this before—in New York, in Los Angeles, in London, in Delhi, in Port of Spain. In the U.S., Jon had been a part of a group to address police brutality against LGBTQ people of color. He had joined the group after witnessing cops pummeling gender-nonconforming friends of his, for absolutely no reason, as they left a Brooklyn gay club one night. We all knew exactly what was happening.

Three more officers arrived, and the situation was mediated, but not before the assaulting officer had asserted increasingly violent levels of authority. Not before the event had been captured on camera phones. Not before Mirla had lost her temper. Not before the crowd narrated its numerous opinions about whose fault it was that the officer had punched her, pushed her, and threatened her and us with their guns.

I shouted over to Mirla and Maribel, "Let's go, *hermanas*. Let's go to the park," and then I called out to D'Lo and Jon in English, "Hey guys, let's get out of here."

D'Lo and Jon looked Dominican, but when I shouted over to them in English, the police officers suddenly and immediately retreated. I did not take time to think through the full implications of that moment until much later. Afterward, I tried to digest the different vectors of power at play: the police authority, the imperial authority of English, the social authority of the crowd. Right then, I just took their retreat as an opportunity to leave. We all climbed back into the car and headed to El Parque. As we wound our way up Lincoln Avenue a second time and then down Independence Avenue, there was neither *soca* nor celebration. Instead, we all sat silent and shaken, and Mirla was in the back scanning the bruises on her body. El Parque would be familiar ground.

At El Parque, I sat on a bench and tried to follow the numerous conversations around me. My mind was on what had just happened and, more importantly, on the fact that the police had written down my license plate number. I was wondering what this might mean. The intergenerational legacy of authoritarian rule is such that my own sense of safety was compromised by the narratives of terror that shaped my childhood experiences. I had grown up hearing stories of Dominican police following people in their cars and killing them. I would not know until the next day that just as we were dealing with officers on the *malecón*, ten blocks away police trailed behind a car carrying several student activists, stopped them in the dark, and executed one of them point-blank (Urbáez 2010).[11] I did not yet know that. I concentrated on the events around me, trying not to worry. But the truth was that my state of joy had been altered. I had been marked. The subjective vertigo that had started earlier in the day had reached a state of full-blown disorientation, mediated by my observation of the strategies that Dominican LGBTQ activists used to address the violence.

In between stories of past protests, people all around us narrated the story of the police officer and Mirla over and over again. Through the process of overlapping, multivocal, continuous narration of protest and injury, Mirla calmed down, and she was publicly exonerated from her outburst of anger. Others who had witnessed the interaction shared their versions and added their own experiences of trauma and anger to the story. Some also discussed other incidents of violence they had suffered. This was done repeatedly over the course of several hours: this process of "faithful witnessing," which Lugones describes as a witnessing of the resistance "against the grain of power" (2003, 7). It was not until a lesbian film crew arrived and interviewed Mirla and Maribel and others who had faithfully witnessed the event that finally the collective process wound down. Everyone agreed that once the incident had been documented on film, it had become fact. And with the documentation of Mirla's narrative in her own words, we had not only proof of her injury—proof, in this instance, being that which was faithfully witnessed—but also testimony that could then circulate within a wider temporal sphere.[12]

After the film crew left, we hung out on the park benches, and someone ordered a round of beers. Someone else distributed plastic cups, and we began to tell stories. A woman and her friend approached my friends and started flirting with D'Lo. After a couple of hours, I was getting tired. I asked D'Lo and Jon if they wanted to go. We piled into the car and began our drive away from El Parque. Just as we left, though, the woman who had been flirting with D'Lo called out to him. I stopped the car so that he could talk with her. That instance would be recounted again and again over the years as the hilarious moment when I stopped the car so that my friend D'Lo could talk with Eleanor. All the folks who had been in the park with us crowded around the car, and we blocked traffic on the street, experiencing—for one more moment—the joy of being *en la calle* together.

The next day, we would learn about the student being assassinated. Mirla and I would go to the courts to try to register a complaint against the police (with no luck). We would call friends to try to get us both lawyers. I would reassure D'Lo and Jon that I was doing the best I could to make sure they got home safely. Someone would post a video of the incident on a gay blog, and international LGBTQ human rights groups would contact the LGBTQ groups in the D.R. to offer their support in filing a case against the state. In this moment, Mirla's experience as a lesbian subjected to state violence made her a universal subject within the realm of human rights. By expanding her personal experience into the spaces of international human rights struggles, international organizations were able to mobilize the universal categories of lesbian and human rights to confront the police and support local attempts at restitution. A month later, the attack against Mirla—along with the student execution[13]—spurred a national protest against police brutality. As the cardinal of the Catholic Church validated the necessity of police action to eliminate social *delinquentes*—and the newspaper printed his decrees—this protest brought together people from across the spectrum of Dominican society, including Mirla and other LGBTQ activists. Unwittingly, this series of events produced a series of *confrontaciones* in *las calles*, where we love and streetwalk.

Conclusion

Confrontación is an important strategy of streetwalking. It is a strategy by which LGBTQ people navigate family, community, and larger publics. Through *confrontación* within our families, LGBTQ activists are able to rehearse the courage, narratives, and practices necessary for navigating broader society. As a strategy, *confrontación* points to the ways in which Christian coloniality suffuses all spaces and places of personhood, undoing the presumptions and false categorizations of private and public. *Confrontar* draws on the psychic posturing of what it means to "deal," to face oneself and others (in Spanish, *enfrentar*). But *confrontar* is explicitly a posture of oppositional consciousness, of streetwalking, in that it entails maintaining an erotic orientation rooted in the possibilities of liberation.

CHAPTER 4

Flipping the Script

I don't ask for anybody's acceptance, or to be tolerated. I ask only to be respected.
—Henry Mercedes Vales, "Sigue creciendo la tasa de homicidios"

"Flipping the script" is a mode of shifting discourse that is often used as a street-walking strategy of *resistencia*. As a strategy of *resistencia*, it enables LGBTQ activists to mobilize Christian colonial logics to confront and overturn the violences enacted against them. It can take the form of speech acts, collective embodied actions, or any combination thereof. In theorizing this strategy, I draw on discussions about Afro-diasporic linguistic practices. Flipping the script is a way of expressing thoughts and feelings rooted in oppositional consciousness and in erotic orientations toward liberation. Flipping the script scrambles relationships of power and ideas of fixedness and stability. Flipping the script unfixes meaning and power. It can entail "testifying" and "signifying" (Gilyard 1996). Flipping the script is a relational process whereby all those involved reread the expected narrative in new forms and thereby imbue those narratives with different, distinct, and often subversive meanings.

Testifying is best described as "a ritualized form of black communication in which the speaker gives verbal [and nonverbal] witness to the efficacy, truth, and power of some experience in which all blacks have shared" (Smitherman 1977, 58). Some examples include a tight-lipped "umm-hmm," tooth sucking, eye cutting, lip pursing, hand-waving, head nodding, finger snapping, hair flipping, lip licking, eyebrow raising, standing up and turning around, giving side-eye, and so on. In Dominican vernacular cultures, subdued laughter, an entirely expansive set of communicative eye gestures, and indirect commentary can also accompany the process of testifying. But most importantly, testifying includes a dialogic process whereby a set of stories and/or interventions or commentary begun by one person is taken up by others.

Relatedly, signifying is "the act of talking negatively about somebody through stunning and clever put downs" (Smitherman 1977, 82), otherwise known as "reading," "shade," or (*en buen dominicano*) *moriqueta*. Reading is a practice that seeks to set a person "'straight,' to put them in their place, or to reveal a secret about someone in front of others in an indirect way—usually in a way that embarrasses a third party. Reading has two modes [in African American gay male culture]: one is serious and one is playful" (Johnson 1995, 126). Shade is rooted in "interpretive and performative black queer practices … [that at times do] not require any specific enunciation to deliver an insult; rather, it uses looks, body gestures and tones to deliver a message at once clear ('ratchet') and open-endedly sneaky ('I didn't say anything')" (Declue 2016, 237). Similarly, *moriqueta* is a non-verbal way of throwing shade that involves eye and mouth gestures; it is a way of saying everything without saying anything at all. Through *moriqueta*, shade, and reading, LGBTQ activists signify value systems, right relationship, and the boundaries around which personhood takes shape and meaning. In flipping the script, LGBTQ activists bring together different techniques of significa-tion in order to reappropriate Christian colonial logics and heteronormative signs, such as ideas of sin, manhood, womanhood, and sexuality. Their *resis-tencia* occurs in the reinterpretation of *respeto* as being *digno de ser* (worthy of existing). Streetwalking, they overturn Christian colonial expectations of who should be and who has a right to exist within the boundaries of the Catholic Hispanic nation-state.

In the discussion that follows, I will theorize and build on streetwalking articulations of *respeto* as they are mobilized by LGBTQ activists across a terrain where respectability politics constitutes yet another mode of Christian colonial sexual terror. In each of the vignettes presented here—in a public retelling of an encounter between a gay man and a heterosexual woman outside of a church, in a confrontation with police during a trans* memorial protest, and in yet another confrontation with the police during a Dominican Pride parade—LGBTQ activ-ists flip the script, producing counternarratives that challenge Christian colonial expectations and streetwalking as a mode of oppositional consciousness where *respeto* is rooted in erotic orientations toward liberation.

"Digno de Ser"

The Catholic Hispanic nation-state, "whose sexual operations are invested with [divinely authorized] political power" (Aretxaga 2003, 403) and whose political power is thoroughly sexualized and heteropatriarchal (Walby 1990; Weeks 1998), has always been and continues to be reliant on the marginalization of those who streetwalk. The creation of punishable categories of people such as *delinquentes* "mark[s] the limits of socio-cultural citizenship that have been rooted in domi-nant nationalist notions related to families, economics, and politics" (D. Thomas 2011, 43). Like the English term "thugs," *delinquentes* is a categorical word used to encapsulate those deemed socially undesirable and unrespectable by the moral authority of the church hierarchy (the cardinal), Christian leaders, state authorities, and elite interests. To streetwalk is to transit through the Catholic Hispanic nation-state's projection of the *delinquente* as the counterpoint to the upright moral citizen.

Despite tensions among Evangelical Christians, Protestant Christians, and Catholics, the churches manage to come together in response to questions of *moralidad pública* and *delincuencia*. The president of CODUE, Rev. Reynaldo Franco Aquino, stated that Evangelical Protestant groups' greatest success has been in "freeing the world of those people [*delinquentes*], each time a *delinquente* or a person who has been in that chaotic world enters our faith, it's one more life that has been changed, transformed, and we are liberating the world of those types of people, and that is happening in an accelerated fashion" (BEREA 2006). Though distinct from the discourse offered by the Catholic Church, Evangelical Protestant groups are equally invested in the elimination of *delinquentes*—those whose streetwalking poses a threat to the moral fiber of the Catholic Hispanic nation-state. The figure of the *delinquente* acts as a common form of subterfuge for the Christian and Catholic Church hierarchies to negotiate with the Dominican government for moral authority and political power. Despite Evangelical Christian struggles over access to political authority, land, and other state resources, the figure of the *delinquente* enables the basis on which to exercise nationalist, right-wing notions of sovereignty that serve to construct a cross-sect alliance between the most conservative bodies within both the Catholic Church and Evangelical Protestant groups.

Between 2009 through 2015, when Cardinal López Rodríguez made declarations about LGBTQ people or Haitian people, he often used the term *delinquente*.[1] This term, also popular in Dominican media, has been used to justify many rash police initiatives—such as neighborhood or street sweeps and extrajudicial executions. In early 2013, a wave of videos circulated through online media networks demonstrating police abuse of people deemed *delinquentes*. These videos often featured young men from impoverished communities whose bodies were marked as racially distinct through either dark skin or stylized features such as cornrows. The landscapes in these videos were inner courtyards and alleyways, areas under bridges, or spaces between shacks. In the mainstream media, the videos were often contextualized through the language of social ills or problems—whereby the figure of the abused bore the onus of the social ill.[2] However, activists took these same videos and circulated them through social media, transforming the conversation from one about the social problem of the *delinquente* to one about the social problem of police abuse.[3]

Similarly, the term *delinquente* has often appeared—and continues to appear—in mainstream newspaper articles covering the murders of gay or trans* people. In 2007, Catholic and evangelical Christian leaders invited youth to "repudiate violence, crime, alcoholism, discrimination, homosexuality" (Padilla and Castellanos 2008, 37), effectively lumping together other social ills with homosexuality, further undergirding the figure of the *delinquente*. The figure of the *delinquente* might signal the murdered streetwalking gay/trans* person directly, or it might signal those associated with them. Similar to the videos of police abuse, photos of murdered gay/trans* people appeared within a landscape of rubble, trash, or alleys between poorly built houses. The figure of the *delinquente* thus transited through the *barrio*, through the streets, through streetwalking bodies in the production of necropolitical excess—that is, deaths produced through the Catholic Hispanic nation-state's exercise of power (Mbembe 2003). The *delinquente*, either beaten, contained, or killed, thereby became a symbol of the Catholic Hispanic state's efficacy, of Christian colonial society's self-management.

LGBTQ activists flip the script on the dominant narrative. Among LGBTQ activists, *delinquente* is mobilized within different registers of meaning. Rather than signaling necropolitical excess, the term is often used to signal behaviors that interrupt a person's inherent right to exist. Streetwalking locates the site of infraction not in the copresence of those who might be deemed *delinquentes* but rather in the infractions that result from the rupture in the logics of transgression. In one interview, a lesbian woman told me, "I was riding the metro and *un delinquente* started shouting homophobic insults." When I asked her to define what she meant by *delinquente*, she responded, "Someone who thinks violence is the best way to resolve things" (Rosanna Marzan, personal communication, February 2013). A gay man shared with me that often when he walks in the city, he is watching out for *delinquentes* who might be a source of random violence (M.C., personal communication, February 2011). In his case, he was indexing the frequent experience of assault and robbery within public transportation but also the specific aggravation that his effeminate masculinity could provoke. In fall 2010, lesbian activists protesting police brutality used the term *delinquentes* in social media and in protest signs to refer to police officers abusing their power. In these instances, the categorical term did not serve as a counterpoint to moral respectability; rather, it referred to people who do not value life, who exercise homophobic *machista* attitudes and behaviors, or who are themselves part and parcel of the Christian colonial necropolitical machinery. *Delinquentes*, in this case, are those who may or may not have social authority but who act with impunity and outright violence from a place of self-decreed moral authority.

The figure of the *delinquente* reframes the basis by which moral and social authority is conferred—in particular, as it refers to social and political negotiations by Dominican LGBTQ activists. Since the mid-1980s, when Dominican LGBTQ activists began to make claims to public political identities, the Catholic Church *jerarquía* has positioned LGBTQ sociality as anathema to *moralidad pública* and national belonging. *Delinquente* became a catchall category that aimed to undermine any efforts by LGBTQ activists in relationships of solidarity among differently positioned, impoverished, and marginalized communities to position themselves as people deserving of *respeto*. To understand what is meant by *respeto*, it is important to delve into the dialectic between notions of respectability and reputation that have informed Caribbean theorizations of gender, race, and class for the better part of the last fifty years.

Anthony Lauria defines *respeto* as "a quality . . . [that] signifies proper attention to the requisite of the ceremonial order of behavior, and to the moral aspects of human activities. This quality is an obligatory self-presentation. . . . The verb form, *respetar*, indicates that in any encounter, one expresses deference to the person whom he confronts. *Un hombre de respeto* . . . can be a proper 'interactant' committed to, and capable of, maintaining another man's image of himself" (1964, 55). This definition of *respeto* iterates three very distinct social possibilities in the Christian colonial context. First, *respeto* can be construed as the embodiment of Christian colonial ideas of morality: biblical manhood and womanhood, proper relations between spouses and between parents and children, and a hierarchy within a God-given ceremonial order in which deference is a cultivated trait. Second, *respeto* can be identified as an internal sensibility akin to dignity, in which one maintains one's composure and/or seriousness in the face of sexual terror. Third, LGBTQ subjects push against these two iterations of *respeto* to generate a third possibility: one in which *respeto* is the adequate recognition from others that one is *digno de ser*[4]—regardless of socioeconomic class, racial/ethnic markers, gendered performance, or reputation. Streetwalking notions of *respeto* defy the logics and structures of domination.

Peter Wilson builds on Lauria's theorization of *respeto* by theorizing respectability and reputation as two distinct and co-constitutive social processes. Wilson defines the difference between respectability and reputation as follows: "Reputation is the key to a social system based on interaction within a community, the internal system, whereas respectability stems from the legal society or the external system" (1969, 79). Deborah Thomas argues that in the context of the Anglo-Caribbean, respectability "is a value complex emphasizing the cultivation of education, thrift, industry, self-sufficiency via land-ownership, moderate Christian living, community uplift, the constitution of family through legal [heterosexual] marriage and related gender expectations, and leadership by the educated middle classes" (2004, 5). As a social mechanism, respectability "is rooted in the system of stratification imposed by the old colonial social order. It was reproduced through the teachings of the colonial church and was associated with 'whiteness,' British culture, and formal authority" (D. Thomas 2011, 143).

Antonio E. de Moya (2004) also takes up the respectability-reputation dialectic. De Moya further theorizes respectability and reputation as gendered and spatialized concepts that define Dominican hegemonic masculinities. He locates the nexus of respectability within the space of the (imagined) sacred ruling class and the heterosexual, patriarchal, and (whitened) home space while locating reputation as a core element of masculinity within the working class and poor, public, (imagined) profane (darkened) streets. In this theorization, de Moya argues, household spaces serve to encompass "social institutions such as marriage, the nuclear family, dominant religions (Catholic and Christian), the formal economy, private and official educational institutions, heterosexual sexual practices, and traditional gender roles and mores." In contrast, the streets are ruled by "practices and situations that are not officially sanctioned, such as the informal economy, the sex industry, extramarital relations and *tigueraje*" (de Moya 2004, 78). Each is informed by the other and forms critical touchstones for the exercise of hegemonic masculinities.

Respectability can be construed as a value complex deeply embedded within Christian colonial vectors of power that produce Catholic Hispanic ethnonationalism. As such, it is then important to think about how respectability politics functions as a mode of sexual terror. When LGBTQ people are deemed incapable of being respectable because of their failure to embody biblical manhood or womanhood or because they—by virtue of who they are, the skin they live in, or the ways they construct sociality—fail to live according to Christian colonial norms of respectability, then it is possible to actively trace how respectability explicitly manifests as a tool of hegemonic social control and epistemic violence. Specifically, the expectation of respectability (and reputation) enacts sexual terror because it embeds Christian colonial mechanisms of social control within logics of personhood and citizenship. This mode of sexual terror explicitly renders streetwalking as an embodiment incapable of containing or enacting respectability and, by extension, personhood or citizenship.

Theories about respectability and reputation have aimed to provide us with frameworks from which to understand social negotiations of colonial hierarchies of power. Deborah Thomas's claim that reputation is a mode of social regulation that relies on "egalitarian" (2011, 144) notions of achievement and performance indexes a counternarrative to the hierarchies of power established through respectability. De Moya's (2004) claims that reputation is a spatialized, classed, racialized, and masculinist set of performances of power highlight how reputation is yet another way in which Christian colonial logics course through the regulatory social mechanisms of those not deemed respectable. If reputation is enacted through explicit heteromasculinist performances of power that seek to replicate Christian colonial ideas of biblical manhood through egalitarian social regulation, then those who fail to embody biblical manhood also fail to garner reputations, except when they are able to enact similar (heteromasculinist) performances of power.

LGBTQ activists' conceptualization of *respeto* as the adequate recognition from others that one is *digno de ser*—regardless of one's ability to enact or embody Christian colonial morality or biblical manhood and womanhood—is critical. Construing *respeto* as an internal sensibility akin to dignity, while also accounting for one's inability to embody either respectability or heteromasculinist reputation, repositions moral authority within another set of logics.

"Look—a Homosexual!"

Since 2010, the national Dominican gay men's network REVASA (Red de Voluntarios de Amigos Siempre Amigos) has been sponsoring an international LGBTQ film festival known as OUTFest in the capital city of Santo Domingo. Each evening, the festival organizers host a preshow teach-in followed by a series of film shorts and two feature films. There is usually a discussion following each film in order to allow space for audience members to air opinions and discuss topics relevant to both the films and LGBTQ communities.

One evening in December 2012, the film that ran was *Call Me Kuchu*, a documentary that delves into the collective struggle of Ugandan kuchu activists facing the Ugandan parliament's debates on whether to assign the death penalty to homosexuality (Zouhali-Worrall and Fairfax Wright 2012). The film also includes footage of the criminal trials along the way, in which individual Ugandan kuchu activists fought off charges of immorality or brought charges against people who had assaulted their person. One of the main people present in the documentary was David Kato, whose murder in 2010 drew international attention, including from many LGBTQ activists in the Caribbean. The documentary was released after his murder, and though it could have become a hagiography of Kato's life, it successfully and carefully skirted this possibility and instead refocused on the continuing struggles of the other activists featured in the film. It also directly engaged the role of both U.S. and Ugandan Evangelical churches in sustaining a culture of homophobia and featured one Ugandan minister who opened his doors to the LGBTQ community. Religion was a central part of the activists' lives and the struggle for civil and human rights in Ugandan society in a way that was readily legible to the Dominican audience.

During the follow-up discussion, I raised my hand and asked, "I am struck [*Me impresionó*] by the conviction the Christians in the film demonstrated that gays are going to bring down the nation, and as a result, gays need to be saved or killed. I am struck by the biblical arguments. How do we argue with the Bible (*¿Como se contradice la Biblia?*)?" My question, which I intentionally framed ambiguously, garnered a series of responses from the festival organizers and fellow audience members. One of the film festival organizers, Deivis, jumped over to the podium to speak. He stated,

> I don't debate about religion—and I'm religious! I go to church with my mother every Sunday. And look, I'm going to tell you a story. One Sunday, I come out of the church, and there is a lady and she says to me, "Wait a minute, I see you in the newspapers. How is it that you do what you do?" And I asked her back, "What is it that I do?" And she won't say, and we continue this way until I decide to go back into the church, at which point she screams, "You are a *homosexual*!!" And I turn around—because I know the commandments

and my religion—and I tell her, "First of all, what you have just done is a sin because the Bible condemns judgment, but I will absolve you. Secondly, my religion is my religion, and I don't have any reason to discuss that with you."...
Being LGBTQ is not a question of religion. It is a question of human rights. It is a civil issue. We are citizens, and we are not asking for special rights; we are asking to have our rights recognized as the rights of all citizens.

In this retelling, Deivis was discussing a time when he had flipped the script. At the moment when Deivis was literally reentering the church and metaphorically repositioning himself vis-à-vis the lady, he was interpellated (Althusser [1971] 2006) as a homosexual. This anecdote recalls Fanon's discussions of blackness; the utterance "Look—a Negro!" ([1952] 2008, 82) is a marker of all that is contained within the moment before one makes oneself known. Though the woman asserted "homosexual" as a critique of Deivis's respectability, Deivis flipped the script and put her in her place by making recourse to his knowledge of Catholic morality. Deivis's response demanded *respeto*. Rather than directly engage with the woman's interpellation of his homosexuality, Deivis turned the situation around and referred to a biblical moral imperative (do not judge), undermining her accusation by eschewing the question of sexuality altogether. But then he also flipped the script on me. When he declared that "my religion is my religion and I don't have any reason to discuss that with you. . . . Being LGBTQ is not a question of religion," he was turning my question inside out and signifying—reading me and the presumptions that religion and religious belief are up for debate while at the same time asserting that his sense of *respeto* is deeply tied to his faith and a sense of authority over what he will or will not discuss with other people.

Deivis further used his position as a leader in the LGBTQ community to emphasize to audience members that he understands the LGBTQ struggle to be about civil and human rights, not about personal matters such as religion or sexuality. Before opening up the floor for others, he went on to say, "There are many Christians, there isn't just one [kind of] Christian, and the interpretation of the Bible is subjective, not objective." His story garnered a laughter of recognition[5] from audience members because it exemplified "flipping the script"— that is, shifting the discourse so as to locate the social transgression (and sin) in the person making the homophobic attack—while also "signifying" by asserting claims to moral knowledge.

After this last predication, received by audience members with many nods, snaps, and other similar expressions of agreement (testifying), one timid older gentleman stood up. He identified himself as Pedro. He first introduced himself as a doctor—a gynecologist. He then went on to say, "These issues touch me very much, because I am a member of a fundamentalist Evangelical church, which preaches against homosexuals, just like in the movie, but we have to know that

God made nothing imperfect, and He put us all on earth just as we are, and that key with key, lock with lock, we love who we love."

Some people in the audience hummed in disapproval, but others nodded in agreement, from which I deduced they either (1) were also members of fundamentalist Evangelical churches, (2) also believed that God made us all perfect, (3) agreed with Pedro's statement that we love who we love, or (4) disapproved of Pedro's Evangelical Christianity. Since I could not distinguish points of agreement and disagreement—a wondrous multiplicity central to signification—I focused more directly on my own personal reactions to what he shared. First, I was struck that he chose to be a member of a *fundamentalist* Evangelical church. In particular, because I had been told by a trans* activist and an HIV advocate that there were some Evangelical churches that were welcoming to gay and trans* members, I wondered if he was a member of one of those congregations. Second, I was reminded of the literature crafted by the local Metropolitan Community Church, which provides the language for LGBTQ Christians and emphasizes God's inability to create imperfection. And third, I was struck by Pedro's management of the contradictions within himself—making room for his *fundamentalist* Evangelical faith as well as his same-sex desire, as articulated through the metaphor "a key with a key." Pedro, in quite a different way from Deivis, challenged the expectations of who might be in the room *and* who evangelical Christianity might contain. As a mode of testifying, Pedro expanded on Deivis's story by adding his own.

As I pondered my own attitudes and assumptions, the discussion continued. Various audience members began to testify, in a sense, similar to testifying in African American religious experience, and that alludes to the kinds of subjective self-representation drawn from this experience (Moore 2005). They were testifying about their own churches and the relative degrees of inclusion or homophobia present within them. And then a young self-identified lesbian woman raised her hand. She changed the conversation by saying that she had left God behind along with her heterosexuality. She then steered the conversation into a sharing of her experiences of discrimination and active self-defensive responses. To each of these testimonies—religious and otherwise—Deivis always made a point of responding (not always affirmatively) in a way that served to highlight how the person's actions were a form of activism. As the conversation wound down, I saw that Pedro was walking out of the auditorium. I quickly followed him so that I could ask him about what he had shared.

I stopped Pedro in the hall and introduced myself as both community member and researcher. I then asked him how he reconciled being part of (*ser parte de*) a fundamentalist Evangelical church with being "who he is" (*quien eres*). His response illuminated the various ways in which tacit subjects often navigate terrains of respectability and reputation. He answered, "Because it's my religion, and it's personal, and I don't have any reason to go into [my sexuality] there.

Besides, I lead a youth circle, so I have to be very careful." Pedro then went on to share a Christian Bible story about Jesus and the adulteress, citing the well-known proverb "Let he who has not sinned cast the first stone." I was set to leave our conversation there, but Pedro continued, adding that for people of faith, the priority was God and then finding someone to be with (*una pareja*), and it was important not to be traipsing through the streets (*pajareando por la calle*) or using boas or false breasts and makeup. He assured me that he was "a proper man." My mind was reeling. Pedro had just articulated some of the primary ways in which respectability functions as a tool of sexual terror: through the mobilization of biblical gender binaries and the relegation of public expressions of difference to the street. This, of course, made sense given his religious subjectivity. But it existed within the contradictions of Pedro's own conceptualization of God's love.

For many Dominicans, sexuality exists within a space of self-protective silence, of a *doble moral* that has allowed for self-preservation in the face of sexual terror. In *Tacit Subjects*, Decena theorizes tacit subjects as those that "not only hold a person or topic from 'falling' by bringing shame on those it concerns; the tacit subject holds the social formation as a whole from falling, moving, getting disordered" (2011, 21). Pedro's tacit subjectivity required positioning himself first as a doctor, then as a fundamentalist Christian, and then as one of God's creations. At no point in time did Pedro ever articulate himself as a gay man or a homosexual. The closest he came to identifying anything about his gender and sexuality were in the direct statement that he was un hombre propio (a "real/ proper man") and through the indirect statement about "keys with keys" in the postfilm conversation.

It is in Pedro's articulation of respectability—through a management of his reputation as an economically successful member of society (*un hombre de respeto*), a good Christian, and a role model of biblical manhood—that it becomes clear how he can so easily lose that same respectability. The first part of his response immediately signaled ideas about homosexuals as sexual predators. He was letting me know that part of maintaining his respectability was in being a doctor and a Christian and, explicitly, being a role model for youth. This role modeling required the suppression of his homosexuality within the space of the church. Employing the deep heteromasculinist logics of respectability and reputation, Pedro clearly articulated his disdain for those who—unlike him—failed to publicly uphold biblical manhood. However, if at any point Pedro failed in his public exercise of biblical manhood and members of his church discovered—through rumor, witness, or any other form—that Pedro was not *un hombre propio*, Pedro's respectability would be shattered. A shattering of his respectability could affect his ability to continue to practice medicine, and he could lose a community of faith that had spiritually sustained him. It would also destroy any potential for his role as a model for youth.

I thanked Pedro and ran outside to say hello to Tania, whom I met at a LGBTQ human rights forum in 2011. Tania is a trans* activist. I had not seen her yet that year and was very happy to encounter her at the film festival. We started discussing that evening's films. We both agreed that we did not like the ending of the Thai film *It Gets Better* (Sukkhapisit 2012) because, stereotypically, the trans* character is killed at the end. Then Tania said, "But if they kill me, I hope it serves a purpose."[6] Her statement gave me pause. Seeing my facial expression—I am quite sure my brows were furrowed in worry and concern—Tania went on to contrast the senseless death of the trans* character in *It Gets Better* with what she saw as the meaningful death of David Kato in *Call Me Kuchu*. I responded by saying I hope she is never killed and that it would be nice to see feature films with trans* characters that are as well developed as people are in real life. Bringing the conversation back to *Call Me Kuchu*, Tania then said, "I have nothing to do with the church, because if they don't want me, I don't want them either." She told me that in her opinion, LGBTQ people are the most religious and then revealed that she herself was a Mormon missionary at one point. "That was how I met Maria. She was also a Mormon," she said. Maria, one of the most vocal radical lesbian activists in Latin America, was a Mormon missionary? I was surprised; I had interviewed Maria and known her for almost eight years, and did not know this about her. "*O, sí,*" Tania responded, "and [this one], she was a priest, and [the other] one a nun, and [this one], he was a Jehovah's witness, and [the other one] *evangélica*. And don't you see that we are the most religious of all? . . . But even so, they attack us." I listened to the list of LGBTQ activists who had been or were deeply religious. And I paused to digest what Tania was telling me.

Tania took my momentary pause as a break to depart and kissed me goodnight. As I waited for my ride, I reflected on that evening's films and discussions. I was reflecting on the ways in which various people had relegated both religion and sexuality to the realm of the personal and how Deivis had then insisted that being LGBTQ is about human and civil rights. This was an articulation of ways of thinking and being that was presciently distinct from the more common "coming out" (Sedgwick 1993) sensibilities present in neoliberal LGBTQ rights discourses. It was clear to me that Deivis and Tania, who are not tacit subjects and rarely enact tacit subjectivity, actively engage in the process of disordering social scripts. They skillfully employ religious motifs such as parables and commandments explicitly, consciously, and with purpose as an effort to counteract Christian colonial respectability's silencing tactics. Their self-conscious articulations also signify a movement out of the space of silences and into the light of public being.

Tacit subjectivity, as in Pedro's case, is one aspect of *respeto* in which both the self and the other are confirmed through a silent acknowledgment of what is already known. To maintain one's *respeto* as a gay man, in this case, requires managing one's reputation so as to maintain respectability.[7] In Deivis's case, as a good Catholic, respectability is eschewed in favor of a *respeto* constructed through the idea of a knowing Christian moral subject. Deivis, in a brilliant play on biblical knowledge, managed to maintain his *respeto* by flipping the script on a woman who called him out as a homosexual.

Pedro's social position compared to Deivis is marked by several visible differences: Deivis is an openly gay, very loud, and very public LGBTQ activist; neither Pedro's faith community nor his professional communities know of Pedro's erotic orientations or identifications. Deivis is a Catholic; Pedro is a fundamentalist Evangelical Christian. Deivis is slight of build and slightly effeminate; Pedro is hypermasculine and muscular. Pedro's reputation is maintained in the performance of biblical manhood, a performance that is essential to maintaining respectability. Deivis's reputation is maintained through both his cisgender masculinity and his unabashed activism and public voice (*voz pública*) on issues related to LGBTQ civil and human rights. But for Deivis, questions of respectability are irrelevant to the construction of LGBTQ rights.

And then there is Tania, whose bodily presentation as a nonpassing trans* person disrupts any likelihood of a socially conferred respectability, though she does indeed desire it. When she states, "I have nothing to do with the church, because if they don't want me, I don't want them either," she is disavowing religion not for its own sake but because of the rejection she experienced during and following the realization of her trans* identity. The embodied knowledge that emerged from her experience as a Mormon and from knowing others who have attempted to exercise religion enable her to claim that LGBTQ people "are the most religious of all." The problem for Tania is not in the free exercise of religion or sexuality but in the experience that *even though* LGBTQ people "are the most religious of all . . . they attack us." Her wish—that should she be killed, it not be in vain—highlighted to me her sense of dignity and the *respeto* she demands through the ways in which she lives her life as a trans* activist. In a society in which trans* people are preordained as *delinquentes*, drug addicts, and prostitutes, death is often senseless. But for Tania, death is one place where she hopes her life can exert some sort of symbolic power that could carry meaning beyond herself. Simultaneously, Tania's demeanor conveys Lauria's notion of *respeto* outside of a normative masculinity or sense of binary gender. Tania's insistence that she would not attend a church because "if they don't want me, I don't want them" eschews tacit subjectivity for a more transgressive assertion of her streetwalking self as a self that deserves *respeto* without the silent ordering of which Decena speaks. For Tania, *respeto* is embedded in her autonomy, defined by an unwillingness to deny oneself or subject oneself to the rejection enacted through Christian (in her case, Mormon) doctrine.

In all three examples, it is possible to see how respectability acts as a socially constraining force that is impossible to inhabit—in particular because LGBTQ subjects are already construed as *delinquentes*. The space afforded by tacit subjectivity is not less violent, for within it lies the potential to be discovered as failing biblical manhood (or womanhood). Reputation, while allowing both Pedro and Deivis (as cisgender men) the direct and mitigated public performances of biblical manhood, requires, in the first instance, the suppression of homosexual identifications and, in the second instance, a recourse to moral authority against and above the figure of the homosexual. For Tania, exercising a heteromasculinist performance of power in order to fortify her social reputation is not only impossible but also anathema to her embodiment of trans* personhood.

Respeto, then, emerges as a mode of LGBTQ transgressive autonomy in which being *digno de ser* supersedes modes of *respeto*/respectability as morally right or *respeto*/reputation as socially mediated. Christian colonial modes of *respeto* enact sexual terror through economic and social violences against streetwalking; they allow for the construction of the *delinquente* as a universalized criminal / disreputable / unrespectable / failed citizen and moral subject. *Respeto* enacted as a mode in which streetwalking enables us to be *digno de ser* affords LGBTQ people the exercise of a moral authority informed by different logics than those embedded within Christian colonial hegemonies. In all three instances, flipping the script—either by the appropriation of Christian moral authority, by a reinterpretation of "God's love," or by the assertion of power over death—reveals the limits of Christian coloniality and its heteronormative presumptions.

RUTA CONTRA LA TRANSFOBIA

When trans* activists mobilize against sexual terror not through erotic performance and sexual lyrics but in performances grounded in Christian colonial rituals of mourning and memorialization, they are enacting a collective *confrontación* that builds on broader social-spiritual logics, further embedding trans* lives within the sociospiritual world of the living and the dead. This *confrontación* entails the appropriation of culturally embedded symbols in order to flip the script across the shared public space of the city. In May 2010, a team of Dominican trans* activists, accompanied by allied gay, lesbian, bisexual, and *quír* activists, performed a public protest titled "Ruta contra la Transfobia y Crimenes de Odio" (TRANSSA 2010).

In this vignette, the term *performance* is not meant to imply a kind of LGBTQ performativity or even to interrogate what performativity might illuminate. Here, I focus on the ways in which the trans* dead animate the LGBTQ living and give meaning to place and relationship. The performance of a public mourning ritual became a form of surrogacy generated by loss and change; as such, it mediated the forgetting that is inherent to memory. Joseph Roach reminds us, "In the life of a community, the process of surrogacy does not begin or end but continues as actual or perceived vacancies occur in the network of relations that constitutes the social fabric. Into the cavities created by the loss through death or other forms of departure . . . survivors attempt to fit satisfactory alternates" (1996, 2).

Whereas "the three-sided relationship of memory, performance, and substitution becomes most acutely visible in mortuary ritual—or mourning of the dead" (Roach 1996, 14)—within the Dominican trans* community, surrogacy is interrupted by the constancy and arbitrary nature of sexual terror enacted on streetwalking bodies: a terror that is mobilized and legitimized by the present-absence of the Catholic Hispanic state and its traces and that aims to discipline the most explicit and profound erotic desires. LGBTQ communities' inability to fill the space of loss created by the murder of friends and loved ones mirrors the space of loss generated by the murder of activists during the Trujillo era and the murder of those presumed to be Haitian along the border and in the wave of anti-Haitian violences of the last two decades. It also ultimately mirrors the genocide of indigenous people and the careless disposal of African bodies into the Atlantic throughout centuries of crossings. For Dominican trans* activists, there is no body to mourn, no casket to gather around, no public place of gathering. Cut out of the fold, silenced, or made invisible by the families of the deceased, trans* activists must create their own places and forms of mourning, acts that generate a countermemory that marks "the disparities between history as it is discursively transmitted and memory as it is publicly enacted by the bodies that bear its consequences" (Roach 1996, 26).

The use of the term *ruta* in "Ruta contra la Transfobia y Crimenes de Odio" made direct reference to the 2004 UNESCO Ruta del Esclavo (personal communication, Mirla Hernández-Nuñez 2010; Comisión Nacional Dominicana de la Ruta del Esclavo 2006), which had been mobilized on national television and in popular memory as the retracing of the slave trade, slave uprisings, and resistance through the geography of the colonial city and nearby countryside. The term simultaneously evokes the notion of a route as a fixed space and of routes as openings for new possibilities. The naming of the walk as such allowed the organizers to position these simultaneous discourses in which they both memorialized the past and presented the possibility for a future without transphobia or hate crimes. The latter terms *transfobia* (transphobia) and *crimenes de odio* (hate crimes) index the position of the organization within a larger context of international LGBTQ activism in which violence against LGBTQ people is marked as explicitly nonarbitrary and motivated by homophobia and—in this case—transphobia.

The performance by trans* and allied activists on the *Ruta* was itself the surrogate for a mourning ritual, simultaneously evoking the lack of bodies (and, in essence, their continued presence and haunting within the spaces of memory and work) and the lack of place. The trans* activists mobilized a streetwalking performance as a space of mourning, in which the memories of a community came to be inscribed upon the city's landscape, the disjunctive voices of trans* activists interrupted the whispers of nighttime sex labor, and the use of traditional mourning symbols repositioned the relationships of power between the community, the Catholic Hispanic nation-state, and the Dominican public. The *Ruta* drew from the national organization's membership and its allies to commemorate the lives and deaths of trans* people who had been brutally murdered by clients, police, and strangers—people whom trans* activists termed *delinquentes* because of their lack of respect for trans* lives. As one of the organization's advocates explained to me, given that the families, police, and judicial authorities had no desire to follow up on the cases as violent crimes, the trans* community, along with lesbian and gay allies, sought this intervention as a way to channel their anger, grief, and sense of helplessness and bring attention to the murders of their community members to a broader public audience.

The action took the form of a Catholic procession in which participants marched through the city bearing the organization's banner, candles, images of the dead, stencils, and spray-paint. They marched at night, symbolically streetwalking and claiming the dark as a space for trans* life. As they marched, they visited the places where trans* people—some of whom were sex workers—were murdered. The names of the dead were spray-painted onto walls at specific sites along the *Ruta*, acting as semipermanent memorials to the collective body of the dead. After the names were written, they were read out loud, and flowers and candles were placed at the foot of the memorial. The procession then continued, its members shouting "No a la transfobia!" and clapping. So it was that the performance of memory called upon not just the visual index of graffiti (which marks both urban space and, in the context of the D.R., left-wing political protest) or other altars (such as those placed for the victims of gun violence or traffic accidents) but also the auditory component of testifying, of calling out names, of stating, "Here died a trans* Dominican as a result of transphobia."

As activists, those on the *Ruta* were also highly self-conscious and aware of the multiple layers of memorialization that were occurring. Not only were there the temporal specificities of the actions and conversations taking place between people in the moments of memorialization, but there were also photography, videography, and narrative voice-over commentaries on the videos being recorded. In one video (TRANSSA 2010), where the ritual is performed specifically for the benefit of the cyberaudience who will see the footage in the future, the seams of the performance are rendered visible. As the shadow of the spray-painter moves outside the frame of the camera, the names of the dead appear on the wall and the center of the screen. The videographer asks one of the activists to read out loud what is on the wall, framing the performance with the statement that "this site marks the death of trans* [people] who have been killed, sometimes because they are doing sex work, which they are forced to do because of social discrimination which limits their opportunities for employment." Just before a trans* activist begins to read the inscription out loud, another trans* activist stands to the side of the memorial, holding a Dominican flag as a camera flash goes off.

The reading of names is interrupted when a police truck pulls up. The camera turns to witness the interaction as a trans* activist and a lesbian activist mediate with the police, asking, "We can't light candles?" This question serves to draw police attention away from the fact that those gathered are LGBTQ—the most likely reason the police have stopped—and to normalize the gathering. The police ask them again what they are doing, and the trans* activist responds, this time verbalizing what has been unspoken up until that moment: "We are lighting candles for the trans* [people] who have been killed."

Another person chimes in, "It's an offering for someone."

A cisgender man holding flowers steps forward. Another voice says, "We are only lighting a candle."

The police, unable to find a reason to continue harassing the group, drive away. The camera immediately focuses on the altar and the shaking heads of the participants, and one of the videographers comments, "See, people, how justice is always taking note of our activities, but they don't do anything about the violations, the aggressions committed against trans* people?"

Continuing and using the moment as an opportunity to document discrimination and violence against trans* people, the narrator states, "Here we saw how a patrol immediately came when we are in the middle of this activity. And yet when the girls are victimized by their clients, or sometimes by the police themselves, they don't appear. For that reason, many of them [our girls] have lost their lives to violence that results from transphobia" (TRANSSA 2010). The videographer's narrative commentary continues, bringing in the language of human rights, critiques of the church, and assertions of the love of country, all of which end in clapping followed by chanting: "No a la transfobia!" As the shouts get louder, the videographer steps out from behind the camera and enters the screen, joining in the chanting as participants gather their belongings to move on to the next location. This series of interactions disorders the power relations between trans* activists and police, flipping the script on how (and which) bodies are authorized within public space. Reading the police officer, the narrator calls attention to the failures of the police to respect their persons in any instance.

Ten other sites were visited throughout the city, though this was the only one recorded on video. The remaining sites were captured in photographs and in the narratives of those who participated and retold the story of the route to others. Invariably, they would list off some of the points where they had built altars. When I revisited these sites one month later, only one graffiti memorial remained; the rest had been painted over or tagged by others. The only remains of these remains were the memories of the people there and the photographs and videos circulating through cyberspace.

Reframing the murders of trans* people not as individual, arbitrary, and untraceable acts but rather as a result of systematic discrimination allowed trans* activists to simultaneously give life to the dead and contextualize the dead within the larger community of the living. The documentation in this case filled the space of memory with things that were not lived personally. They served as stand-ins for particular versions of the stories of what happened. But acting only as a fragment, participation in the procession itself reached into memory through both action and imagination rather than through reference. The work of this performance was not only to document and to memorialize; it was also to deem the dead worthy of remembrance, to give their names life within and on the walls of the city, to mark their deaths as part of a continual haunting that joins the hauntings of all those killed through the violences of colonialism, U.S. occupation, and authoritarian regimes. The procession created an archive in the bodies of the living, inscribing in them the assurance that they, too, will not be forgotten. The *Ruta* marked places of knowing / not knowing, of being / not being. It demonstrated the co-constitution of sexual and racial terror and invoked contours that shape the communities affected by it, giving form to the spaces and modes of being, flipping the script on the media and a society that would just as quickly not remember the trans* dead or living.

In this instance, the trans* and allied activists refused to perform biblical manhood/womanhood. After insisting on their trans* selves, they invoked *respeto* as deeming trans* persons *digno de ser* and worthy of being mourned. By at first only referencing Catholic symbology (candles, flowers) and state symbology (the Dominican flag), those streetwalking used this initial strategy as a way to claim legitimacy within the public space. But when that became insufficient, it was the activist's claim "We are lighting candles for the trans* [people] who have been killed" and the additional testifying "We are making an offering" and "We are only lighting candles," *as well as* the video documentation, that finally pushed the police away. The video documentation, in this instance, became a mode of putting the police in their place. The commentary that followed the police's departure, within the context of the video, was a signification—a reading of the police in which the police's failure to provide protection was marked as the social ill over and against the already preconfigured bodies (both alive and dead) of trans* people.

READING IS FUNDAMENTAL

In June 2012, the Caravana made its way through the main corridors of the city of Santo Domingo yet again. Yori, a young gay activist, rode in the gay bus along with almost one hundred other men, shouting and dancing out of the windows while holding rainbow flags, balloons, and party favors. As they turned the corner off of George Washington Avenue and up Maximo Gomez Avenue, Yori waved a

Dominican flag out the window. Within minutes, the Dominican national police had stopped the Caravan and ripped the Dominican flag out of Yori's hand (Sosa 2012). They would not let the Caravan move forward. Deivis, one of the organizers, made his way up to the police officer.

In this moment, Deivis flipped all registers of masculinity and male respectability. Deivis was dressed in tight red pants and a military captain's hat and, in that mode of dress, both mobilized sass and inverted expectations of what Dominican masculinity is supposed to be. Second, he took the flag back from the police officer, asserting his authority over and above that of the police officer. And through both actions—standing face-to-face with the officer and taking back the flag—Deivis called attention to himself, producing *un show* (a spectacle) that set the stage for him to effectively read the officer from head to toe. The national media immediately flocked around them, capturing the interaction in a video that circulated on TV and online ("Policía Trata Impedir" 2012).

Deivis stated loudly, so everyone around him could hear, "It's because we are citizens of this country that we are vindicating—in our own way—the rights that the Republic's constitution establishes and which also include us." At this point, he held up the Dominican flag for everyone to see. "Nobody can tell us that in this act of faith and for human rights that we can't use this flag, because that would be saying we are not Dominicans. We are Dominicans just like anybody else." Mobilizing public opinion by waving the flag, Deivis called the Caravana "an act of faith and for human rights," at once collapsing the possibility of any critique on the basis of religion *or* law.

Deivis reached back into his right-hand pocket and pulled out his wallet. He searched for his *cédula*—his national identity card—and in a classic act of shade, he pulled out several credit cards before finally locating it. "I have my identity card, which these days is very fashionable, where it says I am a Dominican citizen." He held his *cédula* up to the officer, who stepped back from Deivis, shaking his head.

"Tell me: what have I done wrong, *comandante*?" Deivis stated. "How have I disrespected the nation's honor?"

"No. You can't use [the flag]," responded the officer.

"Ah, I can't use it? Well then show me the legal code where it says I can't. And what will happen to me if I do use it."

"Excuse me," responded the officer. "You can't use it."

"Why can't I use it? Give me the law. Where does it say that I can't use it?"

"No, you can't use it," he repeated.

"But where does it say that? In baseball games, they use flags. The PLDistas (a political party) use flags in their marches. If the PLDistas use the flag, if the Reformistas use the flag, then we as citizens of this country can use the flag, *comandante*," Deivis replied.

"No."

"But why not?"

The officer was cornered. Deivis had revealed the police officer's secret—there was no offense made. This was all just a farce, a performance of police authority. There was no law broken. There was nothing that had been done wrong. Finally, as the media circled the officer, testifying and echoing Deivis's position, the police officer surrendered.

"Yes, yes, you can use it."

"Aaah," said Deivis in mildly irritated triumph.[8]

After the media performance, the officer went on to negotiate the process of saving face (Candelario 2007) by letting Deivis know that he was just doing his job and that if the Caravana participants were going to use the flag, they could not let it touch the ground. The organizers assured the officer that they would follow his recommendations, and the Caravana continued. Had the crowd surrounding Deivis and the officer been in any way hostile, the officer's authority would have been confirmed, and most likely this episode would have had a different outcome. However, the community of LGBTQ activists mobilized their resources immediately, placing one of their most well-trained advocates at the front—a person versed in the law and in flipping scripts—and in so doing, they were able to mediate the encounter.

This recourse to national citizenship among Dominican LGBTQ activists has emerged as LGBTQ *resistencia* becomes increasingly empowered through global human rights processes—processes that include documentation and the sharing of activist toolkits. Following the series of events in 2010 and the subsequent documentation campaigns led by the U.S. embassy, Amnesty International and the EU, LGBTQ activists began to mobilize nationalist discourses to mediate the violence perpetrated against them by state and church authorities. In this instance, we witnessed the dance between Deivis's exercise of power—his self-proclamation as someone of means (credit cards) over the police officer (who makes the legal minimum wage)—and the officer's abuse of his authority by exercising his personal homophobia. The mobilization of the media and the direct interventions by journalists in support of Deivis's claims also reveal the very intimate nature of violence and the fragility and relational nature of citizenship. They demonstrate how Deivis mobilized culturally legible registers of respectability, as defined by Antonio de Moya (2004), within the public space of the streets and the space of the LGBTQ Pride parade. In this instance, however, it was not Deivis's respectability alone that enabled the resolution of the *confrontación*. The negotiation also required the crowd to testify and signify in order to buttress Deivis's advocation. Though the police officer never said why they could not use the flag, it was the officer's recourse to the logics of *moralidad pública* that justified his actions, or the notion that the simple act of a gay person holding a flag was enough of an affront to biblical manhood and, by extension, Catholic Hispanic citizenship. But in the end, Deivis read him—putting the officer in his place and flipping the script on the question of who has the authority to carry a flag.

CONCLUSION

Whereas *confrontación* is a strategy of relational enunciation, in which LGBTQ people express personhood through the unrestrained body and unrestrained speech, flipping the script is a mode of *resistencia* rooted in the appropriation of the Christian colonial signs and symbols of moral personhood and citizenship. In the three examples presented in this chapter, gay and trans* activists utilized Christian colonial logics—and the logics of the Catholic Hispanic nation-state—to carve out a space of *respeto*. Even the terms on which *respeto* is articulated have been inverted from the expectation of a respectability politics or a reputational masculinity into a narrative of what it means to be *digno de ser*. Flipping the script is a powerful strategy of *resistencia* rooted in an erotic orientation toward liberation, where liberation is an understanding that even in streetwalking, we are all worthy of being. In the next chapter, I build on the examination of these strategies to explore the place of *cuentos* in the context of streetwalking.

CHAPTER 5

Cuentos

Cuentos (stories) act as a mode of archiving (Halberstam 2005, 17) and a mode of *resistencia*. *Cuentos* challenge the imposition of gender/sexual categories and reframe the violences experienced by LGBTQ persons in Dominican society. *Cuentos* exist as negotiations over the silencing tactics of the Catholic Hispanic nation-state and are a strategy to enable the transformation of silence. They counteract the epistemic violence of historical erasures of LGBTQ presence and participation within Dominican society. *Cuentos* enable LGBTQ activists to place themselves as protagonists within larger narratives of resistance to anti-LGBTQ state policies, Christian coloniality, and ethno-nationalist Catholic Hispanic narratives of Dominicanness. They occur across various registers of *confrontación*: from the use of the *doble moral* to the documentation of LGBTQ stories in film. In some instances, *cuentos* enable LGBTQ activists to flip the script, and in others, they allow them to simply reimagine streetwalking pasts and futures. The modes in which *cuentos* are shared also complicate the interstices between tacit and streetwalking subjectivities. This chapter is about *cuentos* that streetwalk—that is, *cuentos* that enable LGBTQ activists to transform silence into action that in turn enables the mobilization of that action for liberation.

With streetwalking, the transformation of silence into action is a necessary, almost uncontrollable impulse. Tacit subjectivity, in contrast, layers meaning into silence and creates dark spaces from which knowledge and being can be articulated. The interstices between these two modes of subjectivity reveal how Dominican LGBTQ activists move and manage multiplicity not as an exception to the rule but rather as a central feature of how they understand personhood. In this way, tacit subjectivity gets subsumed by streetwalking and becomes yet another avenue for the encounter with another who is also "at odds with home" (Lugones 2003, 209). On this avenue, the tacit subject is one who chooses, within that space of oddity, to create impermeable boundaries, to spatialize the private, to shelter difference in order to stabilize home at all costs. The subject may even speak the very language and act in the very ways that sustain the Catholic Hispanic nation-state. Between streetwalking and the tacit subject, "there is no common language, no common expectations, no reason to assume trust or trust worthiness, no comfortable womb-warm sense of safety" (Lugones 2003, 229). And yet streetwalking does not preclude us from holding the tacit subject's body against our own, claiming the space between us as one full of potential and possibility. After all has been said and done, we part ways. To others, the tacit subject denies ever having known the street. But the fact of our embrace is imprinted on our beings. The tacit subject resorts to the *doble moral*.

In the practice of the *doble moral*, people exist in public "de la boca pa' fuera"— that is, primarily through speech (Mateo 2004). This expression, which literally translates in English to "from the mouth out," alludes to the ways in which people represent themselves through the performance of conformity through speech; it is in part a masking, a series of hidden transcripts (Scott 1990) that enables people to critique power while also mediating the possibility of death and/or punishment. The *doble moral* is predicated on the denial of violence. People say they support Trujillo because it is required of them. They say they are Catholic or Christian because it is required of them. They say they are heterosexual because it is required of them. They say they are faithfully married while maintaining a cadre of lovers. The *doble moral* calls attention to the contradictions that arise between what people say they do and what they actually do. Enacting the *doble moral* through speech practices means that concepts like the *moral pública* and biblical manhood and womanhood remain intact while people are also able to find meaning and power in what is unspoken, left unsaid, or hidden in farce, metaphor, or *cuento*.

Jaime, a Catholic priest, does not openly critique the Catholic Church because he is still a part of it. When he speaks of the *doble moral* among Dominicans, he speaks of it as a masking: "That comes from Trujillo—the fact that people give you one name, but they have another name." Here, Jaime uses this simple example to talk about the naming practices that took place under the Trujillo regime, in which people had multiple names, a practice that continues today. "They did that because if the *calié* came looking for José Pérez but everyone knows him as Chino, they [the *calié*] couldn't find him."

This practice, I told Jaime, also takes place among Afro-diasporic populations throughout the Americas.

"Maybe," he responded.

But what particularly amused Jaime about my suggestion was, in his words, that "here, everyone practices something. But when you ask them, they tell you they are Catholic or Christian and that they don't believe in all of that. But it's not like that. Everyone practices something."

The *doble moral* extends into broader modes of relationality between people. These modes include the extensive uses of metaphors, stories, and silence as speech acts that serve to preserve relationships. These modes of relationality— of knowing / not knowing, of speaking / not speaking, of revealing / saving face—ostensibly have their roots in many sources, including the silences and indirect communication practices necessary to survive the Trujillato and, later on, Balaguer's regime. But these modes are also informed by centuries of repression of Afro-indigenous spiritual beliefs. The *doble moral* served to both protect the beliefs and strengthen the *santos* through the accumulation generated through their alliance with the figures and stories of the Catholic saints. In all cases, the *doble moral* relies on the use of silence. The *doble moral* is not necessarily celebrated by LGBTQ activists. As stated by Yuderkys Espinosa Miñoso,

> Thanks to this *doble moral* in our society, nobody says anything about the sexist, inappropriate format and content in *Sábado Chiquito de Corporán*, Isha and all of the other shows like this. . . . Thanks to this same *doble moral*, nobody pays attention or regulates the violence communicated in cartoons and stories. . . . Thanks to this *doble moral* our schools expel pregnant girls and youth who are considered degenerates because they transgress the imposed sex-gender system. Nobody denounces, nobody says anything, nobody says anything against sexism, misogyny, violence, racism, compulsory heterosexuality, homophobia, hate of what is different—all of which is transmitted to new generations. (2004, 367)

In this critique, Espinosa Miñoso directly critiques the socially sanctioned practices that sexualize and sustain violence against young girls. This same system stigmatizes young girls' expressions of bodily freedom; it criminalizes abortions in all contexts—including when nine- and eleven-year-old girls are raped. It punishes those who don't conform to biblical gender binaries. This system relies on the silencing of discourses and practices that enable liberation and enable the mobilization of discourses and practices that perpetuate Christian colonial sexual terror.

Through the social vehicle of the *doble moral*, people can construct an image of themselves by mobilizing the public performance of socially acceptable discourses. The *doble moral* is a survival practice that indexes violence. In this context, within the spaces of marginalization and difference, *cuentos* can mobilize power in a way that seeks to counteract the effects of a Christian colonial sexual terror that requires the *doble moral* to substantiate itself. In these instances, *cuentos*, rather than being mobilized to consolidate oppressive power, provide alternative narratives to those that configure streetwalking as already immoral and suspect, as already *delinquente*.

GAY MEN'S CUENTOS

—*What is it to be a man, for you?*
—*It's many things, but for me . . . well, the most beautiful thing about being a man is just that, it's being beautiful, strong, but without having to use force.*

And to be sure of oneself. To walk with confidence, like my man, to speak
without fear, to know what they want and where they are going without fear-
ing anything.
—That's a fantasy, that guy doesn't exist.
—Yes he does, he [my man] is like that.
—Maybe he gives that impression, but inside, in this society, without power
nobody can be sure of themselves—as you say.
—Don't be jealous. One can't speak to a man about another man because he
becomes impossible. In that you men are just like women.

—Manuel Puig, *Beso de la mujer araña*

In 2010, I sat in a secluded restaurant in the capital city of Santo Domingo and
interviewed a small group of homosexual men in their sixties and seventies.
Mind you, none of the men at the table actually told me they were homosexual.
They did not enunciate their subjectivity. However, I was told they were homosexual by Fernando, who gathered them for the express purpose of speaking to
me and documenting their *cuentos*. That evening, as I listened to this group of
tacitly homosexual men (Decena 2011)—Ricardo, José, and Alan—I was witness
to conversations in which they revealed a series of *cuentos* as community history.
These are the counterpoint to the official narratives (and historiography) of Trujillo's authoritarian regime, as told or not told in history books, fictional narratives, and films.[1] These *cuentos*, in contrast to others discussed in other chapters,
mobilize what James Scott discusses as a mode of subordinate discourse. This
mode is one of "disguise and anonymity that takes place in public view but is
designed to have a double meaning or to shield the identity of the actors" (Scott
1990, 19). This mode makes sense in the realm of a tacit subjectivity in which the
actors seek to maintain the Catholic Hispanic order, and their status within it,
while also breaking historical silence through the process of narrativizing, and
thus theorizing, the possibilities of a collective experience.

They did not reveal specific details about their own life experiences. Rather,
these *cuentos* were presented as gossip or amusing stories that in fact diverted
attention away from the men's own painful experiences and allowed them to
avoid implicating themselves in the process of revealing knowledge about people
from this particular era. The use of *cuentos* gave the narrators discursive room
to hide their own participation (or lack of) in Trujillo's world while at the same
time asserting their authority over the official story.

Alan, in his early eighties and the oldest among the men, stared at José, sitting
to his left, as he recalled one of the rumors from the Trujillo era.

ALAN: During the Trujillato, there were rumors of a concentration camp—like
the ones the Nazis had in Germany—for homosexuals. They say it was
on the Isla Saona, because the only way to get there and back is by boat.
There was no escape otherwise. And they left men there to starve.

ME: Is there official proof of this camp?

ALAN: I know men who knew about this camp, but I don't think there are documents. We think that is where people were taken when they were disappeared. They [Trujillo's *caliés*] would generally leave us alone, but every once in a while, men—without uniforms—would sweep through our gatherings and take people away.

ME: Why would they take people away?

ALAN: Well, that's a good question, isn't it?

José, in his sixties, nodded.

JOSÉ: I was too young, but I have heard of this before.

FERNANDO: It was different back then. These days, they just publish your name in the newspaper so that you lose your job, maybe your wife and children and your family. But back then, it was just easier to make you disappear. They were disappearing a lot of people. Not just homosexuals. It's just that they placed homosexuals in a camp, you see.

Ricardo changed the subject.

RICARDO: Nobody wants to admit that the Trujillato was like a golden era for homosexuals.

ME: What do you mean?

RICARDO: See, I was told that the generals would request sexual favors from the madams in the brothels at the edge of town. Here in Santo Domingo and in San Pedro. I know about these cities. They would request all kinds of women and, well—let's just say that hens were not the only dish served. There were roosters there too. So you have all these generals in the Dominican military who are enjoying these delicious dishes: hen, rooster, and even *pollitos* (baby chicks). We had the upper hand.

Alan, visibly disturbed by Ricardo's *cuento*, did not respond. But Fernando picked up on one thread and continued where Ricardo had left off.

FERNANDO: Do you remember the transsexual madam everyone called "La Galla"? She was from the *bateyes* (sugar cane plantations) in San Pedro, very poor and very black. She was famous. People said she was the ruling madam of the barrio.

ME: La Galla? How did she become famous?

FERNANDO: They say she had a performance in a bar and that her outfits were outstanding. She had natural flare, which is hard because she was from a *batey*, you see. She was very poor and very black (*negra*) at a time when being poor and black meant that you could not be a part of society. But because of her performances, men loved her. And then she entered into the brothel business, and the rest is history. Or so they say.

The *cuentos* the men shared with me in 2010 are unofficial and impossible to prove, much like the *cuentos* of Trujillo's sexual encounters. The only archives that can attest to what happened in the detention camps for homosexuals (on the Isla Saona)[2] or the gay bordellos for Trujillo's military officers ("They were on the avenue—a little bit farther up from the cemetery") were the men sitting in front of me, sharing *cuentos* about things that "everybody knows about but nobody speaks about." The *cuentos* also included those of transsexual madams in the *bateyes* of San Pedro de Macorix—a story that is invisible from the public eye because of both its characters (poor and black transsexual madams) and its location (a plantation at the edge of the city of San Pedro). These *cuentos* allowed the men to share some of the sexual geographies that marked homosexual and trans* experiences of sexual terror while allowing them to maintain claims to "not knowing." Even as they shared these *cuentos*, they were explicit in always pointing out that these were stories they heard secondhand. They themselves were not in the bars, or at the bordellos, or at the *bateyes*, or in the camps.

In official Dominican narratives of the Trujillo era, there is little mention of homosexuals, save for Paquita. During the Trujillato, the flamboyant radio personality Paco Escribano,[3] also known as Paquita, a self-proclaimed homosexual who lived in the barrio at the edge of Santo Domingo's colonial city, used the song "Mamita, Llegó el Obispo" as the opening to his national radio show (del Castillo 2013; Mateo 2012). The words to the song are as follows:

Mamita llegó el obispo	Mother, the bishop has come
llegó el obispo de Roma	The bishop has come from Rome
Mamita si usted lo viera	Mother, if you could see him
que cosa linda	What a beauty,
que cosa mona	What a darling.

Sung by Rafael Tavárez Labrador as Paco Escribano.

"Mamita, Llegó el Obispo" was a *plena* written and recorded by the Puerto Rican musician Manuel Canario Jiménez. It was popularized among Afro–Puerto Ricans at the turn of the twentieth century, and its lyrics describe the arrival of a bishop who generates the attention of both women and men (López, n.d.). The plena details the bishop's light skin and blue eyes and how his presence sparked men's jealousy and renewed women's faith. The joke is that bishops are assumed to be both celibate and pious—presumably the furthest from being objects of attraction. The deeper meanings of this song are masked by these tongue-in-cheek lyrics. When Jiménez first wrote "Mamita," he was making an anticolonial, anticlerical critique of the U.S. occupation of Puerto Rico. The new blue-eyed arrivals and the authority behind them (symbolized by Rome in the song) were not necessarily welcomed by Afro–Puerto Ricans.[4] But it was not until thirty years after it was recorded, in 1952, that the song gained broader political currency throughout the Caribbean. "Mamita" moved out of the Afro–Puerto Rican barrios and into the mainstream when Bishop James MacManus arrived on the island in 1947. Paquita picked up where Puerto Ricans left off.

Rumored to be a favorite of Trujillo's mother, Paquita became famous for his political and social *chismes* and his tongue-in-cheek critiques of the Trujillo regime. Each afternoon, he opened his show with this song, and "Mamita," once used to critique U.S. colonialism, was now used to critique Trujillo and his relationship with the Catholic Church. The song gained new social currency within the context of Trujillo's D.R. Paquita's use of "Mamita" marks a social space and time within the Trujillato in which political satire was possible. It was, in many ways, an exceptional space and time: nobody could speak ill of Trujillo's mother, but Paquita often used campy jokes and alternate personas to remark on the social affairs of Trujillo's mother and wife.

In an even more daring fashion, Paquita used the song—and the performance of other openly homosexual characters, like the character Ciprian—as a metonym for his own homosexual desire. He was an effeminate homosexual man who donned the mask of a homosexual character to speak about his homoerotic desires. Because of his ebullient effeminacy, the homosexual character of Ciprian was not taken as a legitimate threat to the Trujillato, despite his outrageous speech acts. And because he was a refraction of Escribano's own homosexuality, Ciprian served to mask Escribano's multiple layers of being, much in the same way that announcing himself as the *obispo* in the song legitimized Paquita's voice as a bishop about to deliver Mass to an awaiting public. The satirical tone of the song only served to couch the truth of his homosexual desire in humor and to point out the ambiguous and problematic nature of him as a pious figure who could do no wrong but who, everyone knew, at times challenged Trujillo and was a sexually active and uninhibited homosexual—or so said la Negra China—another one of Paquita's radio personalities (Veloz Maggiolo 2002; Socias 2001). Escribano risked arrest and death several times throughout his career as a result of his brazenness. In actuality, he died in Puerto Rico. It is impossible to untangle the reason for his departure and subsequent death, whether it was because of his political critiques or his unapologetic and flagrant homosexuality. Historians have claimed he died from kidney failure. But during his tenure on national radio, Paquita's *chismes* served to notify a listening public of the regime's dirtiest social laundry (Coste 2014).

In contrast to the *cuentos* told to me in 2010 or to Paquita's legacy, there exists yet another mode of *cuento* in which LGBTQ subjectivity emerges through the navigation between tacit subjectivities and streetwalking. This other mode is exemplified in Dominican director Osvaldo Añez's theatrical adaptation of Manuel Puig's novel *Kiss of the Spider Woman*. His adaptation allowed the staging of a different *cuento* about Dominican homosexuality. Añez set his adaptation during the Trujillato—a time period known for the disappearance, torture, and execution of hundreds of Dominican political activists (much like Perón's Argentina). In 2004, I went to see the play staged on the Dominican national theater's small stage. For me, the rendition was so powerful that I am able to write about it now, over ten years later, as though I had just seen it yesterday (revisiting my journal and speaking with the director's friends helped too).[5]

The original novel takes place during the Argentinian dictatorship. It features three characters: Molina, Valenzuela, and the prison director. Molina is marked as a homosexual through his narrative voice, his gestures, and his embodiment; he has been arrested for sex crimes and is in the same cell as Valenzuela, a revolutionary political activist who has been detained for his supposed role in a revolutionary conspiracy. The two talk about a range of topics, including sexuality, love, and politics.[6] As the novel progresses, we learn that Molina is spying on Valenzuela on behalf of the prison director in return for favors. But as the two men grow closer—sharing intimacies, having sex—Molina becomes loyal to Valenzuela and even falls in love. Unable to reconcile his love with the director's demands, Molina fails to carry through on his espionage. Eventually, Molina is released and subsequently killed. Valenzuela is left to his fate—in prison.

Añez's adaptation of *Kiss of the Spider Woman* features only two characters: Molina and "El General," the Dominican version of a prison warden who also functions as a stand-in for Trujillo's specter. Molina's character is played by a human being on stage, but the general is a puppet, an unembodied embodiment that serves as a metaphoric reference to all the puppet presidents and puppet *jefes* who ruled during the Trujillo dictatorship. Throughout the play, Molina is both the homosexual and the political activist. His character appears alone in the cell or in the interrogation room with El General. When Molina appears alone, he talks himself through illness, torture, and isolation. El General, on the other hand, attempts to mobilize physical forms of torture (which are forever impossible because of his puppet body but nonetheless appear inscribed on Molina's body as bruises and slashes in clothing) as well as verbal modes of torture, which include references to Molina's *mariconeria*.

Molina is demure and philosophically introspective. In contrast, El General is pure farce: he is crude and almost unintelligible. He dances around the stage, his mustache falling or twirling, his military garb disintegrating. In Añez's retelling, Molina's cunning self-containment as a gay man and a political activist allows him to negotiate both the isolation of his cell and the increasing torture and eventually leads to the revelation that the puppet El General is ultimately just that: a puppet—something that the audience has known all along but that had to be revealed against Molina's political subjectivity in order to be confirmed.

Through his adaptation, Añez asserts a narrative of moral triumph for the human protagonist, locating that triumph within Molina's political agency, an agency informed by the oppositional consciousness and erotic orientations produced by his homosexuality. The structure of theater allows Añez to re-create Molina as both a homosexual and a revolutionary protagonist; the use of farce also allows him to critique the Trujillo regime and its aftermath. He diffuses the sexual binary that generates so much of the tension in Puig's original novel, choosing instead to illustrate revolutionary desire as homosexual desire and vice versa. In addition, Molina's autonomy is defined by how he exercises it, not just within the confines of prison, but within the falsity of the circumstances of dictatorship itself. This is mirrored in Añez's adaptation of the novel as a *cuento* of gay men's political participation and resistance during the Trujillo era—contained and told through the vehicle of theater, a theater operating in the shadows of the Trujillato over fifty years later. The structure of theater allows the director to create and show a gay male protagonist. The use of farce also allows him to critique the Trujillo regime—a strategy Paquita used fifty years earlier but that was still dangerous. It was dangerous not just because of the play's public display of homosexuality but also because of its political references.

Though the staging of Añez's adaptation demarcated a fourth wall between actors and audience, it did so by unbounding the prison walls implicit within the narrative. The set was mostly lighting, with a small window with bars standing in for the cell. We, audience and actors, were in the prison together, encountering each other through the temporal-spatiality of the play. Molina, who made his home in this cell, experienced the violence of the nation-state not as distinct from other forms of violence but rather as an extension of all the possible violences that could be enacted upon him. Though Molina never says "I am a homosexual," his identity as both a revolutionary and a homosexual is implicit to his jailed condition. His character exposes the falsity of the public/private divide, rendering both the fictional cell and the theater in which the play takes place as mutually interchangeable. In this way, Añez's adaptation disrupts not only Christian colonial expectations of what should take place within the confines of the national theater but also the Catholic Hispanic nation-state's expectation of the *doble moral*.

The *doble moral* produces the possibility of conditional truth telling: If it is indeed true that Trujillo frequently slept with young women. If it is true that Trujillo slept with his subordinates' wives. If it is true that there were homosexual bordellos on the edges of the capital city. If it is true that there was a concentration camp for homosexuals on the Isla Saona. If it is true that Trujillo sent militia to murder Haitians along the border. And if it is true that Trujillo was in power for thirty years at all, then the terror provoked by the potential for sexual exploitation and marginalization was in fact a sexual terror that formed part and parcel of the state apparatus of authoritarian rule. Understanding the modes of power represented by the multiple kinds of violences that extended beyond legitimate uses of force allows us to also contextualize the role of *cuentos* in reshaping humanness and human being. *Cuentos* illuminate the intersections where truth cannot be told and history cannot be proven but where meaning is made and life and death are confirmed nonetheless.

While we have no actual records of death camps or sex slaves,[7] Trujillo did effectively legitimate his rule through his continuous presence in the charade of public power while maintaining an apparent absence in the realm of public discipline. Within this dynamic of the ever-present absence of the dictator, the ever-present and possible *cuento* of what might have happened emerges as a discursive strategy for human being beyond the reach of human rights. In a state in which rights are enacted solely through the symbolic and material vector of the dictator, homosexuals were not only invisible but also impossible. These stories, these *cuentos*, are the substance of fear, of terror. These untold narratives, mobilized in a group of tacitly homosexual men and on the stages of national theater, are marks that seep through the fabric of history. They leave traces and shape personal and community memories.

AFUERA HAY AIRE

In 2010, with the assistance and coordination of the Centro Cultural de España (the Spanish Cultural Center) and the Spanish organization Mirada Compartida (dedicated to teaching film throughout the Spanish-speaking world), a group of LGBTQ activists and community members came together to create the documentary compilation *Afuera hay aire* (Outside there is air). The filmmakers included Lolys Mena Elsevyf, Joselina Fay, Henry Mercedes Vales, Carlos Manuel Montilla, Carlos Rodríguez, Darío Pimentel, Elizabeth Ramírez, Cristina Paola Then Payano, and Emil Pimentel Velázquez (2010). The subjects of the film included LGBTQ activists and leaders, including Mirla Hernández Nuñez (longtime lesbian feminist), Wilkin Lara (former priest and current minister of the ICM church), Nairobi Castillo (director of the trans* sex workers organization COTRAVEDT), Joey Nuñez (one of the founding members of the legal education organization IURA), Ileana and Annie (lesbian community members and activists), Michelle Ricardo (well-known experimental sculptor), and other unnamed subjects. Among the unnamed subjects are a young woman and her family who are stitching together the welcome carpet for the 2010 OUTFest, a young painter, an Evangelical schoolteacher, a woman (her face partially hidden) recounting the story of being gay at work, and another woman calling on the audience to "Show your feathers already!" Altogether, the filmmakers and the cast of the documentary compilation worked to create a sense of the quotidian nature of LGBTQ lives in the Dominican Republic.

In the very first moments of the film compilation, we see a pot sizzling with food as Rita Indiana Hernández's song "Guarara" plays in the background. Mirla emerges from one of the houses in the community where she lives. The houses are made of unpainted cement blocks, have tin roofs, and are crowded together behind an unpaved road. Mirla winds her way through the *barrio* to buy a hot dog from a street vendor as she waits for her best friend, Maribel. As we watch her streetwalk through the city, across a geography that is often invisible to foreigners and elite Dominicans, we see her pushing a van, entering a small barbershop with Maribel, purchasing fruit on the street, and sitting down in an alleyway to drink a beer. As the camera follows her throughout the course of her day, Mirla talks about herself as a radical lesbian feminist who embodies *resistencia*. She tells the audience,

> My name is Mirla Hernández Nuñez. I've been using my second last name to recognize my mother in my name. I'm from Neyba, located in the southeast region of the country. It's close to the border with Haiti. I have lived almost half of my life outside of Neyba, living in different places. Recently I have been living here in Santo Domingo. I have self-imposed—rather, chosen—*resistencia*. . . . I have chosen to speak a language that is not Spanish. And because of that I speak Dominican. I have this accent that people can't identify where it is from. And it has to do with the fact that I have been in many places. It also has to do with the fact that I can enter and exit as if it was a linguistic performance. *Resistencia . . . resistencia* is my word. I don't know if you've noticed that I'm always talking about *resistencia*. But it's not a *resistencia* of being stubborn. It has a lot of depth. It's more than a word; it's a concept. It's an ideology. It is the standpoint from which I live my lesbian feminism. (Elsevyf et al. 2010)

Mirla is a self-identified autonomous lesbian feminist. She is explicit in her desire to stay outside of the institutions of feminism. Her lesbian activist erotic orientation is defined by her experiences at the Feria del Libro (an international book festival) in 2001 as someone who was harassed by the police and then outed in the newspapers, as well as her experience at the 2010 Caravana, discussed in chapter 3 (Confrontación). Mirla has traveled and worked internationally and has participated in numerous feminist and lesbian *encuentros* throughout the years. But this *cuento* is not about those experiences. This *cuento* is about Mirla's understanding of *resistencia* and how spirituality, friendship and daily life fit into her conscious decision to *confrontar* the social boundaries established through Christian coloniality. As Mirla arrives at Maribel's house, they sit down to drink a beer and hang out. Mirla speaks as we watch the images:

> Spiritually, I believe in reclaiming everything that was taken from our heritage. In the end, the relationship you have with God or whoever has to be personal. I have left religion, but I am not going to say I deny it, because that would not be accurate. But with a critique of that imposition of a white, bearded, heterosexual, male God. And I look more to the side of my negritude. I look at myself as a woman, but as a woman as an entity of resistance. Not as a woman with an imposed identity. So from that place of being the other, I look for religion from

that standpoint of repression. There are a lot of things about it that I obviously don't understand and that I will obviously critique, but based on my religious identity that stems from my African heritage. I've learned to reencounter my Afro roots and also with our native peoples, the ones that were here during the European invasion because time is not a horizontal line (*la mirada del tiempo no es una linea horizontal*). There is not a linear past, present, and future, but rather it is all a spiral. Everything that happened in the past, everything is connected. What I say now is already in the past. And what I'm about to say is the future, present, and past—it's all at the same time. (Elsevyf et al. 2010)

Kwéyòl news and *bachata* play on the radio behind her. Mirla goes on to discuss solidarity, sisterhood, and family. She locates her radical lesbian politics within a multitemporal framework that I call ubiquitous time (Lara 2013) in order to resuscitate her (Afro, native) female subjectivity. She does this in order to expand the context of agency beyond a linear present into what Paul Gilroy has aptly described as "our various struggles towards emancipation, autonomy and citizenship" (1993, 17). The evocation of God in the context of radical lesbian feminist politics locates Mirla outside of liberal feminist conceptions of secular freedom and complicates the ways in which her own political identity intersects with the state, the church, and sexuality.

As Mirla and Maribel push a van out onto the street, as they sit down and eat lunch together, Mirla's personal understanding of *resistencia*, and her self-fashioning (Allen 2011) as a radical lesbian activist with an African and native heritage come together through her friendship with Maribel. Her *cuento* about Maribel elucidates the way in which Mirla lives *resistencia* through her relationships with other women and other lesbians. As Maribel sits down in a barber's chair to have her face shaved and her afro trimmed, Mirla sits back and reads a newspaper. Her voice provides a narration over the film:

> Maribel is like my sister. We are very different. We don't always have common points in our views. But there are some common points that we do have that have to do with solidarity. Maribel has taught me a lot about giving a shoulder to rely on. Even without a political discourse, without theory, nor any of that. And with a lot of strength (*fuerza*), she has shown me about sisterhood [and about] the solidarity between women. Without even thinking about it. She is my sister and that's it. I love people very much. And I create a code with my friends that I don't even create myself, but those that are part of one's chosen family, one loves them. I care a lot about my friends, the ones that are here. The ones that were here, those that aren't anymore, the ones that are hanging around that are in that continual spiral. With Maribel, one always goes through different things, different stages. She drives me crazy sometimes because she likes to talk a lot. But most of the time, I feel calm. I feel that if something happens, she will

always be there (*que si algo pasa ahi está la loca pa' apoyarme*). But apart from that I have a lot of fun with Maribel. And I can also be very frank and clear with her. I don't have to go around wearing masks to be accepted by anyone. I don't have to use a certain language so that Maribel doesn't get offended. You talk to Maribel, and it's just Maribel. (Elsevyf et al. 2010)

Mirla's story is a powerful streetwalking *cuento* constructed through Mirla's voice and body and Maribel's body moving through the geography of the city—their city—in which they are part of the fabric of community. This is most apparent in the moments when they are pushing the van and talking to the driver, when they are sitting down in an alley to share a beer, when they are at the barbershop, and when they stop to listen to a Kreyol news broadcast. They are part of the landscape; Mirla's voice and her *cuento* are not separate from Dominicanness. As she says herself, she speaks Dominican. This *cuento*, told in a visual format, inserts the personal narrative of a powerful lesbian activist and community leader into a shared, collectivized history. In many ways, Mirla's story actively portrays streetwalking—the ways in which subjectivity is grounded in relationship, how her erotic orientations guide her choices and the way she lives in the world, and her valorization of *resistencia* as not stuck in place but malleable and shifting. That her story is told through the collective process of filmmaking further deepens the power of this story: it is the collectivization of individual speech.

In a quite different evocation of streetwalking, Mirla's story is followed by a montage featuring scenes from interviews with a woman, a self-identified heterosexual Evangelical Christian man, and the trans* activist Nairobi Castillo. In the interview with the woman, we can only see her mouth and chin. Behind her is El Parque, which situates her within the geography of LGBTQ public sociality. The man sits in a sofa in his living room, his legs crossed beneath him, a pillow over his lap. Behind him we see the photos of his family, and we can hear merengue streaming in from outside. As Nairobi speaks to the camera, she sits at her computer, working—a different kind of work than the sex work for which she is an advocate.

The montage begins with the woman sharing a story about her sexist male coworker who hits on her and shares his fantasy of sleeping with two women at once. Immediately, the camera cuts to the man stating, "I have been a professor for over sixteen years, in the area of education. I have had young homosexual students." As he describes a time when he had a homosexual student who came to him, he proclaims,

At that moment, I used the word of God. I had five or six years as a believer. And I told him that homosexuality is not natural. Homosexuality has been a sin, really since antiquity, a sin which does not originate in the present. In truth, God destroyed an entire city because of the sin of homosexuality. Christians have to take what God says about humanity into account. In terms of what God says, homosexuality is grounded in men's attitudes, from which sin is a consequence. . . . . If someone follows the path of God, if they go to church because they feel they need to change their heart, it's because their entire life needs to change. For example, when we have gone to church, we were different people, who were lost. But once we go to church, our whole being changes into a new man as the word of God says. At the beginning it is not easy, because the change is somewhat drastic. But God allows that person to, at a certain point, remove all of those bad and negative things. And he is able to become a new person in the church. And I am positive that he will stop being homosexual. (Elsevyf et al. 2010)

With his statement, the Evangelical Christian man claims homosexuality as a historical fact, preceding the Bible. But, he says, once God enters the picture, once the evidence of homosexuality as a sin emerges, the correct Christian disposition is to "take what God says . . . into account" (Elsevyf et al. 2010). For him, it is at this point that homosexuality then becomes a question of attitude and homosexual acts become the marker of sin—for which there are devastating moral and physical consequences. Because of this conceptualization of homosexuality as a sin, it is a behavior and an attitude that is remediable through Christian intervention.

Though the narrator locates Sodom within the text of the Bible, for many Christians in the D.R., any city contains within it the potentiality of Sodom. This engenders a fear of moral chaos and destruction—and a return to a time before civilization and God. These are some of the underlying warnings and concerns that frame homophobic attitudes. Through church teachings and the shaping of history in educational and religious discourse, these concerns have been reframed within the narration of the destruction of the indigenous populations. Sodom has been transposed onto the constructed images of the savage *indio* and the promiscuous *negro*. In turn, Sodom rises as a specter, a constant threat of destruction, that is used to discipline desires, sexual practices, and embodied ways of being that don't conform to Christian colonial interpretations of biblical truth. The conflation of the biblical story with sexual and racial ideologies enacted within conquest is reinscribed in the national and individual consciousness throughout one's lifetime. As M. Jacqui Alexander points out, "Sodom requires no point of reference other than itself; it can assert authority without comparison, evidence or parallel. Its power lies in its ability to distort, usurp, or foreclose other interpretative frameworks, other plausible explanations for its destruction, or other experiential dimensions of homosexuality that oppose and refuse state constructions of the criminal, presumably reinforced by biblical authority" (2005, 51).

As a Christian metaphor for the island in its premodern state, the city of Sodom is temporally and spatially transposed onto the island and the early moments of conquest. In this Sodom, the "savage," undisciplined sexualities were destroyed for the benefit of civilization, for the creation of the Christian colony of Hispaniola. Because destruction came not once but twice (the first time in Sodom and the second time in Hispaniola), destruction—the Evangelical Christian implies—could come again as a result of unmitigated and undisciplined sexuality.

The images and voice of the Christian Evangelical and racially ambiguous male body is interspersed with images of Nairobi's visibly dark-skinned, biblically transgressive body. Nairobi tells us, "Some of those people that use faggot (*maricón*) might have [hidden] identities within them. They just don't have language for it. . . . Christians do things, but between ourselves we claim ourselves as who we are, and we are God's daughters. We pray to the Lord as everyone can, and God hears us. All of that [saying that we are an aberration] is a lot of religious lies." Her statement "We claim ourselves as who we are, and we are God's daughters," is a direct challenge to Christian concepts of sin and disciplining logics espoused by the Evangelical Christian man. In claiming herself as God's daughter, Nairobi asserts her moral and ethical *being* above and beyond any Christian colonial claims against her person. Because she rests her claim in her belief in God's unmistakable ability to love all creation, her ability to pray and be heard extends beyond any moral claims instituted in the name of religion. She positions her faith as an embodiment that surpasses the powers of a Catholic Hispanic nation-state or its publics. Nairobi concludes by stating, "They act like they don't want to talk to you, because they are embarrassed. They think someone will think that they are gay or lesbian. But these are people that have not decided what they want from life. But we do know what we want" (Elsevyf et al. 2010).

It is enough to consider the juxtaposition of Nairobi's certainty about her own claims to God and her analysis of others' fears with the Evangelical Christian professor's own certainty and biblical interpretations. But the montage includes the third element—the element with which it began—of the anonymous woman's story. As it concludes, the woman tells the last part of her *cuento*:

Until one day he says, "Hey you, I don't know what I'm going to do. But I'm going crazy (*me tiene mal*) for you. I only want a kiss and that's it." [I tell him] "Hey bro, I'm a dyke [*maricona*] and I respect what I am [*lo que yo soy*]." People have to be loyal to what they feel and what they want. If you want to accomplish your socially integrated machismo, believing that men need to be turned on when they see two women together when women shouldn't be turned on by seeing two men, then you're doomed because I do not go that way. The guy

kept on trying until he realized that really, no [it wasn't going to happen], that
I loved my girlfriend and I wasn't going for that. (Elsevyf et al. 2010)

The woman's story of continual harassment at work, of her objectification and
exotification by a male coworker, contrasts starkly with evocation of Sodomic
sin. In her *cuento*, we listen as she recounts how heterosexist "socially integrated
machismo" attitudes, buffered by Christian beliefs, affect a person daily. We also
hear her narrate the ways in which she resists the constant harassment and how
she confronts her male coworker by making recourse to self-respect (*respeto lo
que soy*) and the enunciation of her identity as a *maricona*. Flipping the script on
him, she points out the coworker's hypocrisy and homophobia and ultimately
makes recourse to the evidence of her *mariconeria* through her relationship to
another woman. Her story stands in sharp relief against the Christian's confident
certainty that homosexuals can come to God and leave their homosexual lives
behind. Similarly, it echoes the power of seeing Nairobi's whole person on the
screen in a work space and Nairobi's own self-acceptance and understanding that
"We do know what we want."

In this montage of *cuentos*, LGBTQ life and desires are contrasted with the
Christian colonial beliefs about homosexuality, sin, and moral redemption.
The woman's story locates redemption in a streetwalking notion of *respeto*, where
self-acceptance and being loyal to one's self are greater and more important than
caving to society's expectations. Nairobi's understanding that her relationship to
God is clear, proven, and embodied in realized prayers also undermines Christian
colonial notions of the inherent righteousness of biblical manhood and womanhood. Together, these *cuentos* open up the possibility for audience members to
ask their own questions about their relationship to God and the Bible and their
own complicity in the production and perpetuation of sexual terror. Actualizing
speech and personhood and a clarity about who one is allows streetwalking to
produce new realities that further enable life in a context of enduring violence.

For this reason, *Afuera hay aire* is an important film collection because it
asks audiences to ask questions. In its editorial choices, it confronts us with our
own expectations of what streetwalking narratives are or could be. Rather than
presenting foregone conclusions, it provides a cinematic entrance into LGBTQ
daily life and the preoccupations of LGBTQ activists and leaders as they face discrimination from their families, Dominican society, Christian institutions, and
the Catholic Hispanic nation-state. As an important intervention into messages
disseminated through the religious fundamentalist media, six minutes into the
twenty-five-minute film, the filmmakers turn to the story of Wilkin Lara, minister of the Iglesia Comunitaria Metropolitana (ICM; in the U.S., MCC). As the
camera captures images of him cleaning a storefront space and later of others
laying their hands on his head (thereby consecrating him as minister), Wilkin
states,

My family has always been religious. Principally, my mother has been a faithful follower of the Catholic religion all of her life. This served both my brothers and me in our own formation, in shaping the people who we really are now. . . . For many years in the seminary, because of the Catholic Church's position on homosexuality, I had to repress my sexuality because I had an end goal, and as they say, the end justifies the means, and so I had to repress myself a little bit. They were very hard years, very hard, in which I had support from some people, from some mentors, but not others. So then, there came a moment in which one of my mentors was not sufficiently open minded, and I decided to leave [the seminary], but when I left, I became depressed. Almost all of the Bible is about sexual codes of conduct between people, but they forget that sexuality is one of God's gifts, just as are your eyes or the color of your skin. It's a gift that is yours and yours alone, and in speaking of sexuality in this way, we're talking about the spiritual component of sexuality so that one may live and express one's sexuality. I'm not speaking of religiosity. I'm speaking of the spirituality that emerges when you surrender yourself to someone; in that moment, God is there [with you]. The Bible is a matter of interpretation, but of a healthy interpretation. . . . It is being able to remove those prejudices ingrained in us from the denominations we come from. And to read the Bible in a more spiritual manner, to try to enter into the skin of Jesus. It is much more significant that individuals can now rely on a pastor that comes from the same reality, the same cultural context, as many gays and lesbians here in the Dominican Republic. It is very significant that the LGBTQ community in the Dominican Republic is now able to rely on this space, because it's as if they were able to find an oasis in the middle of the desert, where one can rest, where one can see the Bible from another perspective. Here you are able to see love and experience the love of God in your life without questioning your sexuality. On the contrary, bringing you to the conscious exercise of this, to be able to love without condition. (Elsevyf et al. 2010)

With the assistance of ministers in Puerto Rico and New York, former priest and now minister Wilkin Lara established the ICM. Though designated as an ecumenical Christian church, it draws heavily from the majority Catholic populations as well as some Protestants and Jehovah's Witnesses. Wilkin describes his role as one of interpreting liturgy from a gay perspective. Under his leadership, the ICM provides religious services, counsel, and meeting spaces for LGBTQ activist, social, and support groups. The ICM has been a crucial meeting ground for LGBTQ activists, and the country's Parents and Friends of Lesbians and Gays (PFLAG) chapter—born out of the chapters in South America—is housed there. The ICM and PFLAG are originally U.S. institutions, both of which have been adopted and adapted to meet the needs of local Dominican LGBTQ people and their families. But the organizations' U.S. origins are also a subject of contestation, especially when pronouncements are made—as by Cardinal López Rodríguez in 2004—that all homosexuals should return to their countries of origin in Europe and North America. In those moments, institutions originating in the U.S. are subject to increased scrutiny.

The public advocacy that Wilkin Lara and the ICM carry out on behalf of the LGBTQ community is significant. Wilkin is active in national and international human rights work, appearing in his role as a minister. In this role, he mobilizes both his institutionally legitimated presence as a religious leader and his Christian religious knowledge. In this way, he is able to counter the moral claims by the church and Evangelical Councils. His reframing of Christian theology produces alternative discursive frameworks for those activists seeking to undergird their efforts to diminish sexual terror.[8] Additionally, as an ICM minister, Wilkin serves LGBTQ people from a wide range of Christian sects. In this way, the ICM acts as a religious entity within the Dominican LGBTQ movement. It also acts as an explicitly LGBTQ church within a broader Christian context. Led by a minister trained as a Catholic cleric, the ICM exists at the junction between the social and cultural struggles arising from Christian colonial concerns about morality, spirituality, and the soul.

Wilkin's narration of his own social-spiritual formation within both his family (alongside his mother) and the religious hierarchy foregrounds the ways in which he is a rightful product of the maternal body of the nation, reflecting a Christian colonial social and political logic. Set against the story of his departure from the seminary, this narrative demonstrates how he has reconciled his teachings as a Catholic priest with his reality as a self-proclaimed gay man. He left not because of God but because of other men. He was confident about his moral personhood. By locating spirituality above and beyond the institution of the church as something that exists in the center of who one is as well as a force that manifests within the most intimate moments between people, Wilkin effectively reshapes and recenters Christian teachings in ways that challenge the hegemony of the Catholic Church and Evangelical Christian ministries.

Afuera hay aire circulated through the OUTFest film festival and other film festivals throughout the region, through university spaces in the Caribbean and the U.S., and as part of the educational workshops provided to LGBTQ allies through the organization Individuos Unidos por el Respeto y la Armonía (IURA) and other groups and organizations in the D.R. As the first large-scale collaborative film project by LGBTQ and allied filmmakers and subjects, it represents a significant intervention in the control of narratives about LGBTQ people in the Dominican Republic. The filmmakers, though attributing credit to themselves at the end of the film, did not make distinctions between who filmed what at any point. This highlights the value of the production as a collaborative film project over and above the production as a work that could be attributed to any single author. It represents a community-level *cuento* in which the protagonists are the LGBTQ community in its diversity, its honesty, its courage, and its daily life. Film has proven to be a powerful and effective medium for Dominican LGBTQ activists to tell their *cuentos*, to confront societal attitudes, and to build community. There are some filmmakers, such as Henry Mercedes Valdes, Carlos Rodríguez, and Cristina Paola Then Payano, who have continued to make short feature films, short documentaries, public service films, and announcements and to provide filmmaking expertise to others.

TRANS'IT: A LOVE STORY

Carlos Rodríguez is a force unto himself. He is a friend and colleague, and it is in this context that I speak about his work as a photographer and activist. Trained as a fashion photographer, Carlos has been documenting LGBTQ life and protest in the Dominican Republic for almost a decade. This, here, is a *cuento* of *quír* friendship. In the context of Christian colonialism, the violence of a Catholic Hispanic state, and the challenges of diaspora, our *cuento* of *quír* friendship stands as a testimony to the power of connection in the face of all of these forces. But this *cuento* is one about someone who is a powerful and beautiful *quír* person, whose life has been dedicated to the documentation of LGBTQ life and *resistencia* across the educational, social, visual, and political landscape of the Catholic Hispanic state. His work, in its multiple forms, and his love for *quír* people challenge Catholic Hispanic state repression and fly directly in the face of Christian colonial claims to a totalizing moral authority. Carlos constantly reminds us—through his photographs, his films, and the events he coordinates—that the "deviants" the Christian polity would like to discard and excise from the nation are real people, as are he and I. We streetwalk; Carlos, guided by his erotic orientations toward *resistencia*, toward *quír* liberation, is always already part of a broader collective, temporally complex set of iterations.

In June 2014, Carlos and I sat on the porch of the house where I was staying, overlooking the plants and trees in the distance. We leaned back in our rocking chairs and talked about the world. We reminisced about our friendship, never imagining that we would have the opportunity to spend so much time together over the three years since we had met. I deeply love Carlos, as do many people. By love, I mean that which bell hooks describes as "the will to nurture our own and another's spiritual growth" (2000, 6). By love, I mean that which Audre Lorde describes as the capacity to "share the power of each other's feelings" (1984, 58), thus "form[ing] a bridge between the sharers which can be the basis for understanding much of what is not shared between them" (56). When I speak of loving a friend, I am speaking about a way of connecting with another person that nurtures and enables access to our profound creative sources of power. This love fosters deep friendship, respect, and compassion. That friendship, in turn, feeds and nourishes each of our creative capacities: Carlos's capacity to create worlds through images and community building and my creative power to imagine worlds and to write.

We first met in 2011, when he came to present *Afuera hay aire* at Yale University, where I was a doctoral student. He had come with another *quír* filmmaker and friend, Joselina Fey (codirector of the film and *quír*/black arts initiative Republika Libre), and the queer activist and scholar Dr. Celiany Rivera Velazquez. Earlier that year, Mirla—featured in the film—and Joselina had told me about *Afuera hay aire*. Excited about the development of a Caribbean queer documentary, I had worked diligently with Joselina and others to bring the film to Yale's LGBTQ studies program and to invite these filmmakers to present their work. Their visit to Yale was one in a series of visits to northeastern universities to present the documentary. Carlos accompanied the documentary on its journey, using each opportunity as a teaching moment for other LGBTQ Latin*s and allies. Since then, Carlos has had numerous photographic exhibits in the U.S. and the Caribbean, where he has presented his photographs of Dominican trans* and *quír* activists, fashion models, and artists. In 2015 he debuted his award-winning documentary *Trans'It*, which has shown at film festivals, universities, and community spaces throughout the U.S., the Caribbean, Europe, and Asia. Carlos shared part of his coming out story with me and, in particular, the significance of his trips to New York City and the U.S. to an understanding of his gender, sexuality, and activism:

> I came out when I was thirteen, in high school. I came out as bi[sexual], but I have never been bi. But I saw it as an easier way to fit in. I have learned later on that I don't have to give a fuck about fitting in anywhere. I saw that it was easier with my classmates. Later, I [understood] that I was not really bi and that I have to live my sexuality as I understood it. I came out to my dad at seventeen because they were expecting me to be this straight guy who would bring babies to the house. Those were their expectations of me. . . . As I got older, I wasn't identifying with the gay man identity. I was always very *quír* presenting, and when I started going to New York City—where I could explore a whole diverse spectrum about what it means to be LGBTQ, *quír*—it broadened my perspective on identities and what I could identify with. Growing up, I was always discriminated [against] because I was flamboyant. I found a picture of me with a group of my cousins. They were superheroes and I was like "Ah!" (his hands up and snapping back). When I grew older, I was discriminated [against] a lot because of my feminine gender expression. I was shutting down bit by bit as I grew older. And then at thirteen, I came across Matthew Shepard's story. I was crying the whole night. That was my first reality wake-up call—at the age of thirteen. I realized how, as LGBTQ, we are exposed to so many dangers. At that age, it's what I thought. It opened my eyes to what we are exposed to and the dangers to which the LGBTQ community is exposed every day. I started

to learn more about legal rights. Connecting and being closer with the lesbian and trans* communities helped me understand my privilege as a cisgender (*cisgenero*) and light-skinned man. It helped me learn how to support the community, using that cis-male privilege (*como hombre cis*) to carry a message from the trans* community. . . . Whoever wants to can do it; it's a matter of observing your surroundings and seeing how you can contribute.

As a cofounder of the legal education group IURA along with Joey Nuñez and Amaury Reyes, Carlos has codeveloped a series of workshops to train LGBTQ allies, media, legal teams, and educators throughout the D.R. IURA is self-described as "an organization of volunteers working to advance the rights of the LGBTQI community in the Dominican Republic through educating heterosexual allies about sexual diversity and gender expression and identity, as well as expanding legal and media capacity of other activists and LGBTQI organizations. Its main goal is to promote dignity, respect and equality for LGBTQI people through trainings that adapt to different sectors and strategies of community creation" (AstraeaFoundation.org, n.d.). The documentaries *Afuera hay aire* and *Trans'It*, as well as his photographic documentation, have been key components to the workshops. It was his work with IURA that took Carlos to the fifth forum on LGBTQ human rights, which we both attended in Santiago in 2011. The forum was an important occasion for LGBTQ activists from across the Dominican Republic to come together to learn about the changes then taking place in the offices of the attorney generals. We sat next to each other, learning about our own rights and the initiatives taking place—on city-wide, provincial, and national levels—to address the undue violence toward our communities.

But on that day, in those rocking chairs, in 2014, we were talking about the present of LGBTQ activism in the D.R. and about his vision for a *quír* future. I was sharing with him the plot of a novel I was working on. He had just shown me a series of stunning photographs of trans* models from the Dominican countryside and barrios. In each of them, trans* models composed haute couture from urban and rural detritus. Leftover pleather from an auto body shop became a skirt. A recovered straw placemat became a head piece. Leopard-print pajama pants jumped out against an exposed cement backdrop. Tulle covered a half-naked body, demure and bold against the tussled sheets of a bed pocked with light entering through the clapboard walls. I went through the images over and over again. I was in love with the artistry of both the trans* models and Carlos's composition.

"*Que belleza*, Carlos."

"This is what I want to do. I want to document trans* life in the Dominican Republic," he responded.

"Do it. You should just publish your work," I said to him. "Find a magazine and publish it. You've got this. I've got you too."

We clapped our hands together and Carlos laughed.

"Yeah—OK. I got this."

We often forget how much courage and hard work it takes for artists to materialize the worlds we imagine. It was one thing for Carlos to generate these powerful photographs, but it was yet another for him to imagine that they could have any value or merit in a broader public sphere. As *quír* artists, we can also internalize messages that tell us that not only are our lives worthless—as *quírs* and as artists—but representations of those lives are also worthless. Carlos knew differently. And I supported him. "*Dale*," I told him. "Go for it. We need this. We need to see this beauty." He went for it. Some of the photographs were featured in the online magazine *Remezcla*, with audiences across the hemisphere and Europe (Reynoso 2016). Others he has published as large digital prints, presenting them in exhibits around the Caribbean and in the U.S. His photographs and exhibits have been shown extensively in Dominican newspapers and U.S. LGBTQ online and print media.

Later that same year, Carlos went to work seeking funding to write, direct, and film *Trans'It*, a film that incorporates the testimonies of three trans* activists: Yeisha, Thalia, and Tommy. According to its description, *Trans'It* "explores gender identity in the Dominican Republic through the eyes of Transgender individuals and their daily fight for social inclusion."[9] Carlos's goals for the film included not just the representation of trans* peoples' lives but the creation of a material production that would enable further action and education:

> After *Afuera hay aire*—in 2010—I started engaging more with the [LGBTQ] community and doing more work with IURA, going to Pride and going to the U.S. and New York and promoting *Afuera hay aire*. I saw there was no documentation of the trans* community, nothing that honored the community. I was disturbed by this. In film festivals, I saw there were gay and lesbian stories but zero to none trans* stories. But I wanted these stories to be told from the perspectives of the trans* folks themselves. I first had the idea of telling a trans* story (*de contar una historia trans*), and I started writing the script around three trans*-identified folks in the D.R. The characters were changing. [Tommy and I] met because someone referred me to him. And all of a sudden, he reaches out to me on Facebook, and I see that it's Tommy, and I said, "Ohmigod, I was looking for you to be part of a film. And he says, 'I was looking for you because you could be my husband.'" I knew then this was going to be the most beautiful relationship ever. I was already in conversation with Thalia. The original title was *Chacabana*; it was going to be with la Chaca.[10] I met with Yeisha, and for me it was important to go into their lives and to show the everyday experiences of a trans* person (*mostrar el día a día de una persona trans**). We are not normally exposed to trans* folks and their lives, but we are bombarded when there is a hate crime committed or when a trans* person is misgendered in the media. And so I thought that the film could help

destigmatize trans* lives in the form of a *testimonio* documentary. I wanted
to really humanize these folks, so people could create a connection with the
people [in the documentary] and be sensitized. With the IURA workshops, I
was able to take the documentary to high schools and universities. Whenever
I can find an opportunity to show the documentary, I do it. It has been well
received. A lot of people in Santo Domingo have not known about that reality.

In 2016, Carlos and I spent several days together. Aside from our usual conversations about love interests, life, and spiritual well-being, we also watched epi-
sodes of *RuPaul's Drag Race*, and he showed me *Trans'It*. It was just as he said: it
was the daily lives of three trans* activists. The film portrays their homes, their
loneliness, their friends, their work, their experiences on the street. Following a
similar aesthetic to *Afuera hay aire*, *Trans'It* shares the *cuentos* of these tree trans*
activists in the raw, in the everyday, in the banality of living. The documentary
serves as an important counterpoint to the highly stylized and visually rich aesthetics of Carlos's photographs of trans* models.

In summer 2017, Carlos and I met at the Centro Cultural de España, which
had sponsored, along with the Centro de Orientación e Investigación Integral
(COIN), a photo exhibit about LGBTQ Pride. In the courtyard, we stood in front
of a twenty-five-foot image of a drag queen dressed in yellow Lycra and dia-
monds, with yellow feathers pulsing out of her crown. The image was visible
from the street, and the queen towered over us.

"*Yes*," I said.

"*Yes*," Carlos said back. "I did it on purpose." We laughed together. He did it
on purpose.

How did he do it? Where did he print it? How did he hang it? We ended up
talking about the materiality of the piece itself—questions between artists con-
templating the work of showing our art. But this queen was just a small piece of a
larger picture. In early 2017, Carlos had initiated the public event known as Draguéalo, a space for "art, entertainment, culture events and lifestyle that celebrates
diversity in [the] Dominican Republic for the public in general." In this age of
social media and visual consumption, Draguéalo is not only a lived phenomenon
in which people from all roads come together to don masks and costumes and
explore gender expression and artistry; it is a media phenomenon that inserts
photographs of Dominican club kids, genderqueers, drag queens, and transgender royalty into the international cybersphere. As stated on their social media
advertisements, "La noche empieza temprano! Peina tu peluca, maquíllate y ten
tu look ready con tiempo, que la noche viene cargada de mucho regismo y fabu-
losidad. Are you ready to bring it?! We wanna see you, honey!" Crossing registers
of language and culture, Draguéalo has opened up an important space across
multiple communities and scenes in the D.R. This is Carlos's *cuento* about the
evolution of Draguéalo:

I had a birthday in August 2013; I invited twenty friends. I hadn't had that experience [of *quír* life]. But being in Nueva York expanded my perspectives, and I wanted to dream and create inclusive spaces and not just go to the gay bar. A lot of gay bars here prevent trans* folks from coming in, and a lot of lesbian bars don't allow cismen. So I wanted a space where everyone could come in no matter where they came from and not limited by gender identity and sexual expression or [socioeconomic] class. And right after that first party [in 2013], people kept asking me, When is the next birthday party? And so in 2014, we had the first event for a friend. And we always hosted the parties in friends' homes. Between forty and fifty guests would come, and people would come as dragged up as they wanted to. We had another event in a private residence—I always publicized through social media—and in December 2015, yet another event. Then I let several years pass. Even a small event was a lot of work, and being a Virgo—you know—we are so detail oriented. Then I presented the show D.R.ag—it was a series of photographs about the diverse spectrum of drag identities in the D.R.—while I also held a conversation about what it means to be trans* and making a differentiation between those two [identities]. Then Casa Quien asked if we could do a Draguéalo event there. This was the first public Draguéalo event, and people were *into it* (*y la gente* entregada). People were dancing and expressing themselves like there was no tomorrow, honey. I was amazed and happy about how the night turned out. . . . Casa Quien happened in July 2017. The second official event was in September 2017—that was Caribbean Club Kids. That was beautiful. In December, the leather and lace Christmas theme. When I got the promo for it, the editor and I were like, OK, this is legit. I wanted to be careful though because I didn't want to fall into a cliché about what would happen or what people think happens in LGBTQ events. So I toned it down in the promo. The next event was March 2018. There is a huge cosplay community in the country. I invited folks from this community and called it Cosplay Chic. I am now seeking out sponsors to be able to continue with these events. Draguéalo is a different type of activism—different from photo, film, art exhibits, photo projects, community photoshoots. Draguéalo is interesting as an entertainment event—it is a new form of activism that I am embracing. . . . The beauty of Draguéalo is that I see how it is not only *quír* and LGBTQ folks that attend. There are a lot of straight allies and folks that want to be there. When they enter through the door, they actually see us and remove all of these stigmas that they had [before they entered]. It is a beautiful experience. But in the end, when you see it from the outside, this is helping people destigmatize all these ideas of what the LGBTQ community is. . . . People see that [drag] is an art form.

Carlos and I spoke late into the night. It isn't all fun and games for him. Like most artists, he is often scrambling to find ways to sustain himself and his work.

With events like Draguéalo, Carlos has come across the reality of what it means to do business in the D.R. as a *quír* person. He has had to learn to shift discourse, changing his use of the term LGBTQ to "diverse" and thinking from the perspective of someone responsible for making sure others get paid.

Sometimes we have friends who are mere acquaintances. Sometimes friendships come and go. Like in Mirla's story, sometimes friends are there for you through thick and thin—they are people we can be ourselves around. *Quír* friendship—friendship between folks who are LGBT and *quír*—is something of *cuentos*, of history, and of stories. It is our friendships, and our stories of friendship, that have enabled us to find the strength to *resistir* the many violences produced in the wake of Christian colonial sexual terror. Driven by the deep power rooted in the erotic, in our capacity to transform silence into action, we are the ever already present potential behind all of life's possibilities.

As Carlos would say, "Bring it! Because we are *fierce*."

CONCLUSION

Cuentos are a mode of archiving that allows us to transform silence into an act of power, to transform silence into stories of what was or could have been, to transform silence into being. Building on the discussions about *confrontación* and flipping the script, in this chapter I have considered how *cuentos* emerge from individual and collective experiences that are impossible to tell or to prove, how *cuentos* are a collective evocation of *resistencia*, and how *cuentos* enable us to imagine *quír* friendship as central to the enactment of *resistencia*. The accounting of strategies of *resistencia* need not end here. As articulated in the opening to this section, streetwalking is a malleable disposition rooted in a range of erotic orientations that simultaneously "valorize the logics of resistance" (Lugones 2003, 175) while reconfiguring relations of power. Streetwalking enables us to mobilize universalized political identities, discourses, and structures in order to rupture the infrapolitical, producing new fields for the mobilization of acts of *resistencia*. My hope is that readers take this conversation about streetwalking strategies as an invitation to think through the many ways in which streetwalking might transform the Christian colonial grounds through which sexual terror is produced. My hope is that readers also engage in acts of *confrontación*, flipping the script, and sharing *cuentos* in service of our collective liberation.

Conclusion

ON SILENCE TRANSFORMED

June 2015. I arrive in the Dominican Republic with a heavy heart. For three weeks, I have been following media reports about the human rights abuses against Dominicans of Haitian descent and Haitian migrants. More than that, I have been following the documented reports and legal developments for twenty years, only to see the social and political conditions worsen with each legal battle (Child Rights International Network 2005). These conditions are generating a new kind of urgency. I have visited and revisited *bateyes* in San Pedro and Haina, where I first conducted fieldwork in 1995 and 1996. Many of the people who were there twenty years ago are not there now. Death has claimed quite a few. Many have left or have been forced to leave—either for economic reasons, for health reasons, or because of state repression. The measures assuring that the stateless will remain so and that those who are Dominican by birth and Haitian by heritage become stateless are only increasing. The repression of dark-skinned Dominicans and the general atmosphere of oppression are suffocating. At least that is what I experience living in the diaspora, looking in.

I cross the threshold between the baggage claim and the reception hall. To my left, the Junta Central Electoral (JCE) has set up a temporary station where I can update my national identity card, my *cédula*, to the new format. I am hesitant to go through this process. When I last attempted to get my *cédula*, I was given the runaround for three years. Having been born in the Dominican Republic but raised and living elsewhere, I was a seeming anomaly. Most Dominicans get their *cédulas* when they are eighteen. I got my first one in my thirties. When I attempted to get my *cédula* in the D.R., I was sent to multiple offices, at least four, and no one was ever able to figure out the correct place to process me. I finally went to the Dominican consular office in New York City. In January 2012, after three years of office visits, my *cédula* paper work was finally accepted. But they could not print my card that day. The machine was down. It was an election year. I would have to pick up my *cédula* in the D.R. . . . after the May 2012 elections.

June 2015. I stand in line at the temporary JCE booth as they verify my documents and take my photo, and then fifteen minutes later, just like that, they print my new *cédula*. The young man sitting behind the computer smiles at me. He welcomes me to the country, addressing me as *doña* (Mrs.). I laugh, thank him, and state, "If only things weren't so ugly right now, don't you think?" I walk away from his puzzled expression. I look at myself in the glass window before I walk out into the heat. The JCE agent had insisted on taking a new photograph. I wondered if it was because in the other one, I looked too *macha*.

I am not in the D.R. for a vacation or to participate in nostalgic nationalism. I am there to document the occurrences around the denationalization and regularization processes through my own witness, presence, and conversation. I am there to speak with LGBTQ activists about questions I have about the relationship between the LGBTQ movement and the movement for the rights of Dominicans of Haitian descent. I learn that LGBTQ groups and organizations continue to come together under the name *La Coalición*—The Coalition—signaling an attention to both a collective vision and the imagining of a collective body working together across difference. I learn that lesbians and trans* activists have been developing a series of trainings focused on cultivating a new generation of movement leaders, all the while broadening the discourse on what lesbian and trans* collectivity means for the present moment. I learn that a national gay men's organization has been launching speeches in the national legislature in defense of LGBTQ rights and the rights of those affected by HIV. They are adamant in insisting on a decolonial model. They are adamant about confronting the injustices of the fundamentalist Catholic Church that continues to work with the ultranationalist branches of the Dominican government.

I learn that lesbians are heavily involved in the initiatives to document and fight for the rights of Dominicans of Haitian descent. In June 2015, Rosanna tells me that of the fifty-five thousand Dominicans who had their documents taken from them, fewer than three thousand have been processed. She tells me that Haitians are returning to Haiti voluntarily—that is, to avoid the violence sweeping the country. I learn that trans* leaders are taking a stand in public forums in defense of those who lack proper documentation; they draw connections between the discrimination they face as trans* individuals who cannot petition for documents with their true identities and those who have lost their documents because of their ethnic lineage (TRANSSA 2015). I learn that Dominican LGBTQ activists have been sheltering their lovers, friends, and family who lack documentation. I also learn that no one is immune to the pain produced by ultranationalist, xenophobic racism.

Since I officially concluded my fieldwork in 2013, La Coalición has been meeting with James "Wally" Brewster at the U.S. embassy to discuss the state of LGBTQ human rights. Photos of the LGBTQ leadership with the gay ambassador actively circulate through internet media sites. These meetings fuel homonationalist hopes for LGBT human rights activists as well as the ire of fundamentalist Catholic and Christian leaders who believe that Brewster's presence is an affront to Dominican sovereignty. The meetings have opened up new elements in LGBTQ activism. In 2016, Alex Mundaray and Deivis Ventura ran as the first openly gay candidates. They both ran for the position of *regidor* (local district governor) of the first and second circuits in the capital city of Santo Domingo. Though efforts to legalize gay marriage preceded Brewster's arrival, the presence of the gay U.S. ambassador shored up local efforts. I had heard whisperings of this turn in the LGBT movement's focus in January 2013, but efforts wax and wane. In December 2014, the first same-sex marriage between a British man and his male partner was performed. Despite arguments that the Dominican Constitution does not explicitly prohibit gay marriage (Acento.com 2015), the wedding at the British consulate continues to be denied recognition under Dominican laws (Romero 2014).

Meanwhile, Brewster has also been seen around the Dominican-Haitian border, inspecting the newly constructed detention centers fashioned to hold the thousands of Haitian migrant laborers who are in the D.R. with their families (Lovato 2015). Official reports out of the U.S. embassy in the D.R. and Haiti indicate that no human rights abuses are taking place, but a letter signed by 560 Peace Corps volunteers and sent to the U.S. State Department, as well as reports by organizations on the ground, lawyers, and international human rights agencies, state differently (Carasik 2015). Since June 2015, approximately sixty thousand people have been deported or have left voluntarily. At least two thousand live in the border settlement of Ainse St-Pitre, just a short distance from the border on the Haitian side. Police turn a blind eye to the violence taking place inside poor and marginal communities, attributing xenophobic, racist violence such as lynchings and house burnings to fights between thieves.[1]

The Catholic Hispanic nation-state is predicated on the excision of those deemed "in transit." Yet another iteration of Catholic colonial violence, "in transit" is the constitutional language indirectly designating Dominicans of Haitian descent as temporary visitors, always in transit between seasons of planting and harvest. Reappropriating the idea of "in transit" to mean "on the street" or "in the life," we can reconceptualize the struggles of Dominicans of Haitian descent as grounded in streetwalking. Dominicans of Haitian descent resist the violences of the state in hospitals, on streets, in schools, at home. Unmasking themselves, Dominicans of Haitian descent take over the streets, demanding to be *reconocidos*, recognizing each other in the process as members of a collectivity, that they themselves are always already in relation with each other, with other Dominicans, with international communities of stateless people. Mobilizing international human rights law, Dominicans of Haitian descent reconfigure the relations of power, taking up space—on purpose—and broadening the terms on which Dominican personhood can be defined.

The navigation between homonationalist efforts and the struggle in defense of the rights of Dominicans of Haitian descent should not be complicated. Yet LGBTQ activists find themselves walking in the narrow spaces between their claims for national belonging while negotiating with a nation-state predicated on biblical manhood and womanhood and hetero-complementarity, all rooted in Catholic Hispanic ideologies. It is continuously indicative of the ways in which Dominican LGBTQ activists continue to mobilize strategic universalisms while simultaneously embodying *resistencia* within a more complex understanding of personhood. This balancing act is apparent in the public letter published by La Coalición in January 2016 in response to direct threats from the Coalition of Evangelical leaders against LGBTQ and feminist leaders. Presented here in its totality, it reads,

The Coalition of Lesbian, Gay, Transexual, Transgender and Bisexual activists and organizations in the Dominican Republic calls to the Dominican *pueblo* to not be confused by pseudo-religious leaders in the upcoming elections, scheduled for May 2016.

To the detriment of liberties and in the name of faith, millions of people have been killed, dictatorships have been established, and women have been raped. Our country is no different, and we mention only a few cases and their consequences:

1. Juan Pablo Duarte and his family were the first victims of the Catholic pulpit. Emilio Rodríguez Demorizi brought to light the Pastoral Letter from July 28, 1877, which demonstrates that Archbishop Tomás de Portes e Infante threatened to excommunicate anyone who did not vote for Pedro Santana. This act snatched the presidency from Juan Pablo Duarte, according to the sociologist Argelia Tejada Yangüela (2010, 2012). It allowed for the triumph of Pedro Santana, and it deprived the Dominican nation of a liberal and democratic government, installing in its place an annexationist dictatorship that was responsible for the persecution and assassination of the Trinitarios and the displacement of Juan Pablo Duarte and his family.

2. Juan Bosch was confronted by the Catholic *jerarquía* in 1962. His name rang through all of the country's temples as a name synonymous with Lucifer. The church was even part of the efforts to overthrow him, just seven months after he became president of the Dominican Republic.

3. In the electoral fallout in 2012, the Catholic and Evangelical Christian ultraright stood in their pulpits, list in hand, going against all legislators who defend the right to interrupt a pregnancy. They even went so far as to place posters in the polling stations suggesting a "punishment vote" against Minou Tavárez, Magda Rodríguez, Guadalupe Valdez, and

an entire group of notable people who have defended and continue to defend women's rights, and the rights of all people in our country.

The religious Catholic and Evangelical leaders who have entered the political game standing in alliance with the extreme [political] right, disqualify themselves as potential mediators of the national body. They have abused faith-based organizations, negotiating with detractors of human dignity, and motivating votes for groups that incite hatred, violence, and discrimination against those who go out onto the streets to work for a better country every day.

The freedom of religion is a human right; it is also a right protected by our Constitution, which applies to all. Human rights are for all of us. Freedom of expression is for all of us, but not to incite hatred, racism, and violence.

Church leaders have shown us that they have lost their horizon, by acting like conventional political parties, attacking the common worker, and not attacking the true ills that affect us all: corruption, *delincuencia*, sexual violence against children and adolescents, drug trafficking, murder for money, etc.

We ask our *pueblo* to think, to question; calling for discrimination, violence, and xenophobia is not patriotic. (*ElDesahogoDominicano* 2016)

This letter articulates historical precedents to that political moment. It locates struggles for LGBTQ human and civil rights within broader, deeper struggles against state-sanctioned terror. It is not only symbolic of the continuing repositioning of LGBTQ rights and activism by Dominican LGBTQ activists; it is an act in and of itself.

The D.R., a small country in the Caribbean that shares an island with Haiti, is but a microcosm of the larger processes of Christian coloniality and resistance to its ongoing effects. The struggle of Dominican LGBTQ activists—who are members of families, of ceremonial communities, of the Catholic Church, and of multiple movements—is just one site, one location where the logics of Christian coloniality are negotiated, upended, and reframed. They are well aware that their struggle is part of a larger and longer-term struggle against "fundamentalisms, the Holy Wars, the Inquisition" (Proyecto Ciudadanía 2013), and streetwalking has a great deal to teach us about the ways in which Christian coloniality shapes a modernity that relies on perpetuating sexual terror and the attendant mechanisms of xenophobic racism, homophobia, and transphobia as central components of its civilizing mission.

In June 2015, I hold my *cédula* and my U.S. passport in my hands. I put them safely away. I wander to the warm air outside. I drive into the capital city. The sea salt in the air makes the skin on my face prickle. I am a bundle of mixed emotions. The air smells of burning cane. It is the *zafra*. I drive past the Puerta de la Misericordia (the Door of Mercy), where thousands of enslaved Africans and Aboriginal people were redirected to ships and markets all over the American continent. The specter of sales and the memory of ritual dances before me meld together in ubiquitous time (Lara 2013): from a time when they sold a mother, from the time they hung a maroon's head, from the time a marine shot a Dominican protestor, and from the time a Cuban *santera*, a Dominican *santera*, a Puerto Rican *santera*, and a Haitian vodoun priestess all made offerings. The ghosts compete. On my left, Fray Montesinos shouts into the sky. As I drive down the *malecón*, life moves to its normal rhythms and chaos. I stare at the water to my left. Its teal-blue surface, glistening under the tropical sun, hides the disintegrated remains of ancestors. I turn on the radio, where announcers are espousing xenophobic, racist rhetoric over and over again. I turn the radio off. I pass Club Chic, now abandoned and empty. I turn around and make my way back to La Zona Colonial, down Avenida Independencia. I am in search of *locas*.

Acknowledgments

Each writing project is a world with its own rules and its own people. No author, or scholar, works alone. Even seated at a desk for hours, the voices of all those who have challenged, carried, moved me are right there with me.

This work would not have been possible without the Fund for Lesbians and Gays Grant (FLAGS Grant) at Yale University Women's, Gender, and Sexuality Studies program, which allowed me to visit Port-au-Prince, Haiti, in 2009 for participation in the Ghetto Biennale—an event that became even more significant following the January 2010 earthquake—and allowed me to conduct fieldwork in summer 2011 in the Dominican Republic. Thank you to the Williams Fund at Yale University's Anthropology Department and the African American Studies Department, which together provided funding for fieldwork in summer 2010; the MacMillan Foundation Dissertation Grant, which provided funding for a year of fieldwork in the Dominican Republic from July 2012 to June 2013; the Center for Latina/o and Latin American Studies at the University of Oregon for providing a postdoctoral Visiting Scholars fellowship and intellectual community; and the Center for the Study of Women and Society at the University of Oregon for hosting a workshop of this manuscript.

My most sincere gratitude goes out to all the amazing people who made this research and my dissertation writing possible. Gracias . . .

. . . to the editors at Rutgers University Press, especially Yolanda Martínez-San Miguel and Kimberly Guinta, who gently midwifed this manuscript into the Critical Caribbean Series; to the readers who helped me make this a stronger manuscript; and to Anitra Grisales, who assisted with one of the earlier transformations of this text.

. . . to Erica Lorraine Williams, Ginetta Candelario, Michael Hames-Garcia, Michelle McKinley, and Lynn Stephen, who sat down with me in Eugene,

Oregon, one fall day to provide in-depth feedback on this manuscript, helping me contextualize this work.

... to all the scholars at the Latino Scholars Symposium, beginning with Timothy Matovina, Michelle A. González Maldonado, and Jason Ruiz, who were so generous and amazingly helpful in pushing me to deepen and reconceptualize the history of Catholicism, and to all my fellow scholars at the Young Scholars Symposium 2017—Lauren A. Guerra, Leo Guardado, Melissa Guzman, Rebeca Hey-Colón, and Daisy Vargas.

... to all the scholars who made space for me to think through so many of the ideas that are present in this body of work, including Carlos Ulises Decena, who introduced me to Rodolfo Kusch; April Mayes, who not only lent me her car so that I could complete my fieldwork but has also been a critical interlocutor in my historical analysis; Ralph Nazareth, whose generous suggestion to analyze Catholicism from its Aristotelian and Thomist lineage fundamentally shaped my fieldwork; Michael Hames-Garcia, who sat down with me to parse out decolonial theory, philosophy, and black feminism; J. Kehaulani Kauanui, who pushed me to think through questions of sovereignty and political authority; Marcia Ochoa and Amalia Cabezas, who worked with me to push my thinking on the transnational aspects of my arguments; Kemi Balogun and Margaret Rhee, who read various versions of the manuscript and provided thoughtful feedback and advice on its structure; and Elizabeth S. Manley, who so generously talked through and shared her documents with me.

... to all the professors and researchers in the Dominican Republic who so kindly shared their insights, resources, libraries, and personal intellectual histories with me: Lourdes Contreras (Lulu), Andres L. Mateo, Pablo Mella, Carlos Andujar Persinal, José Alcantara Almanzar, Lourdes Merieles, Tony de Moya, Quisqueya Lora, Roberto Cassá, Ruben Silié, and Maria-Filomena González Canalda. Thank you to the Centro de Estudios de Genero at INTEC, which facilitated a research affiliation, a place to land, a space to teach and learn, and the company of really kind, passionate scholars. And thanks go to my *dos complices* Carolina González and Fatima Portorreal, who over a decade ago introduced me to the robust world of radical political and literary scholarship in the Dominican Republic.

... to Dr. Jafari Sinclaire Allen, Inderpal Grewal and Kamari Clarke, Bernard Bates, and the many amazing faculty in African American Studies and Women, Gender and Sexuality Studies at Yale University, who together pushed me in the development of my theoretical work while I was a graduate student at Yale.

... to the incredible crew that was my incredible Yale African American Studies cohort of grown women, including Sofia Betancourt, Jalylah Burrell, Adom Getachow, Key Jo Lee, and Delaina Price, and the Yale Black Feminist Reading Group—Dana Asbury, Kristin Baxivanos, Diana A. Burnett, Tao Goffe, Sarah Haley, Jennifer Leath, Christine Slaughter, and Heather Vermeulen, among so many others who passed through—to whom I owe my development as a Black feminist scholar. Love through and through and so much love! I was so privileged to have been able to work with you.

. . . to all the Dominican LGBTQ activists and artists who gave of their time to meet with me to share their stories, their opinions, their insights, their visions, their frustrations, their blessings, and their curses. Collectively, this is one of the most brilliant and fierce groups of people with whom I have ever had the privilege to work and to play. I hope this scholarship helps you shape a world in which the struggle for human rights and dignity is made more and more possible, in which your deaths are not in vain, and in which your lives are celebrated, honored, and held sacred. Thank you to all the incredible activists working on the front lines of multiple struggles, but most especially, the badass folks of La Colectiva GLBT, CONAMUCA, Diversidad Dominicana, MUDHA, Kalalú Danza, and La Colectiva Mujer y Salud, among so many others. Wow. That's all I have to say: wow. I am humbled by your power.

. . . to all the Catholic priests and nuns who sat and talked with me even though it was clear I didn't know Catechism from Communion. Thank you for taking the time to share your experiences, your perspectives on faith, and religion, and your own struggles with the intersections of power within the institutions to which you have dedicated your lives. Thank you for helping me see the complexities within your work. Thank you for sharing inside insights—sometimes at risk to yourselves.

. . . to all the fundamentalist Evangelical Christians for your daily, multiple blessings and teaching me about your worldview. Though we disagree on so many things, thank you.

. . . to my amazing, amazing community in Austin, Texas: the brilliant artists, scholars, and activists and the elders and the Native, African American, and Latina/o (Xicana/o) communities that fed me, nourished me, danced with me, made art with me, and told me to go and do good work in the first place. Thank you especially to the Council of Alma de Mujer and to my teacher and *madrina* Abuela Tupina Yaotonalcuauhtli. Thank you for believing in me and sending me off to do my work. Austin is and will always be my home and where I go back to because you are there.

. . . to my parents, who allowed me to test my theories and my thoughts, to bounce ideas off of them, to ask questions about their lives, and to probe into sometimes painful memories. Thank you for receiving me in your home so many weekends when I lived in Connecticut and for all your support and door-opening in the Dominican Republic. Thank you, Mom, for reading through a very early draft and letting me know it was full of jargon. Thank you to my brothers and their families, who bring light to my eyes. Thank you to my queer family, especially D'Lo, Dulani, VictorJose, Lisa, Lisbeth, Sheree, Saray, Jen and Jax, and drea—who helped me keep it real. I hope I have made y'all proud.

. . . to all those who have been with me through this process, mentioned and unmentioned.

. . . to Alaí, who encouraged me the whole way and was so many things at once.

Notes

INTRODUCTION

1. Jacqueline Jiménez Polanco edited a volume of stories and poetry by the same name.

2. In my use of trans* with an *, I am mobilizing Jack Halberstam's use of the * "to open the term up to unfolding categories of being organized around but not being confined to forms of gender variance. . . . The asterisk holds off the certainty of diagnosis" (Halberstam 2017, 4). Solimar Otero takes up Halberstam's suggestion in *Archives of Conjure* (2020) and mobilizes the * as a marker for gender spectrality within AfroLatinx communities.

3. *Avión* is a colloquial term used to refer to a Dominican woman who gives or sells sex to foreign (usually white) men. My aunt, who is married to a white man from the U.S., has repeatedly shared a story with me in which she was walking with her husband through La Zona in the mid-1980s, shortly after they were married. As they were walking, two young boys pointed at her. In an act of shade, one said to the other, "¡Esa avión ya voló!" which directly translates to "That airplane took off!" and signifies a female sex worker's successful pickup of a client. The story is funny to us only because she was already married; their misreading of the situation pointed to the way in which her person (as a dark-skinned *mulatta* woman) always already marks her as streetwalking. Because of her being in relation with a foreign white man, any other script is less visible.

4. The cardinal's full title was Su Eminencia Reverendísima el Cardenal Nicolás de Jesús López Rodríguez, Presidente del Patronato de la Ciudad Colonial y del Fondo para la Protección de la Ciudad Colonial.

5. A deep analysis of the Colonial Fest is outside the purview of this text. However, I must mention that the Colonial Fest was a gross rehearsal of Christian colonial racial and gender logics—complete with the embodied portrayal of white *señoras* dressed in colonial textiles and wigs, *mulatta* house slaves and mistresses dressed in frocks, and dark-skinned, poorly clothed slaves. In other words, someone made a conscious decision to choose people based on skin color and gendered appearance to portray these colonial figures, and again, someone chose to then reenact these relationships within the geography of the colonial city. The purpose of Colonial Fest, as expressed by the organizers, is to celebrate the unique cultural heritage of the Dominican people—in a positive way (and for tourism).

6. In the mid-2000s, there was a very active lesbian direct-action group called Las 3 Gatas. They were well known for public protests using comedy, music, and puns—like their 2011 "Vacunación contra la homolesbotranfobia," drumming sessions, and the purposeful occupation of public space. For more about their history and politics, see Quinn (2015).

7. *Pajaros* and *pajaras* are slang terms for LGBTQ+ people.

8. His exact words were "El parque ha sido tomado por los llamados 'jevitos' y 'metálicos,' pero también por homosexuales y drogadictos que se sientan en el lugar a realizar diversos actos groseros."

9. Thank you to Courtney D. Morrison for reminding me of Essex Hemphill's poem "American Wedding" and the line "Every time we kiss / we confirm the new world coming" (2000).

10. Thank you to Jacqueline Jiménez Polanco, who first explained the concordat to me back in 2011.

11. In chapter 2, "Sexual Terror," I will discuss the particular configuration of Christian coloniality and the actions of the Catholic Hispanic nation-state. In this text, I don't discuss the numerous modes of sexual violence employed by the Trujillato, including rape and pedophilia. In part, Trujillo's masculinity was consolidated through his actual and narrated sex drive and specific "consumption" of young women. There is much work left to be done on this topic. For further discussion and strong historical research on this topic, see Derby (*2000*) and Manley (2012).

12. Frequently, Balaguer justified the necessary territorialization of the border as a sacred patriotic act and paralleled the components of this sacred patrimony to those carried out by Queen Isabel la Católica and the Santo Oficio (the Inquisitorial Courts).

13. Tourism accounted for 17.2 percent of the Dominican Republic's GDP in 2018. In addition, purchases by tourists represented 39 percent of exports, and tourism contributed 37 percent of indirect contributions to the GDP. Read more at WTTC (2018).

14. I have another book titled *Queer Freedom: Black Sovereignty* that takes up these issues and questions. Miranda Ricourt's *The Dominican Racial Imaginary* (2016) also discusses the historical precedents of contemporary life in the Dominican Republic.

15. Some recent and critical texts that do this work include Lorgia García-Peña, *The Borders of Dominicanidad: Race, Nation, and Archives of Contradiction* (2016); Milagros Ricourt, *The Dominican Racial Imaginary* (2016); Raj Chetty and Amaury Rodríguez, eds., *The Black Scholar* (2015); and Dixa Ramírez, *Colonial Phantoms: Belonging and Refusal in the Dominican Americas, from the 19th Century to the Present* (2018).

16. There is a broader and deeper discussion of the term *queer* and what Diego Falconí calls "cuír" subjectivities throughout Latin America and the Caribbean. For an entrée into this conversation, see Viteri (2017); Falconí Trávez (2014); and Falconí Trávez, Castellanos, and Viteri (2014). Thank you to Celiany Rivera Velázquez for helping me understand the distinctions in how *quír* and *queer* are operationalized in the Caribbean.

17. As stated earlier, in my use of trans* with an *, I am mobilizing Jack Halberstam's use of the * "to open the term up to unfolding categories of being organized around but not being confined to forms of gender variance. . . . The asterisk holds off the certainty of diagnosis" (Halberstam 2017, 4). Solimar Otero takes up Halberstam's suggestion in *Archives of Conjure* (2020) and mobilizes the * as a marker for gender spectrality within AfroLatinx communities.

CHAPTER 1 — CHRISTIAN COLONIALITY

1. For more on the construction of pedophilia as a crime, see Hickey (2006) and Mirkin (1999).

2. In November 2013, Pope Francis made a statement to the effect that the church has to stop being involved in social controversies like homosexuality and abortion and instead return to Jesus's mission of serving the poor. See Associated Press (2013).

3. New Ways Ministry, based in the U.S., tracks Pope Francis's trajectory on LGBTQ issues. Compiled by Francis DeBernardo and Robert Shine, their chronology and record attempts to provide a comprehensive overview of the pope's many, sometimes contradictory, positions on LGBTQ issues. New Ways Ministry's mission is to "educate and advocate for justice and equality for lesbian, gay, bisexual, and transgender (LGBTQ) Catholics, and reconciliation within the larger church and civil communities" (New Ways Ministry 2013).

4. This is not to say that there is no homophobia in Afro-Diasporic religions or spaces—quite the contrary. However, theologically—ethically—other possibilities exist besides the model of Sodom and Gomorra. For a discussion about sexuality and gender in Afro-Diasporic traditions, see Méndez (2003).

5. The first evidence of the objectification of indigenous peoples into categorizations as "indias" and "indios" were Cristóbal Colón's navigational diaries and the subsequent travel diaries and chronicles of Christian colonial authorities. Collectively, these documents, their modes, and their content, substantially racialized the indigenous peoples of the Americas and Africa (whose people became identified as "negras" and "negros").

6. See Tortorici (2007, 2012) and Penyak (2008).

7. In June 2016, after the mass shooting at the gay nightclub Pulse in Orlando, Florida, Pope Francis made a public statement affirming the need for Catholics to ask forgiveness from gay people, reiterating his position with the phrase "Who are we to judge them?" This declaration represents a departure from the Vatican's prior positions on homosexuality. See McElwee (2016).

8. Original quote from Pepén (1954).

9. Article 38 of the 1844 constitution states, "The Catholic religion, Apostolic and Roman, is the religion of the State; its Ministers, in exercising an ecclesiastic ministry, depend only on the canonical prelates henceforth instituted" (Asamblea Nacional de la República Dominicana 2010).

10. Article 39 of the 2010 Dominican Constitution establishes equality regardless of religion.

11. Rhoda Reddock (1994) makes a similar argument about marriage.

12. For Ginetta Candelario (2007), the notion of *blancos de la tierra* emerges to differentiate an elite racial identity that stood in contrast to U.S. and Spanish notions of whiteness.

CHAPTER 2 — SEXUAL TERROR

1. As Hartman suggests with her discussion of the word *black*, the words *maricón*, *loca*, and *homosexual* carry within them the multiple registers of violence from which these terms emerge. Though beyond the scope of the current analysis, even a minimal etymological analysis of *marica/maricón* reveals how Christian colonial biblical manhood was constructed against masculinities that deviated from the Christian colonial norm.

In the nineteenth century—with the invention of the (a) criminalized and (b) patholo-gized homosexual subject—*marica/maricón* were scripted as craziness, *locura*, and pro-jected onto sexual difference and the failure of presumably masculine national subjects to embody Christian colonial biblical manhood. In this way, the term *marica/maricón* indexes the inherently violent nature of imposing Christian colonial gender systems in New World contexts as well as the further violence generated through the criminaliza-tion and pathologization of sexual difference that emerged through the consolidation of independent nation-states. Relatedly, for a fantastic read on the mobilization of animal metaphors for queerness/homosexuality, see La Fontaine-Stokes (2007).

2. Tiffany L. King draws on Hartman and Hortense Spillers to argue that blackness is fungible, that "black fungibility recognizes the violence of plantation and its afterlife while simultaneously acknowledging the ongoing capacity for the making and remaking of Black life in the midst of plantation violence" (2016, 1023). My work aligns with King's work in two important ways: the first is that I absolutely agree that onticide is not the primary condition of blackness; the second is that streetwalking is an index of a similar fungibility that complicates the already assumed fixity of subjectivities. Whereas King is arguing for an expansion of our theorizations of black bodies, I am arguing that bodies are only one site for the transformation of silence into power.

3. For early Christian colonial documentation of the success of evangelism, see Pané (1999).

4. The Inter-American Commission on Human Rights (IACHR) published a 284-page report, "Violence against Lesbian, Gay, Bisexual, Trans and Intersex Persons in the Ameri-cas," in 2015. The report provides elaborate legal and anecdotal definitions of violence that take into account social attitudes, social treatment, exclusion, isolation, marginalization, punishment, cruelty, verbal assault, physical assault, rape, and the presence of laws that negatively impact LGBTQ life.

5. In the American and Caribbean regions, St. Lucia was the only state to participate in the drafting of an opposition statement; Peru abstained.

6. See CEDAW, Chapter IV.8. The Dominican Republic became a signatory in 1982.

7. The Concordat and Final Protocol between the Dominican Republic and the Holy See was signed June 16, 1954. This document "promot[es] the fruitful cooperation for the bet-ter good of the religious and civil life of the Dominican Nation . . . establishing the rules that shall govern reciprocal relations between the High Contracting Parties, in accordance with the Law of God and the Dominican Republic's Catholic tradition" (Vatican 1954).

8. I found it troubling that, considering how the positioning of Islam and the East as always temporally backward has been central to Western projects of modernity, both the Christian and LGBTQ views mobilized orientalizing and islamophobic discourses. The use of these discourses signals how homonationalism and the imperial regulation of sexu-ality rear their heads within struggles over discursive and material power.

9. The arbitrary detention of people on the street is a Balaguer-era tactic used to main-tain "public order." It has been applied primarily to sex workers, dark-skinned persons (presumably Haitians), and LGBTQ people. I learned about the arbitrary detention of dark-skinned people from lawyers at MUDHA, who were dealing with the crisis produced by the 2013 Constitutional Court decision across the D.R. (Tribunal Constitucional 2013). Since September 2013, when the Dominican tribunal courts approved the denationaliza-tion of persons with "irregular" migration statuses, TRANSSA has taken a public stance in solidarity with Dominicans of Haitian descent along the lines of a right to identity. Dominican trans* persons of Haitian descent are at a particular disadvantage, as they are

discriminated against not only because of their transgression of biblical gender binaries but also for lacking documents, since an estimated fifty-five thousand Dominicans of Haitian descent had their documents rescinded by the state following a 2007 resolution allowing government institutions to do so.

CHAPTER 3 — CONFRONTACIÓN

1. For a discussion on the complicated interweaving and tensions of revolutionary and lesbian/gay subjectivities, see Howe (2013).

2. All quotes from activists in this chapter are from group interviews conducted at local gay and trans* organizations in Santo Domingo, Dominican Republic, in May 2013.

3. The *colmado* is one of the public spaces that mark the legacy of public sociality theorized in Martínez-Vergne's work. They tend to be hypermasculine, hyperbolically heteronormative sites—men go to *colmados* to drink and play dominos. Loud music is played, and people drink and dance in the street. Women are rarely there except when they join their friends. In some areas of the city, women conduct sex work from *colmados*. There is at least one *colmado* in the city (in El Parque) known for catering to gay clients. Thalia's performances, however, occur not in the gay space of El Parque but in the hypermasculine, heteronormative space of the *barrio colmado*. She has been lauded in gay media for breaking boundaries between heterosexual and gay spaces.

4. A well-known trans* activist died due to medical negligence in January 2014. See Acento.com (2011) and TRANSSA (2014).

5. For discussions on violence in the everyday, see Das (2000, 2007b); Scheper-Hughes (1993); and Thomas (2011).

6. Article 22 of the Concordat specifically states that the state agrees that "all of the institutions and information services under its charge—in particular radio and television programs—will prioritize the exposition and defense of the religious truth, as delivered by priests and religious leaders as designated by the church's representatives" (Vatican 1954).

7. It is outside of the scope of this conversation to compare the ironies and challenges of gender performance in carnivals and the Caravana, but I must mention one thing. In Carnival, drag performances and the presentation of explicit drag characters are part and parcel of farce. The structure of Carnival itself makes one kind of gender rupture acceptable over another. Carnival figures such as Roba la Gallina or La Ciguapa feature men cross-dressing to play off of cultural stereotypes of working-class, rural, and dark-skinned women to critique political corruption, government trickery, and neoliberal working conditions. Trans* and gay activists engage in farce by donning the garb of clergy, the cardinal, or U.S. businessmen. But when they present as themselves, it is an unmasking rather than a masking that takes place. It is by unmasking that trans* activists invert the cultural logics and seek to undo rather than invert the transphobic violence that conditions their lives. The large presence of trans* activists in the Caravana brings attention to the normalization of state and the society's transphobic violence.

8. Mark Padilla (2008) states that the Caravanas began in 1999; Rachel Afi Quinn (2018) claims in 1991. I draw this date from my own archives of the CAP LGBTQIR forum communications as well as interviews with key activists. I see the multiple dates as a signal of internal debates about what constitutes assembly, or the pride parade, generally speaking.

9. Presidente is the national beer. In advertising and cultural events, the color and the beer act as iconic stand-ins for Dominican nationalism.

10. Thomas Aquinas describes pride as an "inordinate self-love [whose] root is found to consist in man not being, in some way, subject to God and His rule" (1997, 77). As such, he identified it as one of the seven deadly sins. This is relevant insofar as LGBTQ activists mobilize a pride discourse that is embedded in transnational notions of liberal queerness, but they also make references to the ways in which "Orgullo LGBT" undermines Christian claims on morality.

11. The victim was Abraham Ramos Morel, a law student at the Universidad Autonoma de Santo Domingo. He was twenty-three years old.

12. Years later, in 2013, at a meeting with trans* activists and Amnesty International (AI), I told this story from my perspective. In my storytelling, I specified the presence of two trans* men in the car. AI's response, and the response of the activists in the room, was that this had already been recorded as Mirla's story. This response essentially rendered the transphobic aspects of the encounter invisible. By reifying the lesbian story as legible and legitimate, the broader context in which two trans* men and three masculine (gender-nonconforming) lesbians were in the car is made invisible.

13. When questioned, the police responsible for the execution of the student responded that they had killed the student because the car refused to pull over when flagged. The police were never tried (Urbáez 2010). These assassinations are part of a larger series of similar incidents for which there was no clear rhyme or reason. Some political activists have labeled these as political assassinations, but neither the courts nor the media will publish opinions to this effect. These opinions have instead been aired in independent YouTube videos. For LGBTQ activists, these assassinations were specifically worrisome because they generated the feeling that LGBTQ persons could be killed "twice"—for being gay and for being activists.

CHAPTER 4 — FLIPPING THE SCRIPT

1. The cardinal was also famed for using the term *lacras sociales*—social waste. Another term used in the past is *vagos* (vagrants). See Quisqueya Lora's *Transición de la esclavitud al trabajo libre en Santo Domingo* (2012) regarding the use of the word *vago/vagrant* following emancipation.

2. There are hundreds of videos, with footage captured on cell phones, that have been posted on YouTube in the last eight years. The killing of young men deemed *delinquentes* goes back at least forty years—to the Balaguerista eras. The capturing of live footage, however, is new to the cell phone video era. The images circulate among millions of viewers as the public attempts to navigate the multiple forms of violence they experience. Digital news stations such as SINoticias and Diario Digital (shut down in 2012) attempt to keep track of these extrajudicial killings.

3. From personal conversations with Y.G.G. (2010–2011), who, along with numerous other LGBTQ activists, used her social media platforms to publish the videos along with commentary about the *delincuencia* of the police. To this day, activists continue to use this strategy to confront abuses by state authorities.

4. This expression comes from a series of LGBTQ media campaigns in 2012. They circulated during the annual OUTFest film festival.

5. I first heard the term "laughter of recognition" in a personal conversation in 2010 with Adelina Anthony about her Hocicona Series and her uses of humor for queer people-of-color liberation. Anthony defines "laughter of recognition" as the laughter that emerges

from seeing the truth of ourselves as queer people of color through humor. She distinguishes it from the "laughter of ridicule," a laughter that emerges from the derisive objectification of queer people, fat people, and people of color.

6. I will revisit this sentiment later in this chapter in my discussion of trans* activists' responses to sexual terror.

7. Carlos Decena (2011) explores this thoroughly in his discussion of *la loca* and normative masculinity.

8. The interaction was captured on video and posted ("Policía Trata Impedir" 2012). I also interviewed Yori about the incident in May 2013. Yori explained to me that he would still like to carry the flag, but he did not want to bring any trouble to the organizers. He told me that in 2013, he was going to wear shorts with the Dominican flag colors that a friend brought him as a gift from New York City.

CHAPTER 5 — CUENTOS

1. Interestingly enough, *cuentos* about the Trujillo regime are rare, as many Dominicans still fear talking about this era, except to reference already known historical facts. In my many attempts to elicit *cuentos* from friends, colleagues, and family members about this era, my respondents will revert to silence, will make platitudes ("we had good schools back then"), or will cite historical texts. Some go so far as to tell me they do not remember. For these reasons, the fact that the gay men I spoke to were explicit in discussing homosexuality in the Trujillo era really struck me. In the many books that discuss the Trujillo era, homosexuality and homosexual communities are not discussed at all.

2. Antonio de Moya and Rafael García (2003) allude to the aggressions against middle- and upper-class bisexual and homosexual men during the Trujillato.

3. Rafael Tavárez Labrador received the name "Paquita" because of his drag shows, in which he would imitate the famous Spanish *cupletista* Paquita Escribano. He was a Trujillo-era radio show personality known for his flagrant homosexuality and crossdressing performances. He also went by the male version of the name, Paco.

4. For a discussion of popular responses to U.S. Empire in Puerto Rico, see Torres (1998) and Briggs (2002).

5. Conversation with filmmaker and activist Henry Mercedes Vales, December 2012.

6. Though I was intrigued by what was taking place in Molina's monologues, an analysis of these monologues is beyond the scope of this book. I was unable to locate feminist analyses—in particular, black feminist or intersectional feminist approaches—to this text in its various forms. For two readings of Molina's monologues, see O'Connor (2004) and Chabot Davis (2007).

7. The novels *In the Time of the Butterflies* by Julia Alvarez (1995) and *La Fiesta del Chivo* by Mario Vargas Llosa (2000) allude to Trujillo's sexual violence toward young women and their families; Balaguer also alludes to Trujillo's sexual excess as a political tool of domination in his *Memorias de un cortesano de la era de Trujillo* (1998).

8. In May 2013, at the annual national LGBT human rights forum, Wilkin gave a keynote speech that tied an interpretation of Christian morality to the efforts of the Procuraduría General (Attorney General) to institute measures aimed at curbing racist, homophobic, and transphobic abuses within the Dominican government and the private sector. He also spoke openly and powerfully about the moral duty to support and sustain the lives of those who are HIV affected.

9. Description presented as part of the Caribbean Fantasy Film Festival in Port-au-Prince, May 2016.

10. La Chaca was a trans* activist and legend in the Dominican *ambiente*.

CONCLUSION

1. There was extensive news coverage of the anti-Haitian violence between 2013 and 2015. See Ponce (2015).

References

Books and Journal Articles

Adorno, Rolena. 2007. *Polemics of Possession in Spanish American Narrative*. New Haven, Conn.: Yale University Press.

Agamben, Giorgio. 2005. *State of Exception*. Chicago: University of Chicago Press.

Ahmed, Sarah. 2006. *Queer Phenomenology: Orientations, Objects, Others*. Durham, N.C.: Duke University Press.

Alexander, M. Jacqui. 1994. "Not Just (Any)*body* Can Be a Citizen: The Politics of Law, Sexuality and Postcoloniality in Trinidad and Tobago and Bahamas." *Feminist Review* 48:5–23.

———. 2005. *Pedagogies of Crossing: Meditations on Feminism, Sexual Politics, Memory, and the Sacred*. Durham, N.C.: Duke University Press.

Allen, Jafari S. 2011. *¡Venceremos? The Erotics of Black Self-Making in Cuba*. Durham, N.C.: Duke University Press.

Althusser, Louis. (1971) 2006. "Ideology and Ideological State Apparatuses (Notes towards an Investigation)." In *The Anthropology of the State: A Reader*, edited by Aradhana Sharma and Akhil Gupta, 86–111. Hoboken, N.J.: John Wiley & Sons.

Alvarez, Julia. 1995. *In the Time of the Butterflies*. New York: Plume.

Aquinas, Thomas. 1997. *Basic Writings of St. Thomas Aquinas*. Vol. 2. Edited by Anton C. Pegis. Indianapolis: Hackett.

Arendt, Hannah. (1968) 2007. "The Origins of Totalitarianism." In *On Violence*, edited by Bruce B. Lawrence and Aisha Karim, 416–433. Durham, N.C.: Duke University Press.

Aretxaga, Begoña. 2003. "Maddening States." *Annual Review of Anthropology* 32:393–410.

Arrom, José. 1973. *Aportaciones lingüísticas al conocimiento de la cosmovisión taína*. Santo Domingo, D.R.: Fundación García-Arévalo.

Artiles Gill, Leopoldo, and P. J. Ortega Espinal. 2008. "Tolerancia y participación ciudadana en el escenario de la democracia." *Global* 1, no. 1: 59–66.

Asad, Talal. 2003. *Formations of the Secular: Christianity, Islam, Modernity*. Palo Alto, Calif.: Stanford University Press.

———. 2015. "Reflections on Violence, Law, and Humanitarianism." *Critical Inquiry* 41, no. 2: 390–427.

Balaguer, Joaquín. 1983. *La Isla al Reves: Haití y el destino dominicano*. Santo Domingo, D.R.: Corripio.

———. 1998. *Memorias de un cortesano de la era de Trujillo*. Santo Domingo, D.R.: Editoria Corripio.

Beam, Joseph. (1986) 2008. *In the Life: A Black Gay Anthology*. Washington, D.C.: RedBone Press.

Bergallo, Paola, and Agustina Ramón Michel. 2016. "Constitutional Developments in Latin American Abortion Law." *International Journal of Gynecology and Obstetrics* 135:228–231.

Betances, Emelio. 2007. *The Catholic Church and Power Politics in Latin America: The Dominican Case in Comparative Perspective*. Lanham, Md.: Rowman & Littlefield.

Blancarte, Roberto. 2011. "América Latina: Entre pluri-confesionalidad y laicidad." *Civitas* 11, no. 2 (May–August 2011): 182–206.

Brennan, Denise. 2004. *What's Love Got to Do with It? Transnational Desires and Sex Tourism in the Dominican Republic*. Durham, N.C.: Duke University Press.

Briggs, Laura. 2002. *Reproducing Empire: Race, Sex, Science and U.S. Imperialism in Puerto Rico*. Berkeley: University of California Press.

Butler, Judith. 1990. *Gender Trouble and the Subversion of Identity*. New York: Routledge.

———. 1997. *The Psychic Life of Power: Theories in Subjection*. Palo Alto, Calif.: Stanford University Press.

Byrd, Rudolph P., Johnnetta Betsch Cole, and Beverly Guy-Sheftall, eds. 2009. *I Am Your Sister: Collected and Unpublished Writings of Audre Lorde*. Oxford: Oxford University Press.

Cabezas, Amalia L. 2009. *Economies of Desire: Sex and Tourism in Cuba and the Dominican Republic*. Philadelphia: Temple University Press.

Candelario, Ginetta E. B. 2007. *Black Behind the Ears: Dominican Racial Identity from Museums to Beauty Shops*. Durham, N.C.: Duke University Press.

Catelli, Laura. 2011. "'Y de esta manera quedaron todos los hombres sin mujeres': El mestizaje como estrategia de colonización en la Española (1501–1503)." *Revista de Crítica Literaria Latinoamericana*, no. 74 (segundo semestre): 217–238.

Cavanaugh, William T. 1995. "'A Fire Strong Enough to Consume the House:' The Wars of Religion and the Rise of the State." *Modern Theology* 11, no. 4: 397–420.

Chabot Davis, Kimberly. 2007. *Postmodern Texts and Emotional Audiences*. West Lafayette, Ind.: Purdue University Press.

Chetty, Raj, and Amaury Rodríguez. 2015. "Introduction: The Challenge and Promise of Dominican Black Studies." *The Black Scholar* 45, no. 2 (May 19): 1–9.

Cohen, Cathy J. 2001. "Punks, Bulldaggers, and Welfare Queens: The Radical Future of Queer Politics?" In *Sexual Identities, Queer Politics*, edited by Mark Blasius, Mark, 200–227. Princeton, N.J.: Princeton University Press.

Comisión Nacional Dominicana de la Ruta del Esclavo. 2006. *La ruta del esclavo*. Santo Domingo, D.R.: UNESCO—Comisión de las Naciones Unidas para la Educación, la Ciencia y la Cultura.

Cvetkovich, Ann. 2007. "Public Feelings." *South Atlantic Quarterly* 106, no. 3 (Summer): 459–468.

Das, Veena. 2000. *Violence and Subjectivity*. Berkeley: University of California Press.

———. 2007a. "Secularism and the Argument from Nature." In *Powers of the Secular Modern: Talal Asad and His Interlocutors*, edited by David Scott and Charles Hirschkind, 93–112. Palo Alto, Calif.: Stanford University Press.

———. 2007b. *Life and Words: Violence and the Descent into the Ordinary*. Berkeley: University of California Press.

Decena, Carlos Ulises. 2011. *Tacit Subjects: Belonging and Same-Sex Desire among Dominican Immigrant Men*. Durham, N.C.: Duke University Press.

Declue, Jennifer. 2016. "Let's Play: Exploring Cinematic Black Lesbian Fantasy, Pleasure, and Pain." In *No Tea, No Shade: New Writings in Black Queer Studies*, edited by E. Patrick Johnson, 216–238. Durham, N.C.: Duke University Press.

de Moya, E. Antonio. 2004. "Power Games and Totalitarian Masculinity in the Dominican Republic." In *Interrogating Caribbean Masculinities: Theoretical and Empirical Analyses*, edited by Rhoda Reddock, 68–102. Kingston, Jamaica: University of the West Indies Press.

de Moya, E. Antonio, and Rafael García. 2003. "AIDS and the Enigma of Bisexuality in the Dominican Republic." In *Bisexualities and AIDS: International Perspectives*, edited by Peter Aggleton, 119–133. Milton, U.K.: Taylor & Francis.

Derby, Lauren H. 2000. "The Dictator's Seduction: Gender and State Spectacle during the Trujillo Regime." *Callaloo* 23, no. 3: 1112–1146.

Díez, Jordi. 2015. *The Politics of Gay Marriage in Latin America: Argentina, Chile, and Mexico*. Cambridge: Cambridge University Press.

Duggan, Lisa. 1994. "Queering the State." *Social Text* 39:5–6.

Edmondson, Belinda. 2003. "Public Spectacles: Caribbean Women and the Politics of Public Performance." *Small Axe: Journal of Criticism* 7, no. 1: 1–16.

Ellis, Nadia. 2015. *Queered Belonging in the Black Diaspora*. Durham, N.C.: Duke University Press.

Espinal, Rosario. 1995. "Economic Restructuring, Social Protest, and Democratization in the Dominican Republic." *Latin American Perspectives* 22, no. 3 (Summer): 63–79.

Espinosa Miñoso, Yuderkys. 2004. "Homogeneidad proyecto de nación." In *Desde la orilla: Hacia una nacionalidad sin desalojos*, edited by Silvio Torres-Saillant, Ramona Hernández, and Blas R. Jiménez, 361–368. Santo Domingo, D.R.: Editora Manatí.

Falconí Trávez, Diego. 2014. "De lo Queer/Cuir/Cu(y)r en América Latina: Accidentes y malos entendidos en la narrative de Ena Lucía Portela." *Revista de pensamiento, crítica y estudios literarios latinoamericanos* 10:95–113.

Falconí Trávez, Diego, Santiago Castellanos, and María Amelia Viteri, eds. 2014. *Resentir lo queer en América Latina: Diálogos desde/con el Sur*. Madrid: Egales Editorial.

Fanon, Frantz. (1952) 2008. *Black Skin, White Masks*. New York: Grove Press.

Finley, Chris. 2011. "Decolonizing the Queer Native Body (and Recovering the Native Bull-Dyke): Bringing 'Sexy Back' and Out of Native Studies' Closet." In *Queer Indigenous Studies: Critical Interventions in Theory, Politics, and Literature*, edited by Qwo-Li Driskill, Chris Finely, Brian Joseph Gilley, and Scott Lauria Morgensen, 31–42. Tucson: University of Arizona Press.

Fleishman, Rishona. 2000. "The Battle against Reproductive Rights: The Impact of the Catholic Church on Abortion Law in Both International and Domestic Areas." *Emory International Law Review* 14:277–314.

Foucault, Michel. 1978. *The History of Sexuality*. Vol. 1. New York: Pantheon.

———. 1982. "The Subject and Power." *Critical Inquiry* 8, no. 4: 777–795.

———. 2010. *The Archaeology of Knowledge*. New York: Vintage Press.

Freston, Paul. 2008. *Evangelical Christianity and Democracy in Latin America*. Oxford: Oxford University Press.

García-Del Moral, Paulina, and Megan Alexandra Dersnah. 2014. "A Feminist Challenge to the Gendered Politics of the Public/Private Divide: On Due Diligence, Domestic Violence, and Citizenship." *Citizenship Studies* 18, nos. 6–7: 661–675.

García-Peña, Lorgia. 2016. *The Borders of Dominicanidad: Race, Nation, and Archives of Contradiction*. Durham, N.C.: Duke University Press.

Garza Carvajal, Federico. 2010. *Butterflies Will Burn: Prosecuting Sodomites in Early Modern Spain and Mexico*. Austin: University of Texas Press.

Gill, Lyndon K. 2018. *Erotic Islands: Art and Activism in the Queer Caribbean*. Durham, N.C.: Duke University Press.

Gilroy, Paul. 1993. *The Black Atlantic: Modernity and Double Consciousness*. Brooklyn: Verso.

———. 2000. *Against Race: Imagining Political Culture beyond the Color Line*. Cambridge, Mass.: Harvard University Press.

Gilyard, Keith. 1996. *Let's Flip the Script: An African American Discourse on Language, Literature and Learning*. Detroit: Wayne State University Press.

Gonçalves Margerin, Marselha and Monika Kalra Varma, and Salvador Sarmiento. 2014. "Building a Dangerous Precedent in the Americas: Revoking Fundamental Rights of Dominicans." *Human Rights Brief* 21:9–16.

Goodpasture, H. McKennie. 2000. *Cross and Sword: An Eyewitness History of Christianity in Latin America*. Eugene, Ore.: Wipf and Stock.

Gregory, Steven. 2006. *The Devil Behind the Mirror: Globalization and Politics in the Dominican Republic*. Berkeley: University of California Press.

Gudorf, Christine. 2014. "Strategic Essentialism and Vatican Policy." *Political Theology* 15, no. 3 (May): 231–238.

Guitar, Lynne A. 2013. "Negotiations of Conquest." In *The Caribbean: A History of the Region and Its Peoples*, edited by Stephan Palmié and Francisco A. Scarano, 115–131. Chicago: University of Chicago Press.

Halberstam, J. 2005. *In a Queer Time and Place: Transgender Bodies, Subcultural Lives*. New York: New York University Press.

———. 2017. *Trans: A Quick and Quirky Account of Gender Variability*. Berkeley: University of California Press.

Hannam, Monique A. 2014. "Soy Dominicano—the Status of Haitian Descendants Born in the Dominican Republic and Measures to Protect Their Right to a Nationality." *Vanderbilt Journal of Transnational Law* 47:1123–1166.

Hartman, Saidiya V. 1997. *Scenes of Subjection: Terror, Slavery, and Self-Making in Nineteenth-Century America*. Oxford: Oxford University Press.

Heger Boyle, Elizabeth, Shannon Golden, and Wenjie Liao. 2017. "The Catholic Church and International Law." *Annual Review of Law and Social Science* 13:395–411.

Hemphill, Essex. 2000. *Ceremonies: Prose and Poetry*. Hoboken, N.J.: Cleis Press.

Hickey, Eric W. 2006. *Sex Crimes and Paraphilia*. London: Pearson Education.

Hird, Myra J. 2000. "Gender's Nature: Intersexuality, Transsexualism and the 'Sex'/'Gender' Binary." *Feminist Theory* 1, no. 3: 347–364.

Hofer, Katharina. 2003. "The Role of Evangelical NGOs in International Development: A Comparative Case Study of Kenya and Uganda." *Africa Spectrum*, February 2003, 375–398.

hooks, bell. 2000. *All about Love: New Visions*. New York: William Morrow.

Horn, Maya. 2014. *Masculinity after Trujillo: The Politics of Gender in Dominican Literature*. Gainesville: University Press of Florida.

Howe, Cymene. 2013. *Intimate Activism: The Struggle for Sexual Rights in Postrevolutionary Nicaragua*. Durham, N.C.: Duke University Press.

Hull, Gloria, Patricia Bell-Scott, and Barbara Smith. 1982. *All the Women Are White, All the Men Are Black, but Some of Us Are Brave*. New York: Feminist Press.

Hurston, Zora Neale. (1935) 1990. *Mules and Men*. Boston, Mass.: South End Press.

Jiménez Polanco, Jacqueline. 2006. *Divagaciones bajo la luna—Musings under the Moon: Voices and Images of Dominican Lesbians*. Santo Domingo, D.R.: Idegraf Editora.

———. 2013. "The Dominican LGBTIQ Movement and Asylum Claims in the US." In *Migrant Marginality: A Transnational Perspective*, edited by Philip Kretsedemas, Jorge Capetillo-Ponce and Glenn Jacobs, 179–199. New York: Routledge.

Johnson, E. Patrick. 1995. "Snap! Culture: A Different Kind of 'Reading.'" *Text and Performance Quarterly* 15, no. 2: 122–142.

———. 2001. "'Quare' Studies, or (Almost) Everything I Know about Queer Studies I Learned from My Grandmother." *Text and Performance Quarterly* 21, no. 1: 1–25.

Johnson, E. Patrick, and Mae G. Henderson. 2005. *Black Queer Studies: A Critical Anthology*. Durham, N.C.: Duke University Press.

Kalyvas, Stathis N., and Kees van Kersbergen. 2010. "Christian Democracy." *Annual Review of Political Science* 13:183–209.

Kempadoo, Kemala. 2004. *Sexing the Caribbean: Gender, Race and Sexual Labor*. Oxfordshire, U.K.: Taylor & Francis.

King, Tiffany Lethabo. 2016. "The Labor of (Re)reading Plantation Landscapes Fungible(ly)." *Antipode* 48, no. 4: 1022–1039.

Kochalumchuvattil, Thomas. 2010. "The Crisis of Identity in Africa: A Call for Subjectivity." *Kritike: An Online Journal of Philosophy* 4, no. 1: 108–122.

Krohn-Hansen, Christian. 2009. *Political Authoritarianism in the Dominican Republic*. London: Palgrave Macmillan.

Kusch, Rodolfo. 2007. *Obras completas, tomos I–III*. Buenos Aires, Argentina: Editorial Fundación Ross.

La Fontaine-Stokes, Lawrence. 2007. "Queer Ducks, Puerto Rican *Patos*, and Jewish American Feygelekh: Birds and Cultural Representation of Homosexuality." *Centro Journal* 19, no. 1 (Spring): 193–229.

Lara, Ana-Maurine. 2005. "Vudú in the Dominican Republic: Resistance and Healing." *Phoebe Journal of Gender and Cultural Critiques* 17, no. 1 (Spring): 1–20.

———. 2009. "Uncovering Mirrors: The Afro-Latina Lesbian Subjects." In *The Afro-Latin@ Reader: History and Culture in the United States*, edited by Miriam Jiménez-Roman and Juan Flores, 298–313. Durham, N.C.: Duke University Press.

———. 2013. "I Think I Might Be Broken: Sharon Bridgforth's Delta Dandi." In *Diasporic Women's Writing of the Black Atlantic: (En)Gendering Literature and Performance*, edited by Emilia María Durán-Almarza and Esther Álvarez López, 34–51. New York: Routledge.

———. 2014. "Moyumba." *Aster(ix) Journal: Ra(i)ces*, Spring 2014. https://asterixjournal.com/moyumba-ana-maurine-lara-guest-editor-print-issue-letter-editor/.

Lauria, Anthony. 1964. "'Respeto,' 'Relajo' and Inter-personal Relations in Puerto Rico." *Anthropological Quarterly* 37, no. 2 (April): 53–67.

Lind, Amy. 2010. *Development, Sexual Rights and Global Governance*. New York: Routledge.

Lora, Quisqueya. 2012. *Transición de la esclavitud al trabajo libre en Santo Domingo: El caso de Higüey (1822–1827)*. Santo Domingo, D.R.: Academia Dominicana de la Historia.

Lorde, Audre. 1984. *Sister Outsider: Essays and Speeches*. San Francisco: Aunt Lute.

Lott, Eric. 2000. "After Identity, Politics: The Return of Universalism." *New Literary History* 31, no. 4 (Autumn): 665–680.

Lugones, María. 2003. *Pilgrimages/Peregrinajes: Theorizing Coalition against Multiple Oppressions*. Lanham, Md.: Rowman & Littlefield.

———. 2007. "Heterosexualism and the Colonial/Modern Gender System." *Hypatia* 22, no. 1: 186–219.

———. 2010. "Toward a Decolonial Feminism." *Hypatia* 25, no. 4: 742–759.

Manalansan, Martin F., IV. 2003. *Global Divas: Filipino Gay Men in the Diaspora*. Durham, N.C.: Duke University Press.

Manley, Elizabeth. 2012. "Intimate Violations: Women and the *Ajusticiamiento* of Dictator Rafael Trujillo, 1944–1961." *The Americas* 69, no. 1: 61–94.

Martínez Fernández, Luis. 1995. "The Sword and the Crucifix: Church-State Relations and Nationality in the Nineteenth-Century Dominican Republic." *Latin American Research Review* 30, no. 1: 69–93.

Martínez Martínez, Julio Luis. 2002. *"Consenso público" y moral social: Las relaciones entre catolicismo y liberalismo en la obra de John Courtney Murray, S.J.* Vol. 1. Madrid: Editorial Universidad Pontifica Comillas.

Martínez-Vergne, Teresita. 2005. *Nation and Citizen in the Dominican Republic, 1880–1916*. Durham, N.C.: University of North Carolina Press.

Mateo, Andrés L. 2004. *Mito y cultura en la era de Trujillo*. Santo Domingo, D.R.: Editora Manatí.

Matory, J. Lorand. 2005. *Sex and the Empire That Is No More: Gender and the Politics of Metaphor in Oyo Yoruba Religion*. New York: Berghahn Books.

Mayes, April J. 2008. "Why Dominican Feminism Moved to the Right: Class, Colour and Women's Activism in the Dominican Republic, 1880s–1940s." *Gender and History* 20, no. 2: 349–371.

———. 2014. *The Mulatto Republic: Class, Race, and Dominican National Identity*. Gainesville: University Press of Florida.

Mbembe, Achille. 2003. "Necropolitics." *Public Culture* 15, no. 1 (Winter): 11–40.

McKittrick, Katherine. 2006. *Demonic Grounds: Black Women and the Cartographies of Struggle*. Minneapolis: University of Minnesota Press.

Méndez, Xhercis. 2003. "Transcending Dimorphism: Afro-Cuban Ritual Praxis and the Rematerialization of the Body." *Power* 3, no. 3: 47–69.

———. 2015. "Notes toward a Decolonial Feminist Methodology: Revisiting the Race/Gender Matrix." *Trans-scripts* 5:41–56.

Meyer, Birgit. 2004. "Christianity in Africa: From African Independent to Pentecostal-Charismatic Churches." *Annual Review of Anthropology* 33:447–474.

Mignolo, Walter D. 2007. "Introduction: Coloniality of Power and De-colonial Thinking." *Cultural Studies* 21, nos. 2–3: 155–167.

Mirkin, Harris. 1999. "The Pattern of Sexual Politics: Feminism, Homosexuality and Pedophilia." *Journal of Homosexuality* 37, no. 2: 1–24.

Molyneux, Maxine. 2000. *Women's Movements in International Perspective: Latin America and Beyond*. London: Palgrave Macmillan.

Moore, Moses N., Jr. 2005. "'Testifying' and 'Testimony': Autobiographical Narratives and African American Religions." In *Teaching African American Religions*, edited by Carolyn M. Jones and Theodore Louis Trost, 95–107. Oxford: Oxford University Press.

Muñoz, José Esteban. 2009. *Cruising Utopia: The Then and There of Queer Futurity*. New York: New York University Press.

Nikolas, Rose. 1987. "Beyond the Public/Private Division: Law, Power and the Family." *Journal of Law and Society* 14, no. 1 (Spring): 61–76.

O'Connor, Patrick. 2004. *Latin American Fiction and the Narratives of the Perverse: Paper Dolls and Spider Women*. London: Palgrave Macmillan.

O'Flaherty, Michael, and John Fisher. 2008. "Sexual Orientation, Gender Identity and International Human Rights Law: Contextualising the Yogyakarta Principles." *Human Rights Law Review* 8, no. 2: 207–248.

Oppenheim, Claire E. 2012. "Nelson Mandela and the Power of Ubuntu." *Religions* 3, no. 2: 369–388.

Otero, Solimar. 2020. *Archives of Conjure: Stories of the Dead in AfroLatinx Cultures*. New York: Columbia University Press.

Oyěwùmí, Oyèrónké. 1997. *The Invention of Women: Making an African Sense of Western Gender Discourses*. Minneapolis: University of Minnesota Press.

Padilla, Mark. 2008. *Caribbean Pleasure Industry: Tourism, Sexuality, and AIDS in the Dominican Republic*. Chicago: University of Chicago Press.

Padilla, Mark, and Daniel Castellanos. 2008. "Discourses of Homosexual Invasion in the Dominican Global Imaginary." *Sexuality Research and Social Policy: Journal of NSRC* 5 no. 4 (December 2008): 31–44.

Pané, Fray Ramón. 1999. *An Account of the Antiquities of the Indians: A New Edition, with an Introductory Study, Notes, and Appendices by José Juan Arrom*. Durham, N.C.: Duke University Press.

Pateman, Carole, and Charles Wade Mills. 2007. *Contract and Domination*. Cambridge: Polity Press.

Penyak, Lee M. 2008. "Temporary Transgressions, Unspeakable Acts: Male Sodomy in Late-Colonial Mexico, 1744–1843." *Colonial Latin American Historical Review* 17, no. 4: 329–359.

Pepén, Juan F. 1954. *La cruz señalo el camino: Influencia de la iglesia en la formación y conservación de la nacionalidad dominicana*. Santo Domingo, D.R.: Editorial Duarte.

Pérez, Sara. 2004. "La iglesia patriarcal dominicana." In *Desde la Orilla: Hacia una nacionalidad sin desalojos*, edited by Silvio Torres-Saillant, Ramona Hernández, and Blas R. Jiménez, 269–276. Santo Domingo, D.R.: Editora Manatí.

Puar, Jasbir K. 2007. *Terrorist Assemblages: Homonationalism in Queer Times*. Durham, N.C.: Duke University Press.

Puig, Manuel. 2002. *Beso de la mujer araña*. Buenos Aires, Argentina: Archives de la Littéra-
ture Latino-Américaine, des Caraibes et Africaine du XXe Siècle.

Quijano, Anibal. 2000. "Coloniality of Power, Eurocentrism, and Latin America." *Nepantla:
View from the South* 1, no. 3: 533–580.

Quinn, Rachel Afi. 2015. "Black Lesbian Feminist Activism in Santo Domingo." In *Transatlantic Feminisms: Women and Gender Studies in Africa and the Diaspora*, edited by Cheryl R.
Rodriguez and Dzodzi Tsikata, 25–32. Washington, D.C.: Lexington Books.

———. 2018. "Dominican Pride and Shame: Gender, Race, and LGBT Activism in Santo
Domingo." *Small Axe: A Caribbean Journal of Criticism* 22, no. 2: 128–143.

Radford Ruether, Rosemary. 2008. "Women, Reproductive Rights and the Catholic Church."
Feminist Theology 16, no. 2: 184–193.

Ramírez, Dixa. 2018. *Colonial Phantoms: Belonging and Refusal in the Dominican Americas,
from the 19th Century to the Present*. New York: New York University Press.

Reddock, Rhoda. 1994. *Women, Labour and Politics in Trinidad and Tobago a History*. London: Zed Books.

Reddy, Chandan. 2011. *Freedom with Violence: Race, Sexuality, and the US States*. Durham,
N.C.: Duke University Press.

Reyes-Santos, Alaí. 2015. *Our Caribbean Kin: Race and Nation in the Neoliberal Antilles*. New
Brunswick, N.J.: Rutgers University Press.

Richards, David A. J. 1999. *Identity and the Case for Gay Rights: Race, Gender, Religion as
Analogies*. Chicago: University of Chicago Press.

Ricourt, Milagros. 2016. *The Dominican Racial Imaginary: Surveying the Landscape of Race
and Nation in Hispaniola*. New Brunswick, N.J.: Rutgers University Press.

Roach, Joseph R. 1996. *Circum-Atlantic Performance*. New York: Columbia University Press.

Robbins, Joel. 2004. "The Globalization of Pentecostal and Charismatic Christianity." *Annual
Review of Anthropology* 33:117–143.

Robotham, Don. 2005. "Cosmopolitanism and Planetary Humanism: The Strategic Universalism of Paul Gilroy." *South Atlantic Quarterly* 104, no. 3: 561–582.

Rodriguez, Jenny K. 2010. "The Construction of Gender Identities in Public Sector Organisa-
tions in Latin America: A View of the Dominican Republic." *Equality, Diversity and Inclusion: An International Journal* 29, no. 1: 53–77.

Rodríguez, Juana María. 2003. *Queer Latinidad: Identity Practices, Discursive Spaces*. New
York: New York University Press.

———. 2011. "Queer Sociality and Other Sexual Fantasies." *GLQ: A Journal of Lesbian and
Gay Studies* 17, no. 2: 331–348.

Romany, Celina. 1993. "Women as *Aliens*: A Feminist Critique of the Public/Private Distinc-
tion in International Human Rights Law." *Harvard Human Rights Journal* 6:87–126.

Ryall, David. 2001. "The Catholic Church as a Transnational Actor." In *Non-state Actors in
World Politics*, edited by Daphné Josselin and William Wallace, 41–58. London: Palgrave
Macmillan.

Sáez, José L. 1987. *Cinco siglos de la iglesia dominicana 1*. Santo Domingo, D.R.: Editora
Amigo del Hogar.

Sandoval, Chela. 2000. *Methodology of the Oppressed*. Minneapolis: University of Minnesota
Press.

Scheper-Hughes, Nancy. 1993. *Death without Weeping: The Violence of Everyday Life in Brazil*.
Berkeley: University of California Press.

Schwaller, John Frederick. 2011. *The History of the Catholic Church in Latin America: From
Conquest to Revolution and Beyond*. New York: New York University Press.

Scott, James C. 1990. *Domination and the Arts of Resistance: Hidden Transcripts*. New Haven,
Conn.: Yale University Press.

Sedgwick, Eve Kosofsky. 1993. "Epistemology of the Closet." In *The Lesbian and Gay Studies
Reader*, edited by Henry Abelove, 45–61. New York: Routledge.

Sierra Madero, Abel. 2004. "Sexualidades disidentes en el siglo XIX en Cuba." *Estudios Inter-disciplinarios De América Latina y El Caribe*, 16, no. 1. http://www1.tau.ac.il/eial/index.php?option=com_content&task=view&id=360&Itemid=188.

Simmons, Kimberly Eison. 2012. "Constructing and Promoting African Diaspora Identity in the Dominican Republic: The Emergence of Casa de la Identidad de las Mujeres Afro." *African and Black Diaspora: An International Journal* 5, no. 1: 123–133.

Simpson, Audra. 2007. "On Ethnographic Refusal: Indigeneity, 'Voice' and Colonial Citizenship." *Junctures: The Journal for Thematic Dialogue* 9 (December): 67–80.

———. 2014. *Mohawk Interruptus: Political Life across the Borders of Settler States*. Durham, N.C.: Duke University Press.

Smitherman, Geneva. 1977. *Talkin and Testifyin: The Language of Black America*. Detroit: Wayne State University Press.

So, Mia. 2011. "Resolving Conflicts of Constitution: Inside the Dominican Republic's Constitutional Ban on Abortion." *Independent Law Journal* 86, no. 2: 713–734.

Spillers, Hortense J. 1987. "Mama's Baby, Papa's Maybe: An American Grammar Book." *Diacritics*, Summer 1987, 65–81.

Spivak, Gayatri Chakravorty. 1988. "Can the Subaltern Speak?" In *Marxism and the Interpretation of Culture*, edited by Cary Nelson and Lawrence Grossberg, 271–313. Champaign: University of Illinois Press.

Stoler, Ann Laura. 1995. *Race and the Education of Desire: Foucault's History of Sexuality and the Colonial Order of Things*. Durham, N.C.: Duke University Press.

Tejada Yangüela, Argelia. 2010. "Destrujillización inconclusa: El estado confesional." *Boletín del Archivo General de la Nación* 35, no. 127: 99–162.

Thomas, Deborah A. 2004. *Modern Blackness: Nationalism, Globalization, and the Politics of Culture in Jamaica*. Durham, N.C.: Duke University Press.

———. 2011. *Exceptional Violence: Embodied Citizenship in Transnational Jamaica*. Durham, N.C.: Duke University Press.

Thompson, Krista A. 2006. *An Eye for the Tropics: Tourism, Photography, and Framing the Caribbean Picturesque*. Durham, N.C.: Duke University Press.

Torres, Arlene. 1998. "La Gran Familia Puertorriqueña 'ej prieta de beldá' (The Great Puerto Rican Family Is Really Really Black)." In *Blackness in Latin America and the Caribbean*, edited by Norman E. Whitten and Arlene Torres, 285–306. Bloomington: Indiana University Press.

Tortorici, Zeb. 2007. "'Heran todos putos': Sodomitical Subcultures and Disordered Desire in Early Colonial Mexico." *Ethnohistory* 54, no. 1: 35–67.

———. 2012. "Against Nature: Sodomy and Homosexuality in Colonial Latin America." *History Compass* 10, no. 2: 161–178.

Vargas Llosa, Mario. 2000. *La fiesta del chivo*. Santo Domingo, D.R.: Editora Taller.

Viteri, María Amelia. 2017. "Intensiones: Tensions in Queer Agency and Activism in Latino América." *Feminist Studies* 43, no. 2: 405–417.

Walby, Sylvia. 1990. *Theorizing Patriarchy*. London: Basil Blackwell.

Walker, Alice. 1995. "Only Justice Can Stop a Curse." *Race, Poverty and the Environment* 5, no. 3/4 (Spring/Summer): 41–42.

Weeks, Jeffrey. 1998. "The Sexual Citizen." *Theory Culture Society* 15, no. 3–4: 35–52.

———. 2002. *Sexuality and Its Discontents: Meanings, Myths, and Modern Sexualities*. New York: Routledge.

Whitehead, Neil L. 2011. *Of Cannibals and Kings: Primal Anthropology in the Americas*. University Park, PA: Penn State University Press.

Wilderson, Frank B., III. 2011. "The Vengeance of Vertigo: Aphasia and Abjection in the Political Trials of Black Insurgents." *InTensions Journal*, no. 5 (Fall/Winter): 1–41.

Wilson, Peter. 1969. "Reputation and Respectability: A Suggestion for Caribbean Ethnology." *Man* 4, no. 1 (March): 70–84.

Wynter, Sylvia. 1984. "The Ceremony Must Be Found: After Humanism." *Boundary* 2:19–70.

Wynter, Sylvia, and Katherine McKittrick. 2015. "Unparalleled Catastrophe for Our Species? Or, to Give Humanness a Different Future: Conversations." In *Sylvia Wynter: On Being Human as Praxis,* edited by Katherine McKittrick, 9–89. Durham, N.C.: Duke University Press.

Zeller, Neici M. 2010. *The Appearance of All, the Reality of Nothing: Politics and Gender in the Dominican Republic, 1880–1961.* Champaign: University of Illinois Press.

Documents and Reports

Amnesty International. 2011. "Dominican Republic Urged to Tackle Alarming Levels of Police Abuse." *Amnesty International Reports,* October 25, 2011. http://www.amnestyusa .org/research/reports/dominican-republic-urged-to-tackle-alarming-levels-of-police -abuse.

Asamblea Nacional de la República Dominicana. 2010. *Constitución Dominicana.* Santo Domingo, D.R.: Asamblea Nacional de la República Dominicana.

AstraeaFoundation.org. n.d. "IURA-Individuos Unidos por el Respeto y la Armonía." *Astraea Lesbian Foundation for Justice.* https://www.astraeafoundation.org/stories/iura-individuos -unidos-por-el-respeto-y-la-armonia/.

Balaguer, Joaquín. 1993. *Decreto No. 220-93 que crea el Patronato de la Ciudad Colonial.* Gaceta Oficial Número 9865, August 31, 1993.

Bureau of Democracy, Human Rights and Labor, U.S. Department of State. 2010. *International Religious Freedom Report,* November 17, 2010. http://www.state.gov/j/drl/rls/irf/ 2010/148751.htm.

Camara de Diputados. 2016. *Código Penal de la República Dominicana.* https://www .camaradediputados.gov.do/masterlex/mlx/docs/1D/121E/1259.htm.

Center for Research on Population and Security. n.d. *Church or State? The Holy See at the United Nations.* http://www.population-security.org/crlp-94-07.htm.

Child Rights International Network. 2005. "Yean and Bosico V. Dominican Republic." CRIN .org, September 8, 2005. Accessed November 12, 2013. http://www.crin.org/en/library/legal -database/yean-and-bosico-v-dominican-republic.

CLADEM. 2011. *Impacto socio-jurídico de la nueva Constitución en los derechos de las mujeres en República Dominicana: Análisis de algunas de las implicaciones socio-jurídicas de la nueva Constitución en la vida de las mujeres.* República Dominicana: CLADEM, Foro de Mujeres. http://library.fes.de/pdf-files/bueros/fescaribe/08594.pdf.

Colección de Leyes and Decretos, Consultoría Jurídica del Poder Ejecutivo. 2008. *1844 Constitution of the Dominican Republic.* Accessed September 18, 2013. http://www.consultoria .gov.do/constituciones%201844-2008/Constitucion%201844.pdf.

Cote-Muñoz, Natalia, and Verónica Alma Rosario. 2015. "Human Rights under Threat: Denationalization and Dominicans of Haitian Ancestry." *SAIS Review of International Affairs,* February 25, 2015. http://www.coha.org/human-rights-under-threat-denationalization -and-dominicans-of-haitian-ancestry/.

EU Council—Working Party on Human Rights. 2010. *Toolkit to Promote and Protect the Enjoyment of all Human Rights by Lesbian, Gay, Bisexual and Transgender (LGBT) People,* October 2010. Accessed April 24, 2011. https://www.consilium.europa.eu/en/documents -publications/publications/promoting-enjoyment-all-human-rights-lesbian-gay-bisexual -transgender-people/.

Holy See. n.d. "Our History." The Permanent Observer Mission of the Holy See to the United Nations. https://holyseemission.org/contents//mission/our-history.php.

———. 1983. *Charter of the Rights of the Family,* October 22, 1983. Accessed January 15, 2017. http://www.vatican.va/roman_curia/pontifical_councils/family/documents/rc_pc_family _doc_19831022_family-rights_en.html.

IACHR. 1969. "American Convention on Human Rights." Organization of American States. November 22, 1969. https://www.cidh.oas.org/basicos/english/basic3.american %20convention.htm.

———. 2015. "Violence against Lesbian, Gay, Bisexual, Trans and Intersex Persons in the Americas." Organization of American States, OAS/Ser.L/V/II. Doc. 36/15 Rev. 2, November 12, 2015. http://www.oas.org/en/iachr/reports/pdfs/ViolenceLGBTQQIPersons.pdf.

Jiménez Polanco, Jacqueline. 2004. "DR LGBT Movement—a Sociopolitical and Cultural Approach." Paper presented at CUNY Graduate School, New York, New York, October 11, 2004.

Ministerio de Economía, Planificación y Desarrollo, Oficina Nacional de Estadística, Republica Dominicana. 2010. *IX Censo nacional de población y vivienda 2010, informe general,* June 2012. http://censo2010.one.gob.do/volumenes_censo_2010/vol1.pdf.

New Ways Ministry. 2013. "The Many Faces of Pope Francis: A Timeline of His LGBTQ Record." March 13, 2013. https://www.newwaysministry.org/resources/pope-francis-LGBTQ-issues/.

Pérez, Celso. 2015. "We Are Dominican: Arbitrary Deprivation of Nationality in the Dominican Republic." *Human Rights Watch,* June 30, 2015. https://www.hrw.org/report/2015/07/01/we-are-dominican/arbitrary-deprivation-nationality-dominican-republic.

Proyecto Ciudadanía Activa de las Mujeres. 2013. *Boletín Trimestral,* April 3, 2013.

Rodríguez Morel, Genaro. 2011. *Cartas de la Real Audiencia de Santo Domingo, 1547–1575.* Santo Domingo, D.R.: Archivo General de la Nación.

SASOD-Guyana. 2011. "Caribbean Groups Join International Community in Saluting Murdered African Human Rights Worker." February 1, 2011. Accessed February 18, 2011. https://www.sasod.org.gy/sasod-blog-caribbean-groups-join-international-community-saluting-murdered-african-human-rights.

Tribunal Constitucional, República Dominicana. 2013. "Pierre v. No. Judgment 473/2012, Judgment TC/0168/13." September 23, 2013. http://noticiasmicrojuris.files.wordpress.com/2013/10/sentenciatc0168-13-c.pdf.

U.N. 1979. "Convention on the Elimination of All Forms of Discrimination against Women." December 18, 1979. https://treaties.un.org/Pages/ViewDetails.aspx?src=IND&mtdsg_no=IV-8&chapter=4.

———. 2015. "70 Ways the UN Makes a Difference." Accessed January 15, 2014. https://www.un.org/un70/en/content/70ways/index.html.

UNHRC Report. 2010. "Suggested Recommendations on Human Rights Issues Related to Sexual Orientation and Gender Identity." Arc-International.net, December 1, 2010. https://arc-international.net/wp-content/uploads/2013/02/UPR15-Suggested-SOGI-recommendations.pdf.

United Nations News Service. 2011. "UN Issues First Report on Human Rights of Gay and Lesbian People." UN.org, December 15, 2011. Accessed March 23, 2012. http://www.un.org/apps/news/story.asp?NewsID=40743.

U.S. Department of State. 2012. "2011 Report on International Religious Freedom—Dominican Republic." Refworld.org, July 30, 2012. Accessed July 15, 2013. http://www.refworld.org/docid/502105c67d.html.

U.S. Embassy. 2010. "Informe de derechos humanos en la República Dominicana—2010." *US Embassy Annual Reports.* Accessed May 13, 2011. http://spanish.santodomingo.usembassy.gov/hr2010-repdom-s.html.

Vatican. 1954. *Inter Sanctum Sedem et Rempublicam Dominicianam Sollemnes Conventiones: Concordato entre la Santa Sede y la República Dominicana,* June 16, 1954. Accessed May 29, 2020. https://www.vatican.va/roman_curia/secretariat_state/archivio/documents/rc_seg-st_19540616_concordato-dominicana_sp.html.

———. 2008. *Statement of the Holy See Delegation at the 63rd Session of the General Assembly of the United Nations on the Declaration on Human Rights, Sexual Orientation and Gender Identity,* December 18, 2008. Accessed December 10, 2013. http://www.vatican.va/

roman_curia/secretariat_state/2008/documents/rc_seg-st_20081218_statement-sexual
-orientation_en.html.

World Health Organization, World Health Assembly. 1987. *Resolution WHA 40.26, Global
Strategy for the Prevention and Control of AIDS.* Geneva: WHO, May 5, 1987.

WTTC. 2018. *Distribution of Dominican Republic's Total Contribution of Travel and Tourism
to GDP in 2017,* Chart, Statista, March 15, 2018. Accessed October 8, 2019. https://www
.statista.com/statistics/874522/dominicanrepublic-travel-tourism-total-contribution-to
-gdp-by-share/.

Newspaper Articles

7dias.com.do. 2013. "Vargas Llosa desea el reemplazo del Cardenal López Rodríguez."
December 30, 2013. Accessed February 18, 2017. http://www.7dias.com.do/el-pais/2013/
12/30/i154772_vargas-llosa-desea-reemplazo-del-Cardinal-lopez-rodriguez.html#
.WKiqCPLeo8c.

Abbey-Lambertz, Kate. 2013. "Allen Vigneron, Detroit Archbishop: DOMA Proposition 8
Rulings 'Hurt Us All.'" *Huffington Post,* June 26, 2013. Accessed February 24, 2017. http://
www.huffingtonpost.com/2013/06/26/allen-vigneron-detroit-archbishop-doma-prop-8
_n_3506316.html?1372288833.

Abreu, Teofilo. 2007. "Consejo Evangélico plantea reforma: Carta se base en conseno may-
oría." *Hoy Digital,* February 27, 2007. Accessed January 20, 2018. http://hoy.com.do/consejo
-evanglico-plantea-reformacarta-se-base-en-consenso-mayora/.

Acento.com. 2015. "Constitución dominicana no prohíbe el matrimonio entre personas
del mismo sexo." January 12, 2015. Accessed January 23, 2016. http://acento.com.do/2015/
actualidad/8212087-constitucion-dominicana-no-prohibe-el-matrimonio-entre-personas
-del-mismo-sexo/.

Arias, Aurora. 2013. "Besatón 2013: El beso que llegó para quedarse." Acento.com.do, April 10,
2013. Accessed April 10, 2013. http://acento.com.do/2013/opinion/208719-besaton-2013-el
-beso-que-llego-para-quedarse.

Associated Press. 2004. "Cardenal dominicano arremete contra gays." ElNuevoHerald.com, April
2004. Accessed October 10, 2013. http://www.nuevoherald.com/2004/6/4/cardenal-dominicano
-contra-gays.

———. 2013. "Pope Francis: I Prefer a Church Which Is Bruised, Hurting and Dirty." *USA
Today,* November 26, 2013. Accessed February 15, 2018. https://www.usatoday.com/story/
news/world/2013/11/26/pope-francis-poverty/3759005/.

BEREA. 2006. "Lideres evangélicos cuantifican aportes sociales en República Dominicana."
Diario Evangélico Digital, August 26, 2006. Accessed January 28, 2012. http://ceirberea
.blogdiario.com/1156562760/.

Bonilla, Teofilo. 2010. "Migración se lleva haitiano besando su esposa; ella huye." *El Nacional,*
May 28, 2010. https://elnacional.com.do/migracion-se-lleva-haitiano-beso-a-su-esposa-ella
-huye/.

Brydum, Sunnivie. 2013. "Pope Francis Says He Won't Judge Gay Priests." *Advocate,* July 29,
2013. Accessed February 24, 2017. http://www.advocate.com/politics/religion/2013/07/29/
pope-francis-says-he-wont-judge-gay-priests.

Carasik, Lauren. 2015. "The End of U.S. Complicity in the Dominican Republic: How Washington Should Respond to the Humanitarian Crisis." *Foreign Affairs,* August 20, 2015.
Accessed September 5, 2015. https://www.foreignaffairs.com/articles/dominican-republic/
2015-08-20/end-us-complicity-dominican-republic.

Catholic League. 2009. "Vatican Rejects U.N. Declaration on Gays." *Catholic League Newslet-
ter,* January 17, 2009. Accessed February 13, 2017. http://www.catholicleague.org/vatican
-rejects-u-n-declaration-on-gays/.

Colectivos LGBT. 2013. "Comunidad Gay Dominicana defiende a embajador James Brewster." Diariohispaniola.com, July 1, 2013. Accessed September 5, 2013. https://www.diariohispaniola .com/noticia/404/sin-clasificar/comunidad-lgbt-en-republica-dominicana-defiende-a -embajador-de-ee.uu.-.html.

Coste, Carlos. 2014. "Biografía de Paco Escribano 'El más grande humorista dominicano de los años 40–50.'" Villaconmundial.com, November 18, 2014. Accessed August 10, 2015. http://villaconmundial.blogspot.com/2014/11/biografia-de-paco-escribano-el-mas.html.

Cristianodigital.net. 2013. "Católicos y Evangélicos Dominicanos rechazan embajador gay de Estados Unidos." June 26, 2013. Accessed July 13, 2013. http://www.cristianodigital.net/ catolicos-y-evangelicos-dominicanos-rechazan-embajador-estados-unidos/.

Cruz Benzán, Ramón. 2013a. "Fijan para las 4:00 de la tarde de hoy lectura de la sentencia caso Iglesia y Profamilia." Listindiario.com, May 20, 2013. https://listindiario.com/la -republica/2013/05/20/277642/print.

———. 2013b. "Jueza falla a favor de la campaña de Profamilia." Listindiario.com, May 21, 2013. https://listindiario.com/la-republica/2013/5/20/277709/Jueza-falla-a-favor-campana -de-Profamilia.

del Castillo, José. 2013. "Mamita llegó el obispo." DiarioLibre.com, July 13, 2013. Accessed September 5, 2013. http://www.diariolibre.com/jose-del-castillo/2013/07/13/i392629_mamita -lleg-obispo.html.

El Caribe. 2013. "Tribunal Constitucional: Hijos de extranjeros en tránsito no son dominicanos." September 25, 2013. Accessed September 27, 2013. http://www.elcaribe.com.do/2013/ 09/25/tribunal-constitucional-hijos-extranjeros-transito-son-dominicanos.

———. 2014. "Embajador De EE.UU. En RD recibe grupo de gays." February 13, 2014. Accessed February 13, 2014. http://www.elcaribe.com.do/2014/02/13/embajador-.-recibe-grupo-gays.

ElDesahogoDominicano. 2016. "Coalición GLBT Dominicana responde a las amenazas del CODUE." January 18, 2016. Accessed January 23, 2016. https://scharboy2009.wordpress .com/2016/01/18/coalicion-glbt-dominicana-responde-a-las-amenazas-del-codue/.

El Día. 2013. "Grupos en RD rechazan embajador gay de EEUU." July 1, 2013. Accessed July 8, 2013. http://eldia.com.do/grupos-en-rd-rechazan-embajador-gay-de-ee-uu/.

Gettleman, Jeffrey. 2011. "Ugandan Who Spoke Up for Gays Is Beaten to Death." New York Times, January 27, 2011. Accessed January 28, 2011. http://www.nytimes.com/2011/01/28/ world/africa/28uganda.html?_r=0.

Grindley, Lucas. 2016. "Pope Francis Says Jesus Would Not Abandon Transgender People." Advocate, October 3, 2016. Accessed September 28, 2016. http://www.advocate.com/ religion/2016/10/03/pope-francis-says-jesus-would-not-abandon-transgender-people.

Gutiérrez, Tony. n.d. "Algunas reflexiones sobre estado, religión y laicismo." Monografias.com. http://www.monografias.com/trabajos82/reflexiones-estado-religion-laicismo/reflexiones -estado-religion-laicismo.shtml.

Herrera, Mairobi. 2010. "El Parque Duarte es un centro de promiscuidad." Listindiario.com, April 5, 2010. http://listindiario.com/la-republica/2010/4/4/137227/El-parque-Duarte-es -un-centro-de-promiscuidad.

Horowitz, Jason, and Laurie Goldstein. 2018. "Pope Francis Summons World's Bishops to Meet on Sexual Abuse." New York Times, September 12, 2018. https://www.nytimes.com/ 2018/09/12/world/europe/pope-bishops-conference.html.

Hoy Digital. 2012. "Vicepresidenta se reúne con Cardenal López Rodríguez." October 2, 2012. http://hoy.com.do/vicepresidenta-se-reune-con-cardenal-lopez-rodriguez/.

Jiménez, Ulises. 2012. "Cardenal critica matrimonio gay, llama 'farsantes' a quienes favorecen esta práctica." Noticias SIN, January 27, 2012. http://www.noticiassin.com/2012/01/cardenal -critica-matrimonio-gay-llama-farsantes-a-quienes-favorecen-esta-practica/.

Lavers, Michael K. 2015. "Dominican Cardinal Describes Gay US Ambassador as 'Wife.'" Washington Blade, December 2, 2015. http://www.washingtonblade.com/2015/12/02/dominican -cardinal-describes-gay-u-s-ambassador-as-wife/#sthash.uSCGnaEw.dpuf.

Leclerc, Isabel Leticia. 2013. "Evangélicos se oponen a la designación de embajador."
    Listindiario.com, July 11, 2013. http://www.listindiario.com/la-republica/2013/7/10/284043/
    Evangelicos-se-oponen-a-la-designacion-de-embajador.
Listindiario.com. 2013. "Iglesia Católica desaprueba nominación de embajador gay."
    June 27, 2013. http://www.listindiario.com/la-republica/2013/06/27/282225/iglesia-catolica
    -desaprueba-nominacion.
————. 2014. "Victor Grimaldi defiende al Cardenal López Rodríguez." February 14, 2014.
    http://www.listindiario.com/la-republica/2014/02/14/310624/victor-grimaldi-defiende-al
    -Cardinal-lopez-rodriguez.
López, Ramón. n.d. "Bembeteos del obispo." Bembeteo.com. http://www.bembeteo.com/
    bembeplena/bembeplena5.pdf.
Lovato, Robert. 2015. "U.S. Complicit in Dominican Republic Mass Haitian Deportations."
    Compton Herald, July 14, 2015. http://comptonherald.com/u-s-complicit-in-dominican
    -republic-mass-haitian-deportations/.
Mateo, Andrés L. 2012. "¡Mamita llegó el obispo!" Hoy Digital, July 11, 2012. http://hoy.com
    .do/mamita-llego-el-obispo/.
McElwee, Joshua J. 2016. "Francis: Christians Must Apologize to Gay People for Marginalizing
    Them." National Catholic Reporter, June 26, 2016. Accessed June 26, 2016. http://www.ncronline
    .org/news/vatican/francis-christians-must-apologize-gay-people-marginalizing-them.
Mejía, Odalis. 2013. "Tribunal dará a conocer fallo de caso Iglesia Católica versus Profamilia a
    las cuatro de la tarde." Hoy Digital, May 20, 2013. http://hoy.com.do/tribunal-dara-a-conocer
    -fallo-de-caso-iglesia-catolica-versus-profamiliaa-las-cuatro-de-la-tarde/.
Ministerio de la mujer. 2010. "Analizan avances y desafíos de los derechos de las mujeres en
    nueva Constitución." Listindiario.com, April 15, 2010. https://listindiario.com/la-republica/
    2010/4/15/138523/print.
Nuestro Tiempo. 2015. "Del manifiesto del placer al beso micropolítico." August 14, 2015. http://
    nuestrotiempo.com.do/2015/08/14/del-manifiesto-del-placer-al-beso-micropolitico/.
Paiewonsky, Denise. 2009. "'Modernidad democrática' y represión homofóbica en RD."
    DiariodigitalRD.com, June 29, 2009. http://www.diariodigital.com.do/articulo.42293.html.
————. 2013. "Caso Profamilia: Una muestra de debilidad de la Iglesia Católica." Acento
    .com, May 11, 2013. http://www.acento.com.do/index.php/news/78072/56/Caso-Profamilia
    -Una-muestra-de-debilidad-de-la-Iglesia-Catolica.html.
Paredes, Julieta. 2012. "IX Encuentro de lesbianas feministas-Abya Yala." La Razón, November 18,
    2012. http://www.la-razon.com/opinion/columnistas/IX-Encuentro-lesbianas-feministas
    -Abyayala_0_1726027483.html.
Pérez Reyes, Ramón. 2016. "El Senado convierte en ley nuevo código penal: Mantienen
    penalización aborto y sube pena máxima de 30 a 40 años." Listindiario.com, December 15,
    2016. Accessed December 15, 2016. http://www.listindiario.com/la-republica/2016/12/15/
    447016/el-senado-convierte-en-ley-nuevo-codigo-penal.
Peters, Edward. 2013. "A Primer on Church Teaching regarding 'Same-Sex Marriage.'" In the
    Light of the Law: A Canon Lawyer's Blog, March 27, 2013. Accessed August 8, 2016. https://
    canonlawblog.wordpress.com/2013/03/27/a-primer-on-church-teaching-regarding-same
    -sex-marriage/.
Ponce, Miguel. 2015. "Matan hombre y lo cuelgan en parque de Santiago." El Caribe, Feb-
    ruary 11, 2015. Accessed February 23, 2105. http://www.elcaribe.com.do/2015/02/11/matan
    -hombre-cuelgan-parque-santiago.
Pullella, Philip. 2008. "Vatican Attacked for Opposing Gay Decriminalization." Reuters,
    December 2, 2008. Accessed February 11, 2017. http://www.reuters.com/article/us-vatican
    -homosexuals-idUSTRE4B13QA20081202.
RB News. 2013. "Nominación embajador gay de Estados Unidos en Dominicana: Polémica."
    June 29, 2013. Accessed July 18, 2013. Laromanabayahibenews.com/2013/06/nominación
    -embajador-gay-de-estados-unidos.

Religión Digital. 2013. "El cardenal de Santo Domingo insulta al embajador gay USA." July 5, 2013. Accessed July 13, 2013. http://www.periodistadigital.com/religion/america/2013/07/05/el-cardenal-de-santo-domingo-insulta-al-embajador-gay-usa-iglesia-religion-isla-dominicana.shtml.

Reynoso, Pamela. 2016. "Through These Gorgeous Portraits, Photographer Carlos Rodríguez Is Giving Visibility to DR's Trans Community." Remezcla.com, May 31, 2016. http://remezcla.com/features/culture/photographing-dr-trans-community-carlos-rodriguez/.

Romero, Argénida. 2014. "Embajada británica en Santo Domingo celebra matrimonio gay." *Diario Libre,* December 30, 2014. Accessed January 23, 2016. http://www.diariolibre.com/noticias/embajada-britnica-en-santo-domingo-celebra-matrimonio-gay-EFDL947641.

Rosario Adames, Fausto. 2014. "Grimaldi ahora le responde al Gobierno de Danilo y dice que él respeta la Constitución" Acento.com, February 14, 2014. Accessed February 18, 2017. http://acento.com.do/2014/actualidad/1165413-grimaldi-ahora-le-responde-al-gobierno-de-danilo-y-dice-que-el-respeta-la-constitucion/.

Said Ceballos, Aileen. 2012. "Feministas denuncian reforma código penal sería grave retroceso." Acento.com, November 15, 2012. Accessed November 15, 2012. http://www.acento.com.do/index.php/news/24319/56/Feministas-denuncian-reforma-Codigo-Penal-seria-grave-retroceso.html.

Socias, Augusto. 2001. "Paco Escribano: El más grande humorista dominicano." *Revista Ahora: Bono Cimarrón Pensamiento Crítico,* October 29, 2001. Accessed September 18, 2016. https://bonoc.wordpress.com/2011/07/18/paco-escribano/.

Sosa, José R. 2009. "Vecinos hacen policía interrumpa acto gay." *El Nacional,* June 30, 2009. Accessed June 20, 2010. http://elnacional.com.do/vecinos-hacen-policia-interrumpa-acto-gay/.

————. 2010. "En RD han asesinado ya 10 transexuales." JoseRafaelSosa.blogspot.com, April 1, 2010. Accessed September 28, 2013. http://josersosa.blogspot.com/2010/04/nueve-de-los-diez-transexuales.html.

————. 2012. "Caravana gay cruzó banderas y banderas." JoseRafaelSosa.blogspot.com, July 3, 2012. Accessed November 13, 2013. josersosa.blogspot.com/2012/07/caravana-gay-cruzo-banderas-y-banderas.html.

Tavarez Mirabal, Minou. 2011. "Culpables de ser inocentes." *Diario Libre,* March 8, 2011. Accessed March 14, 2011. http://www.diariolibre.com/noticias_det.php?id=282052.

Tejada Yangüela, Argelia. 2012. "República Dominicana: Constitución y derechos de la mujer." Acento.com, January 25, 2012. Accessed February 2, 2012. http://awid.org/esl/Nuestras-Iniciativas/Resistiendo-y-Desafiando-a-los-Fundamentalismos-Religiosos/Republica-Dominicana-Constitucion-y-derechos-de-la-mujer2.

Thomas, Juan Eduardo. 2015. "López Rodríguez arremete contra embajador James Brewster." Listindiario.com, December 1, 2012. Accessed December 1, 2015. http://www.listindiario.com/la-republica/2015/12/01/398571/lopez-rodriguez-arremete-contra-embajador-james-brewster.

TN.com.ar. 2010. "Dura condena del cardenal Bergoglio al matrimonio gay." July 8, 2010. Accessed March 13, 2013. http://tn.com.ar/politica/dura-condena-del-cardenal-bergoglio-al-matrimonio-gay_038359.

Urbáez, Ramón. 2010. "Policias matan de un balazo a joven estudiante de derecho." Listindiario.com, June 28, 2010. https://listindiario.com/la-republica/2010/06/28/148050/policias-matan-de-un-balazo-a-joven-estudiante-de-derecho.

Vargas, Tahira. 2010a. "El Parque Duarte y las 'buenas costumbres.'" *Clave Digital,* April 10, 2010. Accessed June 12, 2010. http://www.perspectivaciudadana.com/contenido.php?itemid=32694.

————. 2010b. "Criminalización de la homosexualidad en la sociedad dominicana." *Clave Digital,* July 7, 2010. Accessed July 7, 2010. http://www.perspectivaciudadana.com/contenido.php?itemid=32675.

Veloz Maggiolo, Marcio. 2002. "Don Paco Escribano 'El rey del disparate' y 'el archipámpano de la carcajada.'" *La Nación Dominicana*, November 2, 2002.

Weber, Courtney. 2014. "'Lacras sociales': Iglesia y homosexualidad en República Dominicana." 8ogrados.net, February 14, 2014. Accessed February 14, 2014. http://www.8ogrados .net/lacras-sociales-la-iglesia-y-la-homosexualidad-en-la-republica-dominicana/.

VIDEO AND FILM

Acento.com. 2011. "Centenares de miembros de la comunidad LGBT dominicana marcharon por la igualdad." YouTube video, 5:00 min., July 4, 2011. Accessed January 23, 2014. http:// www.youtube.com/watch?v=geD7HgVJa1g&feature=youtube_gdata_player.

———. 2014. "'Me lo dejaron morir por negligencia médica' madre de Paloma Sody." YouTube video, 5:49 min., January 23, 2014. Accessed January 23, 2014. http://www.youtube .com/watch?v=JnQ6lF4mdBw.

"El cardenal, la primera dama y los evangélicos en pleito con la comunidad gay." 2012. YouTube video, 3:43 min., January 28, 2012. Accessed January 23, 2014. http://www.youtube .com/watch?v=8i-kqYJBJxo&feature=youtube_gdata_player.

Elsevyf, Loly Mena, Joselina Fay, Henry Mercedes Vales, Carlos Manuel Montilla, Carlos Rodríguez, Darío Pimentel, Elizabeth Ramírez, Cristina Paola Then Payano, and Emil Pimentel Velázquez, dirs. 2010. *Afuera hay aire*. Santo Domingo, D.R.: Asociación Miradas Compartidas. DVD.

Fortunato, René, dir. 1991. *El poder del jefe*. Vols. 1–3. Santo Domingo, D.R.: Corporán. DVD.

Mercedes Vales, Henry. 2012. "Mi Escuelita." YouTube video, 3:15 min., November 28, 2012. http://youtu.be/KrUxRgpyDLI.

"Policía trata impedir uso bandera dominicana en marcha orgullo GLBT." 2012. YouTube video, 1:34 min., July 2, 2012. Accessed January 23, 2014. http://www.youtube.com/watch?v =_S6hcPyo47c.

Rodríguez, Carlos. 2015. *Trans'It*. Santo Domingo, D.R.: Rodríguez, Brea & Terrero. Digital short film.

Sukkhapisit, Tanwarin. 2012. *It Gets Better*. Bangkok, Thailand: Amfine Productions. DVD.

TRANSSA. 2010. "Ruta contra la transfobia y los crímenes de odio—mayo 2010 1/3." YouTube video, 3:18 min., May 25, 2010. http://www.youtube.com/watch?v=DpG5LPORup8.

———. 2014. "Mujeres Trans=Derecho a la Salud." YouTube video, 1:37 min., September 9, 2014. https://youtu.be/u-MfXTdioog.

———. 2015. "Foro 'La situación de las personas LGBTI Afrodescendientes en América Latina y El Caribe.'" YouTube video, 17:33 min., June 20, 2015. https://youtu.be/UFagoSnXvmk.

Zouhali-Worrall, Malika, and Katherine Fairfax Wright, dirs. 2013. *Call Me Kuchu*. Los Angeles: Cinedigm. DVD.

Index

About the Author

ANA-MAURINE LARA is a scholar, novelist, and poet. Her scholarship has been published in *Small Axe, Sargasso, Feminist Review*, and numerous anthologies. Lara's work asks questions about what it means for black queer folks/women to be free. She is currently a faculty member in the Department of Women, Gender, and Sexuality Studies at the University of Oregon.